Dostoevsky and the Ethics of Narrative Form

SRLT

Dostoevsky and the Ethics of Narrative Form

Suspense, Closure, Minor Characters

Greta Matzner-Gore

NORTHWESTERN UNIVERSITY PRESS / EVANSTON, ILLINOIS

Northwestern University Press
www.nupress.northwestern.edu

Studies of the Harriman Institute
Columbia University

The Harriman Institute, Columbia University, sponsors the Studies of the Harriman Institute in the belief that their publication contributes to scholarly research and public understanding. In this way the Institute, while not necessarily endorsing their conclusions, is pleased to make available the results of some of the research conducted under its auspices.

An earlier version of part of chapter 3 was published as "Kicking Maksimov out of the Carriage: Minor Characters, Exclusion, and *The Brothers Karamazov*," *Slavic and East European Journal* 58, no. 3 (Fall 2014): 419–36. Reprinted here with permission of the publisher.

Printed in the United States of America

10 9 8 7 6 5 4 3 2 1

Library of Congress Cataloging-in-Publication Data

Names: Matzner-Gore, Greta, author.
Title: Dostoevsky and the ethics of narrative form : suspense, closure, minor characters / Greta Matzner-Gore.
Other titles: Studies in Russian literature and theory.
Description: Evanston, Illinois : Northwestern University Press, 2020. | Series: Studies in Russian literature and theory | Includes bibliographical references and index.
Identifiers: LCCN 2020002301 | ISBN 9780810141971 (paperback) | ISBN 9780810141988 (cloth) | ISBN 9780810141995 (ebook)
Subjects: LCSH: Dostoyevsky, Fyodor, 1821–1881—Criticism and interpretation. | Literature and morals.
Classification: LCC PG3328.Z6 M285 2020 | DDC 891.73/3—dc23
LC record available at https://lccn.loc.gov/2020002301

Contents

Acknowledgments

I CAME UP with the idea for this book soon after receiving my Ph.D. My adviser, Irina Reyfman, warned me that writing a book from scratch would be difficult and, as always, she was right. Then she made it possible. She read draft after draft of my work in progress and cheered me on with her unwavering faith in the project, even when I had temporarily misplaced my own. She is the model of a devoted, compassionate, and intellectually hard-nosed mentor, and I am forever in her debt.

Several other people read and commented on large portions of the manuscript. Deborah Martinsen was there every step of the way, helping me express my ideas more clearly and cutting out the clutter. Time and again, Anna Berman and Chloë Kitzinger provided moral and intellectual support. I am proud to call them my peers and my friends. The introduction benefited from a writing workshop with Matt Elia, Ashleigh Elser, Joe Lenow, and Kris Norris in the summer of 2018. I had the opportunity to present variations of chapter 1 at the University of Virginia; the University of Wisconsin–Madison; University of California, Berkeley; and Stanford University, and the thoughtful, thought-provoking questions from those audiences helped shape the final version. The early versions of chapter 3 took shape under the tutelage of Cathy Popkin, Eric Naiman, and Liza Knapp, and I am grateful for their help and advice. I would also like to thank the reviewers from Northwestern University Press for their generous suggestions for revision. I have tried my best to follow their recommendations, and I know the book is better for them.

A Columbia University Harriman Institute postdoctoral fellowship gave me the year I needed to conceive, research, and write this book, and the institute's publishing grant has supported its publication. I am grateful to the institute's wonderful faculty and staff. It will always feel like home.

Finally, I want to thank the people who have been there for the long haul. My eighth-grade teacher, Peter Valdez, got me hooked on Sergei Eisenstein and sparked a lifelong love of Russian culture. I owe an enormous debt of gratitude to my parents, who humored my obsessive childhood reading habits, the many, many copies of *The Brothers Karamazov* I littered throughout the house, and summer after summer of Russian-language programs.

This book is dedicated to my husband, Paul, who helped me write it, and to my daughter, Ramona, who gave me no choice but to finish it.

Note on the Text

FOR TRANSLITERATION OF Russian words, I follow a modified version of the Library of Congress guidelines. When giving Russian names, however, I use the version most likely to be familiar to American readers: Dostoevsky rather than Dostoevskii, Alyosha rather than Alesha, Golyadkin rather than Goliadkin, Gogol rather than Gogol' (except in the citations, which adhere to the Library of Congress system).

When referencing Dostoevsky's works, I generally provide page numbers for a published English translation (occasionally modified to bring it closer to the Russian original) and for his collected works, the *Polnoe sobranie sochinenii v tridtsati tomakh* (*PSS*). Both sets of references appear parenthetically in the text, with page numbers for the translation preceding those for the *PSS*. References to Bakhtin's *Problems of Dostoevsky's Poetics* follow a similar system. Uncredited translations are my own.

Dostoevsky makes frequent use of ellipses. (I discuss some of the reasons why in chapter 2). In order to distinguish ellipses in the original from my own omissions, I have marked mine with square brackets. Dostoevsky also makes frequent use of italics. All emphasis in quotations is in the original unless otherwise noted.

Abbreviations

A Fyodor Dostoevsky. *The Adolescent*. Translated by Richard Pevear and Larissa Volokhonsky. New York: Vintage Classics, 2003.

BK Fyodor Dostoevsky. *The Brothers Karamazov*. Translated by Richard Pevear and Larissa Volokhonsky. New York: Farrar, Straus and Giroux, 1990.

CP Fyodor Dostoyevsky. *Crime and Punishment*. Translated by Oliver Ready. London: Penguin Books, 2014.

D Fyodor Dostoyevsky. *Demons*. Translated by Robert A. Maguire. Edited by Ronald Meyer. London: Penguin Books, 2008.

I Fyodor Dostoevsky. *The Idiot*. Translated by Richard Pevear and Larissa Volokhonsky. New York: Vintage Classics, 2003.

PDP Mikhail Bakhtin. *Problems of Dostoevsky's Poetics*. Edited and translated by Caryl Emerson. Minneapolis: University of Minnesota Press, 1984.

PSS F. M. Dostoevskii. *Polnoe sobranie sochinenii v tridtsati tomakh*. Edited by V. G. Bazanov, V. V. Vinogradov, F. Ia. Priima, G. M. Fridlender, and M. B. Khrapchenko. 30 vols. Leningrad: Nauka, 1972–90.

SS Mikhail Bakhtin. *Sobranie sochinenii v semi tomakh*. Edited by S. G. Bocharov et al. 6 vols. Moscow: Russkie slovari, 1996–.

WD1 Fyodor Dostoevsky. *A Writer's Diary: Volume One, 1873–1876*. Translated by Kenneth Lantz. Evanston, Ill.: Northwestern University Press, 1993.

WD2 Fyodor Dostoevsky. *A Writer's Diary: Volume Two, 1877–1881*. Translated by Kenneth Lantz. Evanston, Ill.: Northwestern University Press, 1994.

Dostoevsky and the Ethics of Narrative Form

Introduction

DOSTOEVSKY'S NOVELS ARE designed to draw you in. They are not only exciting, suspenseful, and compulsively readable, they also blur the boundaries between fiction and reality, reader and text. Take his political thriller *Demons*, for example. It "exceeds even the bloodiest melodramas in its abundance of horrors and deaths," each of which attracts a crowd.[1] Where there is a rumor to be heard, scandal to be seen, or corpse to be gaped at, curious townsfolk throng around. They hurry to the governor's gala, gleefully expecting mayhem to unfold there, the "'denouement' [*razviazka*], as some people put it, rubbing their hands in anticipation" (*D*, 509; *PSS*, 10:354). The literary term "denouement" should make us stop short, because it suggests a parallel between the townsfolk's anticipation and our own. Caught up in this fast-paced, suspenseful novel, haven't we also been awaiting this very denouement, perhaps even "rubbing [our] hands in anticipation" of the next catastrophe?[2] The narrator—a curious townsperson in his own right—declares that "in every misfortune that befalls one's neighbor there is something that gladdens the bystander's eye, it doesn't make any difference who you may be" (*D*, 364, translation modified; *PSS*, 10:255). We are not actual bystanders to the novel's gruesome events, but we are bystanders by proxy. Do they "gladden" us on some level as well? Do we derive aesthetic pleasure and excitement from reading about them? Should we?

Dostoevsky loves to put his readers in morally compromising positions, and some readers don't like it. In 1875, Alexander Skabichevsky compared reading a novel by Dostoevsky to going to the theater and finding yourself an unwitting, and unwilling, player in the performance. Instead of depicting a thunderstorm onstage, the director dumps water straight into the dress circle. Instead of firing blanks, the actors use real bullets, which fly whizzing over your head. Skabichevsky complains, "It always seemed to me that Mr. Dostoevsky crosses this line in art and does not limit himself to presenting you with a set of poetic images but instead makes you participate in the moral sufferings of his heroes yourself."[3] In 1882, Nikolai Mikhailovsky dubbed Dostoevsky a cruel talent whose works make their *readers* cruel, too.

In novels like Dostoevsky's, Mikhailovsky wrote, "they beat a person who is guilty of nothing for no reason, but at the same time they beat him so artistically that the reader begins to find watching this revolting spectacle pleasant [*liubo*]; simply pleasant, without the slightest partaking of other feelings or thoughts."[4] According to Mikhailovsky, Dostoevsky's gruesome spectacles "torture" us precisely *by* gladdening us, by making us take pleasure in them whether we would or no.

For Mikhailovsky, Dostoevsky is simply a sadist who likes to make his characters (and his readers) squirm. But other critics have seen Dostoevsky's attempts to implicate readers "in the moral sufferings of his heroes" as marking the very core of his artistic-ethical endeavor. As early as 1847, Valerian Maikov suggested that Dostoevsky's novels work like moral mirrors. Look into the hearts of his least-likable characters, and you will see yourself there.[5] Maikov writes that it is "impossible" not "to sympathize" with even the morbidly vain, envious, and self-conscious protagonist of *The Double*—Golyadkin. "Ask yourself," he inquires, "isn't there anything Golyadkin-like in you yourself, which no one wants to own up to but which fully accounts for the wonderful harmony reigning in human society?"[6] Maikov implies that there is, and so the not-so-wonderful harmony in human society comes down to us.

Contemporary scholars have followed Maikov's lead. According to Robert Belknap, *Crime and Punishment* "programs" its readers "to participate actively in a vicious murder" and then exposes their complicity. By keeping the narrative claustrophobically close to the murderous Raskolnikov's thoughts and feelings and then ratcheting up the suspense, Dostoevsky encourages us to root for his many narrow escapes from justice "and then suddenly realize that we are accessories after the fact."[7] Robin Feuer Miller makes a complementary argument about *The Idiot*. In that novel, she contends, "Dostoevsky sought to move his reader beyond mere engagement: he attempted to make him actually share responsibility with the characters in the novel for the moral and ethical judgments with which the characters, often tragically, affected each other's lives." Dostoevsky not only describes the psychological phenomenon of "double thoughts," he also creates them in the reader, who feels tempted to agree with, or at least smile at, the narrator's cruel, dismissive remarks.[8] Alexander Spektor takes Miller's argument a step further. He claims that in *The Idiot* Dostoevsky represents "any kind of finished interpretation" (including the act of interpreting *The Idiot* itself) as "morally inadequate." The very process of reading the novel, then, "is a participatory experience that engages our sense of duty. Zosima's beloved formula in which our sense of mutual responsibility is awoken through the acknowledgment of our personal guilt *before* each other—'each of us is guilty before everyone, for everyone and everything'—finds its realization diachronically in our involvement with the text."[9] According to critics like

Belknap, Miller, and Spektor, Dostoevsky draws us into the rain, thunder, and lightning *by design*, pushing us to recognize that his characters' moral dilemmas are our dilemmas too.[10]

This book takes their insights as its jumping-off place. It asks *how* Dostoevsky draws us into the storm. How does he design his novels to make them maximally interactive, to make readers participants in (rather than mere observers of) the moral dramas that play out on their pages? What experiments with narrative form allow him to do so, and how did he develop them? What can Dostoevsky contribute to debates about the ethical dimensions of narrative technique that are ongoing to this day?[11] Attempting to answer these questions takes me in three directions at once: deep into Dostoevsky's creative process, into the narrative structure of his finished works, and into the ethical questions that they raise. All three avenues of exploration repeatedly intersect and sometimes even merge, because for Dostoevsky problems of narrative form and morality were always inextricably interconnected.

From the outset, Dostoevsky had a penchant for the metaliterary. (His first novella, *Poor Folk*, stars an impoverished civil servant who reads tales about other civil servants and complains about how they are portrayed.) This book does not attempt to cover Dostoevsky's entire metaliterary career, however. Instead it focuses on the 1870s, the decade in which he wrote his last three great novels: *Demons* (1871–72), *The Adolescent* (1875), and *The Brothers Karamazov* (1879–80). This was also the decade when his formal innovations reached their peak as he put ever new genres, literary styles, and methods of engaging reader response to the test.[12] During these years Dostoevsky was particularly preoccupied with the three formal problems that anchor this study: how to build suspense, how to end a novel effectively, and how to distribute narrative attention between major and minor characters. His letters and notebooks reveal how frequently he thought about all three. How could he spark his readers' curiosity and then keep their attention? How could he conclude his novels in a way that both does justice to the complexity of the questions they raise and provides an adequate sense of closure? How could he keep readers from becoming "confused" by the proliferation of characters and subplots in his works?

These questions dogged Dostoevsky, I suggest, because their implications reach far beyond the realm of narrative structure to the very nature of human cognition. Building suspense requires more than just maintaining an air of mystery. It also requires the author to consider what piques our curiosity and why. Developing an effective novelistic ending demands more than either tying up loose plot ends or intentionally leaving them untied. It also prompts the author to contemplate how endings shape our thinking, how they push us to reconsider everything that has come before, to make summations and draw conclusions. Deciding how many characters to include in a single narrative obliges the author to reflect on something more fundamental: how many people, things, and ideas readers can hold in their minds and memories at one time. When will they start getting confused? These are questions about how human attention, judgment, and memory work—the structures of thought that govern not only the way we read novels but also, and more essentially, how we understand and interact with the world around us.

Dostoevsky's experiments with narrative form ultimately led him to another set of questions. Given our cognitive limitations, how can we nevertheless lead ethical lives? Given our finite attention spans, where should we direct our focus first and foremost, and what can we put off thinking about until later? Some things (especially scandalous, violent, and destructive things) grab our interest quickly and hold it fast. Should we indulge our curiosity about them? Or try to resist it? And if we do indulge that curiosity, what sort of conclusions can we draw about the things we learn? What are the dangers of rushing to judgment? What are the dangers of suspending it entirely? The more Dostoevsky struggled with the questions about suspense, closure, and narrative focus that obsessed him, the more interested he became in their ethical ramifications—for how he interacted with his readers, for how his readers interacted with his characters, and, if reading fiction is the morally formative experience that Dostoevsky hoped it could be, then perhaps even for how his readers interacted with one another after they put his novels down.

THREE NOVELS, THREE FORMAL-MORAL PROBLEMS

Each of this book's three chapters focuses on one formal problem that preoccupied Dostoevsky, the moral dilemmas that it raised for him, and the novel in which he foregrounds both. Chapter 1 explores the ethics of curiosity and suspense in *Demons*. As Dostoevsky endeavored to maintain reader interest in his long, dense novels—which were published in irregular serial installments, sometimes over the course of several years—he experimented with multiple techniques for building suspense. He filled his works with ominous foreshadowing and cliff-hanger chapter endings and employed gossipy narrators adept at making readers want to know more. By the time Dostoevsky began working on *Demons*, however, he had begun to wonder what *sort* of interest his exciting, scandalous plots would evoke in their readers: compassionate concern about the characters' plight or "greedy curiosity" about what thrilling thing would happen next, the desire to know more for the sake of knowing more? As I argue in this chapter, *Demons* not only asks what kind of interest its readers will take in its suspenseful, grisly story line; it prompts readers to ask this question of themselves as well.

Chapter 2 examines Dostoevsky's experiments with endings and narrative closure in *The Adolescent*. If in *Demons* Dostoevsky warns of the dangers of excessive curiosity (the desire to overcome suspense hastily and absolutely), in his next novel he warns of the dangers of going to the opposite extreme: of disavowing *all* certainty, to the point of losing one's ability to tell right from wrong. *The Adolescent* tells the story of Arkady Dolgoruky, a young man trying to find his way through the social chaos of 1870s Russia, a world in which, as Dostoevsky once wrote, "everything [will be] topsy-turvy for a thousand years" (*WD1*, 122; *PSS*, 21:6). Arkady realizes that in order to develop a clear moral vision, he must endeavor to look beyond the state of historical suspense in which he finds himself. He must imagine how human history can and will finally come to an end. Once he determines where humanity is (or should be) heading, he will know how to help it get there; once he discovers the ultimate goal of life on earth, he will know how he can contribute to its achievement. Over the course of the novel, Arkady listens to several different accounts of human destiny, ranging from the radically open-ended and ethically confused to tales of universal redemption achieved prematurely, without suffering or sacrifice. Arkady must evaluate them all, and then decide which to adopt for himself.

While Arkady is searching for a compelling vision of the end, his creator was looking for an ending of a different but related kind. For a long time, Dostoevsky remained unsure how to conclude the novel: With Arkady's death? With his resurrection to new life? With a massive conflagration? With something else entirely? Like his protagonist, Dostoevsky was seeking a finale that balanced open-endedness with closure, that both respected the disorderly nature of contemporary Russian life *and* provided readers with ethical direction, an idea of where Russia could and should go next. In both its form and its content, thus, *The Adolescent* suggests that our "sense of an ending" and our ethics cannot be parsed apart: how we imagine our stories will end fundamentally shapes the choices we make today.

Chapter 3 looks at the problem of minor characters in *The Brothers Karamazov*. During the 1870s, a growing chorus of critics complained that Dostoevsky "overloaded" his works with characters and subplots, to the point that readers could barely follow along. Dostoevsky took this criticism to heart, worried that if his readers became distracted by "secondary things" they might miss his "main aim," his most important social, ethical, and philosophical points. He promised not to make the same "mistake" again, and while he was working on *The Adolescent* strove to limit the novel's scope. That meant not only constructing an ending that would grant form and shape to the whole but also carefully considering which characters and story lines to include and which to exclude, what to place in the foreground and what to leave in the background of the narrative. This time, Dostoevsky assured himself, he would center the action on the hero and keep "secondary things" firmly on the periphery where they belong.

In his next novel—*The Brothers Karamazov*—Dostoevsky investigated the ethical ramifications of that formal choice. As the novel emphasizes, deciding what (or who) is more or less important is an ethically fraught process, and one necessarily subject to error. Our social prejudices can warp our judgment, leading us to regard entire categories of people as being of minor or secondary significance *habitually*. The novel's narrator struggles, and frequently fails, to sort the major from the minor, the essential from the ancillary elements of his tale, and he is not the only one. The character that nearly everyone in *The Brothers Karamazov* dismisses as secondary—the lowly, illegitimate servant Smerdyakov—in fact requires the other characters', the narrator's, and the *reader's* primary attention.

DOSTOEVSKY AND NARRATIVE THEORY

My approach to Dostoevsky's last three novels has been inspired by rhetorical narrative theory. As two of its chief representatives, James Phelan and Peter Rabinowitz, explain, rhetorical narrative theorists are "concerned with narrative's affective, ethical, and aesthetic effects."[13] They begin from the premise that

> texts are designed by authors (consciously or not) to affect readers in particular ways; that those authorial designs are conveyed through the occasions, words, techniques, structures, forms, and dialogic relations of texts as well as the genres and conventions readers use to understand them; and that since reader responses are ideally a consequence of those designs, they can also serve as an initial guide to (although, since misreadings are possible, not as a guarantee of) the workings of the text.[14]

In short, they are interested in textual design and its potential impact on readers. Their methods are particularly well suited to studying Dostoevsky, because he thought constantly about narrative effect as well. From questions as minor as whether part 2 of *The Adolescent* would appear in two or three installments and how this would alter its "effect" (*PSS*, 29.2:25) to as major as whether the indirect answer to the Grand Inquisitor in book 6 of *The Brothers Karamazov* would "be understood and will I achieve even a drop of my goal" (*PSS*, 30.1:122)—Dostoevsky considered the impact of all his formal decisions, great and small.

Dostoevsky was not trying to affect just any readers, of course. He was targeting a very specific audience. He wrote *Demons*, for example, for a readership that was intimately familiar with the "Nechaev affair"—the real-life political conspiracy, murder, and ensuing public trial that inspired the novel's plot. *Demons* was "ripped from the headlines": the suspenseful introductory chapters to part 2 came out in July of 1871, the very month in which the trial was taking place. The trial (and the media storm around it) would have served as a constant reminder that the violence in the novel was not a figment of the author's imagination but a stark reality of Russian political life. Dostoevsky's original readers would never have lost sight of the fact that *Demons* was a work of fiction, not journalism, and that it described the lives and deaths of literary characters, not people. But they would also have been painfully aware that the novel's blood and chaos were only one step removed from contemporary fact.[15]

My interpretations of Dostoevsky's novels are attentive to his original readers and the historical environment in which they encountered his works. Yet I am also interested in what makes his novels relevant to new readers in new contexts. The plot of *Demons* may not be as immediately recognizable to an American audience today as it was to a nineteenth-century Russian one, but the questions it poses—about how to read, hear, and tell stories of scandal and violence compassionately, rather than curiously—remain as topical as ever.[16] Dostoevsky's experiments with narrative form remain relevant as well. Narrative theorists continue to debate the questions about reader interest, narrative closure, and the differences between major and minor characters that Dostoevsky posed a century and a half ago. In each chapter I place Dostoevsky in dialogue with different sets of contemporary critics—from Martha Nussbaum and Suzanne Keen to Wayne Booth and Alex Woloch—who share his interest in the ethical dimensions of novelistic technique. His works can enrich their inquiries and help sharpen their disputes. Dostoevsky may have been speaking to a historically specific audience, but the questions he raises about the limitations of human attention, memory, and judgment—and how they shape the stories we tell—are universal.

PROBLEMS IN *PROBLEMS OF DOSTOEVSKY'S POETICS*

Alongside several major works of narrative theory, this book engages with perhaps the most influential piece of Dostoevsky criticism ever written—Mikhail Bakhtin's *Problems of Dostoevsky's Poetics* (first published in 1929 and revised and retitled in 1963).[17] Throughout his analysis, Bakhtin insists that he is concerned only with Dostoevsky's artistic innovations, not with his ideology or even the subject matter of his novels. There is an obvious reason for the omission: Dostoevsky's Christianity was a taboo topic in Soviet literary studies, and any work that discussed it in depth risked never being published. (Apparently, the need to dance around Dostoevsky's "main questions" about faith and the existence of God pricked Bakhtin's conscience.)[18] And yet *Problems of Dostoevsky's Poetics does* treat Dostoevsky's central moral and philosophical concerns, if only indirectly. Despite Bakhtin's assurances that he is focusing on questions of form—not content—he repeatedly suggests that the two cannot be separated.[19] Again and again, he implies that the literary structure *of* Dostoevsky's works reflects the ethical principles that the author champions *in* them. He tries to show that Dostoevsky's fundamental moral principle—"the affirmation of someone else's 'I' not as an object but as another subject"—is likewise "the principle behind Dostoevsky's *artistic* visualization of the world, the principle behind his artistic structuring of a *verbal* whole, the novel" (*PDP*, 11; *SS*, 6:15).

In order to realize this new, ethically inflected artistic vision, Dostoevsky had to invent a new kind of literary structure: what Bakhtin calls the polyphonic novel. In contrast with writers like Lev Tolstoy, who write *about* their characters (all of whom fill set functions in the novel's predetermined ideological design), Dostoevsky attempts to speak *with* his, allowing them to become "*not only objects of authorial discourse but also subjects of their own directly signifying discourse*" (*PDP*, 7; *SS*, 6:11). Instead of enforcing a literary structure from above, as it were, Dostoevsky allows his self-directed characters—who engage one another in ongoing, open-ended dialogue—to organize the plot for him. As for the author himself, he maintains "a *fully realized and thoroughly consistent dialogic position*, one that affirms the independence, internal freedom, unfinalizability, and indeterminacy of the hero. For the author the hero is not 'he' and not 'I' but a fully valid 'thou,' that is, another and other autonomous 'I' ('thou art')" (*PDP*, 63; *SS*, 6:74). Dostoevsky relates to his characters in the way that he believes God relates to us, and in the way we should relate to one another, respecting their autonomy and inherent spiritual worth.[20]

As influential as Bakhtin's work on Dostoevsky continues to be, it has also received serious criticism. Scholars have attacked it from all sides. Some have argued that Bakhtin underestimates Dostoevsky's tendentiousness; others that he underplays "the negative, destructive potential of dialogic discourse" in Dostoevsky's fiction; still others that Bakhtin's argument is based on a faulty premise: how can an author engage in meaningful "dialogue" with characters that are ultimately figments of his own imagination?[21] This book examines a different set of lacunae in Bakhtin's argument, lacunae that remain largely unexplored. Chapter 1 challenges Bakhtin's claim that neither Dostoevsky nor his narrators "spy" on his characters. Chapter 2 tests Bakhtin's assertion—albeit one made with several caveats—that Dostoevsky's novels are distinguished by a "rigorous unfinalizability [*nezavershennost'*] and dialogic openness [*otkrytost'*]" (*PDP*, 272; *SS*, 6:300). It asks if there are limits to the open-endedness of Dostoevsky's fiction and if so what they are and what artistic purposes they might serve. Chapter 3 addresses a question that Bakhtin comes close to raising but never definitively answers: whether all of Dostoevsky's characters are full participants in the "great dialogue" of his novels or if only the "major characters" (*glavnye geroi*) enjoy this privilege (*PDP*, 7; *SS*, 6:10). If the latter is true, and not all of Dostoevsky's characters are created equal, then what role do the nonparticipating, "object" characters play in his works?

Because Bakhtin concentrates so intently on the *correlation* between Dostoevsky's poetics and ethical worldview, he tends to overlook those moments when they come into *conflict*, when Dostoevsky's narrators belittle his characters, silence their voices, or gossip about them. Yet such conflicts are practically inevitable. As *Demons*, *The Adolescent*, and *The Brothers Karamazov* repeatedly remind us, narratives are written by and for fallible people. They are subject to limits of time, space, and selection, and they are driven forward by discord and disharmony, which is what attracts us to them in the first place. Narratives are necessarily imperfect, and that is precisely what makes them, in Dostoevsky's eyes, the perfect art form for exploring the imperfections of human existence—something he called "only developing on earth, and therefore not finished, but transitional" (*PSS*, 20:173). Bakhtin's "benevolent" reading of Dostoevsky does not always map easily onto the author's tortured and torturous prose.[22] But even those places where Bakhtin's argument breaks down point to key tensions in Dostoevsky's works.

ARTISTIC FORM AND MORAL FORMATION

Dostoevsky believed that great art has great moral power. Following in the footsteps of one of his favorite writers, Friedrich Schiller, he insisted that formally beautiful works of art are both good in and of themselves and can have a morally beneficial effect on the people who come in contact with them.[23] In his 1861 polemic against utilitarian literary criticism, "Mr. ——bov and the Question of Art," he imagined the profound transformation a young man might undergo upon seeing the Apollo Belvedere:

> And because the youth's impression was, perhaps, an ardent one, convulsing his nerves and making his epidermis turn cold; perhaps—who knows!—perhaps as a result of such sensations of higher beauty, as a result of this convulsion of the nerves, some sort of internal change even takes place in the person, some sort of shifting of particles, some sort of galvanic current, which, in one instant, makes the past not what it was before, turns a piece of ordinary iron into a magnet. (*PSS*, 18:78)

Twenty years later, this former youth may still feel the magnetic attraction of that "majestic and infinitely beautiful image" (*PSS*, 18:78). Now a major player on the world stage, he may still be subject to its influence in ways that he himself does not fully recognize or understand. As Dostoevsky wrote in another article from that same year, "I always believed in the power of a humane, aesthetically expressed impression. These impressions accumulate little by little, and with development break through the exterior of the heart, pierce the heart itself, into its very core, and form the person [*formiruiut cheloveka*]. The word, the word is a great undertaking! [*Slovo,—slovo velikoe delo!*]" (*PSS*, 19:109). This is why, he explained in an 1880 letter to a father, young people should be exposed to literature that "creates *beautiful impressions and gives birth to great thoughts*" (*PSS*, 30.1:237). These childhood shocks could transform them for life: an early love of aesthetic harmony could awaken their desire for *social* harmony as well.

As Robert Louis Jackson has shown, however, there was always an unresolved tension between Dostoevsky's artistic ideals and his literary practice, "between a classical aesthetic which acknowledges only one beauty, and a practical poetics (his own) which seeks out the inner shape, rhythmic proportions, and dynamics of change of a disfigured reality."[24] Few of his characters look anything like Apollos: they have swollen, greenish, sallow, and asymmetrical faces, limps, hunches, and squinted eyes. With rare exceptions they neither "create beautiful impressions" nor model "humane" interactions. They congregate in rainy town squares, stinking taverns, and filthy huts rustling with cockroaches, where they debase, bite, and murder one another. His novels have never been known for their formal beauty either. Dostoevsky may have admired Pushkin's laconic prose style, but his own works are disorderly and disorienting, swollen with minor characters, myriad subplots, and layer upon layer of unreliable narration. No wonder Dostoevsky hesitated to recommend his novels to very young readers. "[As for] my works, I don't think that all of them would prove useful to her," he warned the parent of a young girl (*PSS*, 30.1:212). To the father who inspired his words about the importance of "beautiful impressions," Dostoevsky recommended Pushkin, Turgenev, Tolstoy, and Dickens, passing over his own novels in silence.

If Dostoevsky did not think that his own works would necessarily create "beautiful impressions" or inspire "great thoughts" in the minds of the young, how did he hope they *would* form his readers, at least those of a certain age? In his own disharmonious, less-than-beautiful novels, Dostoevsky undertakes a much riskier aesthetic and ethical endeavor. He challenges readers to confront their own moral deformations. After being arrested for the murder of his father, Dmitry Karamazov has a sudden realization. "I'm not good myself, gentlemen, that's the thing," he admits to his interrogators.

"I'm not so beautiful myself, and therefore I had no right to consider him repulsive, that's the thing" (*BK*, 462; *PSS*, 14:417). Dostoevsky's works are designed to prompt readers to similar recognitions: we have an ugly side, too.[25]

For Dostoevsky, such realizations are no small feat. In fact, he believed that they were at the root of all positive social change. Only by facing our own moral weaknesses can we hope to repair them; only by recognizing what makes us ugly can we begin to cultivate the qualities that make us beautiful. Once enough of us do, human life as a whole will finally begin to improve. In an 1880 entry of his *Writer's Diary*, Dostoevsky claimed that personal acts of self-discipline and self-control are the one true catalyst of social transformation: "Where is the source of the ideal of civic organization in human society? If you follow it historically you will see at once where the source is. You will see that it is solely and exclusively the product of the moral betterment of individuals; this is where it begins, and so it has been from time immemorial, and so it shall remain for all time to come" (*WD2*, 1317; *PSS*, 26:165). By pushing readers to confront their own moral limitations—their *Schadenfreude*, their desire for power, their habits of social stereotyping—Dostoevsky asks us to begin the reform at home.

There is a passage in "Mr. ——bov and the Question of Art" that bears a much closer resemblance to a novel by Dostoevsky than the static Apollo Belvedere does. In it, the author tries to explain why we love and appreciate beauty:

> Because the need for beauty develops to the greatest extent when a person is in discord with reality, in disharmony, in a struggle, that is, when he is *most alive*, because a person is most alive precisely when he is searching and striving for something; that's when there most appears in him the natural desire for everything harmonious, for calm, and in beauty there is both harmony and calm. (*PSS*, 18:94)

Dostoevsky's novels are neither formally harmonious, nor do they contain much in the way of social harmony or calm. Instead, they are written both *about* and *by* people at their "most alive." Both his characters and his narrators "are in a struggle," doing battles with ideas, with one another, and with the chaotic stories they endeavor to tell. Dostoevsky hopes to spark the struggle in his readers as well. By confronting us with discord, both within and without, he tries to whet our desire for ideals, for the moral beauty that is so often lacking in everyday life.

Chapter One

Curiosity, Suspense, and Dostoevsky's *Demons*

> It's all very well for you to shout about gossip and spying, but observe that it's after you've squeezed everything out of me, and with such an excess of curiosity besides.
> —Liputin, *Demons*

> When a so-called political affair is being investigated, when everyone has abandoned themselves to reading about it with more or less zeal, the observer of daily life must speak about it as well . . .
> —Feuilleton about the Nechaev affair in the *Saint Petersburg News* [*Sankt-Peterburgskie vedomosti*]

> Your novel [i.e., *Demons*] is being read with avidity [*s zhadnost'iu*].
> —Nikolai Strakhov to Dostoevsky (1871)

DOSTOEVSKY IS A MASTER of suspense. Yet few scholars have studied how suspense functions in his works. As Caroline Levine has argued, for much of the twentieth century literary theorists associated suspense with popular, middlebrow, and even socially conservative fiction.[1] E. M. Forster expressed his disdain in especially colorful terms, calling suspense a "weapon" fit for use on "tyrants and savages," and the curious interest that it inspires "one of the lowest of the human faculties," incompatible with critical judgment or aesthetic appreciation.[2] By contrast, Leonid Grossman, the scholar who has studied Dostoevsky's use of suspense in the greatest depth, suggests that it is incompatible with neither. Grossman calls *zanimatel'nost'*—which can be translated as "engagement," "interest," or "entertainment"—the "highest principle of Dostoevsky's art," arguing that the author strives to provoke readers' "terrible curiosity" about what will happen next. Yet even Grossman suggests that Dostoevsky's exciting story lines are ancillary to his major moral and philosophical concerns. They are the spoonful of sugar to make the medicine go down, mainly a tool Dostoevsky uses to keep readers reading his long, intellectually challenging novels.[3]

Dostoevsky did indeed understand the practical importance of an engaging plotline. In an article on reading primers for peasants, he argued that such collections should be *interesting*, first and foremost. No one wants to read boring, moralizing tales about the hazards of laziness and drink, least of all peasants, who have better things to do. Unless editors choose stories for their "engagement and entertainment value" (*zanimatel'nosti i zavlekatel'nosti*), they will fail in both their aims: the peasants will neither learn how to read nor receive the intended moral instruction (*PSS*, 19:52). "The very best book, no matter what kind it may be or what subject it may treat, is an engaging one [*zanimatel'naia*]," Dostoevsky declares (*PSS*, 19:51).

As for Dostoevsky, whether or not readers found his works "engaging" was a matter of financial survival. Deeply in debt throughout the 1860s, he received most of his income in the form of cash advances from the "thick journals" that published his novels in serial form. Editors paid because his novels attracted subscribers; if his readership declined, his advances would decline too.[4] No wonder he had a habit of assuring friends and publishers that whatever he was currently writing would be interesting, if nothing else. When he conceived his quasi-memoiristic account of life in a Siberian prison camp, *Notes from the House of the Dead*, he had high financial hopes for the project. "I understand the curiosity and the *significance* of this article and I don't want to lose my own," he wrote to his brother. If he sold it to a journal in time for the January issue (when editors were trying their hardest to attract subscribers for the year), he was sure to make a profit. They "understand what kind of curiosity such an article could arouse," Dostoevsky concluded, and they will be willing to pay for it (*PSS*, 28.1:353).[5] A few years later, when he and his brother began editing their own journal, *Time*, he got the chance to put this principle of curiosity provocation into effect for himself. *Time* regularly published the proceedings of famous European murder trials, but—as Dostoevsky promised his readers—"only the most engaging ones [*samye zanimatel'nye*]. That we can guarantee" (*PSS*, 19:90). The first trial featured a criminal Dostoevsky described as "phenomenal, enigmatic, terrible, and interesting" (*PSS*, 19:90). He published the proceedings of another under the exciting title "A Mysterious Murder: From the Criminal Cases of France in 1840" (*PSS*, 19:284).

Yet Dostoevsky's preoccupation with reader engagement—what would make readers turn another page, devour one more chapter, run to purchase the next installment—was never purely pragmatic either. By the time he began writing *Demons*, he had become increasingly interested in the underlying intellectual and spiritual impulses that make suspense possible in the first place. What undergirds human curiosity, our desire to learn and know, especially our desire to know about other people? Why do we love listening to gossip about our neighbors, especially when something bad happens to them? What makes uncertainty so agitating, and the desire to overcome it so strong, that some of us would rather stay up all night reading than put a novel down before learning how it ends? *Demons* implicitly raises all these questions. A story about revolutionary conspiracy, political scandal, suicide and murder, it is also a story about the ethics of reading and writing an "engaging" novel about human suffering—a novel like *Demons* itself.

In October 1870, Dostoevsky admitted to feeling dissatisfied with part 1 of the novel. "For all that I am not worried about the continuation or the ending," he wrote. "At least it will turn out to be engaging [*zanimatel'no*] (and I have come to the point that I place entertainment [*zanimatel'nost'*] higher than artistry)" (*PSS*, 29.1:143). Dostoevsky had made this promise before, but his use of these particular words to describe *Demons* is nevertheless discomfiting, because they have highly negative connotations in the novel itself. In one scene, a lady voyeur urges her friends to go gawk at the corpse of a young suicide: "Everything's become so boring," she complains, "there's no point in being fastidious about one's amusements, as long as they are engaging [*zanimatel'no*]" (*D*, 362, translation modified; *PSS*, 10:254). The echo between her words and her creator's raises troubling questions. What, if anything, distinguishes the feeling of engagement that the lady voyeur derives from gawking at the corpse from the feeling of engagement Dostoevsky hoped to evoke in his readers as they encountered this same corpse on the printed page? What differentiates the "avid curiosity" with which "everyone" in the scene stares at the dead young man from the curiosity readers feel as they turn the pages of this violent and suspenseful novel (*D*, 364; *PSS*, 10:255)?

Some of Dostoevsky's critics have suggested that the answer is not very much. According to Dmitry Merezhkovsky, Dostoevsky's "insatiable curiosity" about the "most frightening and shameful ulcers of the human soul" crosses a moral and aesthetic line.[6] Merezhkovsky calls the graphic description of Kirillov's suicide in *Demons* "cynical, cruel, maybe criminal, not just artistically but morally criminal."[7] Even worse, Dostoevsky's "criminal" curiosity has a way of infecting his *readers* as well, who follow the "final shudderings" of Kirillov's soul "with revulsion and the curiosity of horror [*liubopytstvom uzhasa*]."[8] In a similar vein, Gary Saul Morson has called reading Dostoevsky's works a "vicarious act of voyeurism." Those readers "who respond to the irresistible attraction of Dostoevsky's novels (as almost everyone does)," he contends, "become living examples of sociality in its primary, voyeuristic form."[9]

In this chapter, I argue that the dynamics of curiosity in *Demons* (and that Dostoevsky provokes in readers of *Demons*) are more complex. With the help of a gossiping narrator who half reveals, half conceals the details of the scandalous story line, Dostoevsky does indeed whet his readers' curious interest. But then he takes another step. By highlighting the similarities between the novel's most "greedily curious" characters and its most avid *readers*, he pushes us to consider what kind of curiosity we feel: compassionate concern about the characters' fates or simply a passionate desire to know what will happen next? Dostoevsky suggests that reading a violent novel like *Demons* can provoke multiple types of interest in quick succession and on a sliding scale—from compassion for the characters' suffering at one end of the spectrum to voyeuristic pleasure at the other.

PUBLIC CURIOSITY ABOUT THE NECHAEV AFFAIR

Part of what makes reading *Demons* so ethically messy is that its scenes of suffering and scandal were inspired by historical events. When we read Dostoevsky's description of Shatov's murder, we are not just reading about the hypothetical death of a hypothetical person that could have hypothetically occurred sometime in 18—; we are reading Dostoevsky's fictionalization of a real murder that took place on November 21, 1869, just outside Moscow. On that night, the revolutionary conspirator and con man Sergei Nechaev and his followers killed a member of their own group and dumped the corpse in a pond. The body was soon discovered and the murderers apprehended, all save Nechaev, who had already fled abroad. The ensuing criminal and political investigation made international headlines and enthralled the Russian reading public, including Dostoevsky, who first learned of it in Europe. When the trial of the coconspirators began in the summer of 1871, it was the talk of the entire country, and regular publication of the court transcripts heightened interest in the case all the more. As Mikhail Saltykov-Shchedrin wrote in September of that year, the Nechaev affair had "engaged public attention for almost two months straight."[10]

Scholars have long studied how Dostoevsky incorporated details from the Nechaev affair into the plot of *Demons*, which he was in the process of writing and publishing before, during, and after the trial. But he incorporated the feverish public *reaction* to the affair into his novel as well.[11] *Demons* includes a host of observer characters whose main and sometimes only function is to watch and listen with bated breath as the dramas of the protagonists unfold: the tragic romance between the impulsive Liza and the enigmatic Stavrogin; the strained relationship between the former professor, Stepan Trofimovich, and his ingratiating son, Pyotr Verkhovensky; and the political ambitions of the governor's wife, Yulia Mikhailovna. When Liza first bumps into Stepan Trofimovich on the street, she notices a young woman "admiring" them from a window (*D*, 119; *PSS*, 10:87). When the "mysterious lame woman" (Stavrogin's secret wife, Maria Lebiadkina) falls on her knees before Stavrogin's mother in church, spectators immediately encircle them. Some look on with surprise, some start to giggle, and others stare with what the narrator calls "sly curiosity [*lukavym liubopytstvom*] and, at the same time, with the innocent desire for a juicy little scandal" (*D*, 173, translation modified; *PSS*, 10:124). And it is not only the immoderate who express this not-so-very-innocent desire. Even the most dignified and serious-minded of the townsfolk listen "with relish" (*s appetitom*) to rumors about Stavrogin's slap, Liza's mysterious fainting spell, and what may or may not have happened between the two of them in Switzerland (*D*, 233; *PSS*, 10:168).

The word "curiosity" (*liubopytstvo*) and its cognates appear in the novel more than eighty times (not counting the excised chapter "At Tikhon's," in which it appears several times more). Curiosity is called "sly" (*lukavoe*), "greedy" (*zhadnoe*), "unconquerable" (*nepreodolimoe*), and even "pitiless" (*bezzhalostnoe*). Several scenes prove just how dangerous it can be. The former governor of the province, who is called "extremely curious," inclines his ear to Stavrogin's mouth in the hope of hearing an "interesting secret" but receives a painful bite instead (*D*, 56; *PSS*, 10:42–43). His replacement, von Lembke, is even more curious, and it gets him into an even pricklier situation. Out of a "healthy curiosity" (*iz poleznogo liubopytstva*), he has amassed a collection of revolutionary pamphlets, a foible that leaves him vulnerable to blackmail (*PSS*, 10:245).

At other points in the novel curiosity takes on an even more sinister aspect. Suffering provides a spectacle for inquisitive eyes, and the novel's most curious characters take pleasure in the sight of other people's pain. When fires begin to rage across the river, spectators flock in from all over town. Some of them try to help put the fire out, but others just stand and stare, "gawking like tourists [*kak liubiteli*]" (*D*, 569; *PSS*, 10:394). The novel's narrator, Anton Lavrentyevich G——v (whose full last name is never revealed), uses the scene as an opportunity to muse over what makes watching someone else's house burn to the ground so intoxicating. He blames the "destructive instincts" that "lurk in every heart" and repeats something Stepan Trofimovich once told him: "I don't know whether one can look at a fire without a certain pleasure" (*D*, 569; *PSS*, 10:394).

CURIOSITY IN THE GARDEN

In dramatizing the dangers of uncontrolled curiosity, Dostoevsky was drawing on an ancient tradition. According to Plutarch, the curious mind "fears and shudders at what lies within, and rushes outside to roam over strange ground, feeding and fattening its malice."[12] Tikhon of Zadonsk—the eighteenth-century Orthodox bishop who inspired the character Tikhon in *Demons*—warned of the "hateful curiosity" that draws our eyes to other people's sins while leaving us blind to our own. Instead of gawking at your neighbors, Tikhon admonishes his audience,

> Know and examine yourself. First remember your former sins and cleanse them with repentance and with the rending of your heart, and then you will not look to see what other people are doing. Look more frequently into your own heart, and examine how much pernicious evil is hiding within it—and you will have plenty to examine. For we can never completely sound our hearts, but we know that they contain every possible evil.[13]

Dostoevsky gave *Demons* two epigraphs, which I discuss later in this chapter. This quote from Tikhon of Zadonsk could have served as the third.

There is ample biblical support for Tikhon's warning. After all, an act of illicit curiosity was humankind's first sin. In Genesis, Adam and Eve break the one rule that God has given them—not to eat from the Tree of Knowledge of Good and Evil. The cunning serpent spins a seductive tale, promising Eve that the fruit will open her eyes and make her "like God" in wisdom. Transfixed by the fruit's beauty (most accurately translated from Hebrew as "a lust to the eyes"), Eve eats, Adam eats, and both are expelled from their garden home.[14] The theologian Vladimir Lossky provides an Orthodox perspective on the nature of their transgression and why it costs them so much. Neither the desire for knowledge nor the aspiration to be godlike is inherently wrong or sinful, Lossky explains. To the contrary, the call to *theosis*—to realize, as fully as possible, one's potential likeness to God—is a central tenet of Orthodox theology:

> In fact the fruit was good in itself, but everything hinges on the personal relationship of man and God. And when Eve sees that the tree is beautiful, a value outside of God appears. "You will be like God," says the serpent. He does not altogether deceive man: for the latter is called to deification. But here "like" signifies an equality, through resentment, of him who stands up to God: autonomous god against God, god by himself, god of the earthly cosmos isolated from God.[15]

The sin, thus, lies not so much in *what* Adam and Eve want as in *how* they try to achieve it. Instead of communing with God in an ever more perfect way—the only path toward true knowledge—they abandon their relationship with him. They set themselves outside of and against God, trying to learn about him and his creation on the sly, without allowing themselves to be seen in turn. (Recall how they try to hide their naked bodies from God's sight). Adam and Eve achieve the opposite of what they hoped, however: they become *less* godlike, since God is loving and seeks a relationship with humankind, and *less* knowledgeable, because they have abandoned the one source of truth.

In *Demons*, the "greedily curious" characters reenact the original transgression again and again. Stepan Trofimovich—the representative of 1840s Russian liberalism and the source of intellectual and moral disorder in the novel—is also the first to commit this sin. In his youth, he wrote a poem that expresses a distinctly Adam and Eve–like desire:

> And finally, in the very last scene, the Tower of Babel suddenly appears, and some athletes are busy bringing it to completion, with a song of fresh hope, and when they reach the very top, the lord of—let's say it's Olympus—runs off in comical fashion, and mankind, which has grasped the situation, occupies his place, and immediately begins a new life with a new and deeper understanding of things [*s novym proniknoveniem veshchei*]. (*D*, 11; *PSS*, 10:10)

Like Adam and Eve before him, Stepan Trofimovich dreams that humankind can achieve ultimate knowledge outside of and in contradiction to its relationship with God.[16] In fact, if we have enough moxie, we can replace God entirely, assuming his place and acquiring his omniscience. Mankind will look down from the heights of Olympus or the Tower of Babel with a totalizing gaze that sees, and sees through, everyone and everything.[17]

THE SPECTACLE VERSUS THE ICON

If Adam and Eve's transgression serves as the archetype for the many instances of "greedy," "sly," and "pitiless" curiosity in the novel, then the path to knowledge that Adam and Eve should have taken, but did not, can illuminate the other side of the coin: what a *moral* attempt to learn and know might look like for Dostoevsky. A recent study of the intellectual appetites by the Catholic theologian Paul Griffiths helps clarify how this mode of learning might work. Building on the writings of Augustine, but drawing on Orthodox thinkers such as Pavel Florensky as well, Griffiths elaborates on the difference between the Christian virtue, *studiositas*, and the vice, *curiositas*.[18] Although these two "appetites" resemble each other superficially, the latter is in fact the "deformed kissing cousin" of the former.[19] The curious seek knowledge for the power it confers. They see the world as a place "in which ownable objects are mathetically arrayed before the aspiring owner's gaze."[20]

The studious, by contrast, seek knowledge in order to achieve "*closer reflexive intimacy*" with God's world, because they know that learning about it can teach them something about themselves (as they are God's creatures, too).[21] In his most succinct formulation, Griffiths writes that "the curious seek and find the spectacular and the studious the iconic."[22] Even the most spectacular scenes of gore and violence contain "iconic traces" that are visible to studious eyes; they can see the reflection of Christ's wounds in the lacerations of even the most sinful sufferers.[23]

"The Spectacle and the Icon" could stand as the subtitle of Dostoevsky's entire collected works. Some of his characters treat the people around them as spectacles—something to gawk at, preferably from the anonymity of a crowd or the shadow of a corner.[24] Others treat their neighbors as beings made in the image of God just like they are, who can teach them about themselves and whose pain hurts them, too. *The Idiot*'s Prince Myshkin, for example, "knows how to look" at scenes of violence and suffering. Robert Louis Jackson compares the way Myshkin looks at and thinks about a man condemned to death with the way Ivan Turgenev does the same in "The Execution of Troppmann," an 1870 article in which Turgenev describes attending the public execution of a famous murderer. According to Jackson, Turgenev "remains the quintessential observer," viewing the murderer/victim "almost as a scientific curiosity, an aberration, that is, precisely as a being *not* like us."[25] When Myshkin attends an execution, by contrast, he never loses sight of the spiritual ties that bind him and the condemned man together. He describes looking into the prisoner's face and trying "to imagine everything that went before, everything, everything" (*I*, 64; *PSS*, 8:55). Myshkin envisions every detail of the prisoner's day, from how he is surprised by the news of his execution at five o'clock in the morning to how he bargains for more time as he approaches the scaffold. Myshkin can even imagine what it would feel like to lie under the guillotine and hear the knife falling overhead: "You're bound to hear it! If I were lying there, I'd listen on purpose and hear it!" he cries (*I*, 64; *PSS*, 8:56). Rather than looking at the condemned man from a bystander's point of view, "as a being *not* like us," Myshkin tries to imaginatively live in and through his mental torture.

It is no coincidence that the painting Myshkin dreams of composing on the basis of this scene bears a muted resemblance to an icon. Set seconds before the execution, the painting will depict the prisoner kissing the cross held out for him by a priest. Although the priest and the executioner hover in the background, the central focus of the painting will be, as Myshkin puts it, "the cross and the head—there's the picture" (*I*, 66; *PSS*, 8:56). The prisoner's face is discolored, with bluish lips that "greedily" stretch toward the cross without any genuine religious feeling. But the way Myshkin frames the painting draws attention to the "iconic traces" the prisoner still possesses.

Some of the most famous icons of Jesus depict a cross and a head as well: the face of Christ laid over the schematic outline of a cross. Myshkin can see the likeness to God in even this murderer's hideous features.

WISE SERPENTS: LIPUTIN, VERKHOVENSKY, DOSTOEVSKY

In *Demons*, however, *curiositas* rules. In the distorted provincial garden where the novel takes place, characters often inhabit multiple roles: they play both Eve *and* the Serpent, the tempted and the tempter. The most excessively curious are also the best at provoking the curiosity of others and using it to their advantage. The town gossip, Liputin, is a "genuine born-spy," who "knew all the very latest news and all the ins and outs of our town, primarily where abominations were concerned" (*D*, 93; *PSS*, 10:68). He is also a dangerously compelling storyteller who has perfected the art of stimulating interest. As G——v puts it, he has "the gift of compelling people to listen to him, especially when he [is] very angry at something" (*D*, 92–93; *PSS*, 10:68). Liputin creates intrigue by provoking but never fully satisfying his listeners' curiosity, always leaving them hungry for more. "Well then, as a punishment I'm not going to say another word to you!" he teases G——v at one point. "And how you'd love to hear more, right? [. . .] I'm not lying! I've just found out—and from a most reliable source. Well, now go ahead and poke around for the rest yourself, I'll say no more. Goodbye!" (*D*, 132; *PSS*, 10:96).

Liputin paves the way for the appearance in the novel of Dostoevsky's Nechaev figure, Pyotr Verkhovensky, who possesses an even greater desire for omniscience than his father, Stepan Trofimovich, does. When Stavrogin calls Verkhovensky "the sort of little man who perhaps even now is eavesdropping on us, using his own ears or someone else's, right here in your own entryway, perhaps," he is not exaggerating (*D*, 268; *PSS*, 10:192). Verkhovensky has an "unpleasantly curious gaze that dart[s] to every corner" and assures the obedience of his fellow conspirators by spying on them (*D*, 336; *PSS*, 10:237–38). He knows that Liputin pinches his wife before bed. He knows that Tolkachenko incited a factory worker to arson, even though they were speaking in whispers, in a dark corner, in the middle of the night. "I was sitting there under the table. Don't worry, gentlemen, I know every step you take," Verkhovensky warns them (*D*, 605; *PSS*, 10:418).

Like Liputin, Verkhovensky is a tempting storyteller, but his methods are subtler and therefore more insidious. He enters the novel in a chapter titled "The Wise Serpent"—a name given to Stavrogin but one that fits Verkhovensky equally well. His speech is revoltingly rapid and smooth, his tongue almost snakelike: "You somehow began to imagine that his tongue must be of some special shape, unusually long and thin somehow, terribly red and extraordinarily sharp, its tip in constant and spontaneous movement" (*D*, 199; *PSS*, 10:144). And in his debut scene, Verkhovensky shows just what his tongue can do. When Stavrogin's mother, Varvara Petrovna, asks Stavrogin point-blank whether or not he is married to Maria Lebiadkina and Stavrogin leaves the room without answering the question, Verkhovensky takes advantage of the general mood of anticipation. He promises to tell the group "a rather interesting little thing [. . .] I'm sure that Lizaveta Nikolaevna would be curious to hear it" (*D*, 206; *PSS*, 10:148). The story he tells about Stavrogin's good deeds and Maria Lebiadkina's madness is not really meant to convince, however, but to create still more uncertainty. By comparing it to a "novel" and making a public show of intimidating the one witness who can attest to its truth, Pyotr Verkhovensky sows seeds of doubt into his listeners' minds even as he reassures them. Stepan Trofimovich says of his son's performance that "it was all deliberately made too obvious [*sshito belymi nitkami*—literally, 'it was sewn together with white thread'] so that it could be noticed by those . . . whom it concerned" (*D*, 238; *PSS*, 10:171). In short, Verkhovensky *wants* his listeners to see the stitching, to recognize his story for the construction that it is, and realize that they still do not know the whole truth.

"For them to believe it, it has to be as vague as possible [*kak mozhno temnee*]," Verkhovensky says when dictating Kirillov's false confession of murder. "With just hints. You have to show only a corner of the truth, just enough to pique them" (*D*, 687; *PSS*, 10:473). These words could stand as his manifesto, and he continues to live by them right up to his final scene in the novel. Fleeing town after the murder, Verkhovensky weasels his way into a first-class train car using this very strategy. When he promises to tell a wealthy fellow traveler "a little something" (*koe-chto*) about Stavrogin, Yulia Mikhailovna, and a certain Prince K., "though only as far as chivalry permits," the young man invites him into his carriage, and Verkhovensky escapes abroad in style (*D*, 696; *PSS*, 10:478).

Yet Verkhovensky's many tempting narratives are little more than trial runs for the one he plans to use to bring all of Russia under his control. First, he and Stavrogin will "unleash chaos" (*pustim smutu*) throughout the Russian lands (*PSS*, 10:324). The word *smuta*, which can be translated as "unrest" or "trouble," evokes the seventeenth-century Time of Troubles (*Smutnoe vremia*), when a crisis of succession led to a Polish invasion and the appearance of several pretenders to the Russian throne. But *smuta* also suggests haziness and darkness, a time when the formerly visible has become obscure and uncertainty reigns. After initiating this new dark age, Verkhovensky will start spreading rumors that Stavrogin is the legitimate heir: "Listen, I won't show you to anyone, to anyone," he tells his idol. "That's how it should be. He exists, but no one has seen him; he's in hiding. And you know, he might even be shown to one person out of a hundred thousand, for instance. And word will spread across the entire earth: 'We've seen him, we've seen him'" (*D*, 468; *PSS*, 10:326). By provoking curiosity about Stavrogin but keeping him hidden—or revealing him in such brief flashes that his power to fascinate becomes all the stronger—Verkhovensky will establish absolute allegiance to himself, the only point of access to the new tsar. Stavrogin will become the new "god of the earthly cosmos isolated from God," and Verkhovensky will be his omniscient, omnipotent high priest.

THE GOSSIP G——V

The narrator, G——v, professes his dislike for Verkhovensky and Liputin, but he resembles them in more ways than one. He attends Yulia Mikhailovna's disastrous gala, not in order to prevent the disaster but out of what he calls "an irresistible curiosity [*nepreodolimogo liubopytstva*] to listen in on what was happening (without asking any questions): how were people in our town in general talking about all these events? Besides, I wanted to have a look at Yulia Mikhailovna, if only from a distance" (*D*, 555; *PSS*, 10:385). G——v claims to hold Liza's secrets "sacred," but, as Malcolm Jones quips, he spends his entire narrative "engaged in the wholesale betrayal of personal confidences," Liza's and everyone else's.[26] To quote Slobodanka Vladiv-Glover, the entire novel "could be classified, in an extreme view, as one huge piece of local provincial gossip."[27]

Like Liputin, G——v has mastered the art of "compelling people to listen" to his stories, or, rather, compelling people to *read* them.[28] His frequent but obscure references to some future crisis help create the sense of foreboding that permeates the text. He closes one chapter by posing an intriguing question about Stepan Trofimovich: "Did he have a premonition that evening of the colossal test that was being prepared for him in the very near future? (*D*, 70; *PSS*, 10:53). He concludes a later chapter even more provocatively: "An uproar followed, but just then a remarkable incident which absolutely no one could have anticipated suddenly broke upon all of us" (*D*, 224; *PSS*, 10:163). For the novel's original readers, who read *Demons* in serial installments, G——v's cliff-hangers would have had an even more powerful effect than they do on readers today. Most of the novel's installments end either at the climax of a terrible scandal or by hinting at scandal to come. The February 1871 issue concluded with Varvara Petrovna's terrified reaction to Maria Lebiadkina's limp. G——v notes Varvara's surprised, fearful response but declines to explain the cause of her fear: "Everyone noticed it at the time, but didn't understand it . . ." (*D*, 175; *PSS*, 10:126).

The July 1871 installment ended on a similarly suspenseful note. In its final scene, Stavrogin unbinds the escaped convict Fedka—who has just offered to kill the Lebiadkins for a cash advance—and throws a wad of money into the air, leaving Fedka to interpret the gesture as he will. Readers would have been left in a state of tense uncertainty: has Stavrogin agreed to Fedka's proposition or not? But the conclusion to the penultimate, November 1872, installment was the most nail-biting of all. In it, a gloomy mob, rustling with rumors about Stavrogin's guilt, gathers around the corpses of the Lebiadkins and their maid. The chapter concludes with a tradesman's frantic address to the crowd: "'Brothers, what is this? Is it really going to be like this?' and as he said this he waved his arms" (*D*, 574, translation modified; *PSS*, 10:397). Dostoevsky's readers would *also* have been left wondering whether it was "going to be like this," for an entire suspenseful month. And, as we know, Dostoevsky's original readers really did experience painful feelings of anticipation. One fan of *The Brothers Karamazov* accused Dostoevsky's editor of intentionally delaying the next installment in order to generate interest: "No one taunts the public like he does, making the entire intellectual population of Russia wait with bated breath."[29]

On top of cliff-hangers, G——v fills his story with doubts and misgivings that rival Pyotr Verkhovensky's in their obscure provocativeness. His knowledge of the events he describes is emphatically partial, and he casts doubt on even those facts that he does reveal, making readers wonder if they are facts at all. He peppers his narrative with phrases such as "I'm sure I'm not lying" (*D*, 228; *PSS*, 10:166), "I know almost for certain" (*pochti polozhitel'no znaiu*) (*D*, 484; *PSS*, 10:337), and, in a half attempt to explain his sources, "I know from rumours of a most intimate sort (well, you may assume that Yulia Mikhailovna herself [. . .] subsequently told me a small part of this story)" (*D*, 485; *PSS*, 10:337–38). His defense raises more questions than it answers, however: why must we "assume" that she told him the story? Did she tell him, or didn't she? And if she told him only a "small part" of it, where did he get the rest?[30]

While G——v's partial knowledge can frustrate, it is also a remarkably effective tool for provoking interest. Take for example his attempts to describe a (potentially) violent meeting between Liza and Stavrogin:

> I saw their encounter in the doorway; it seemed to me that they both paused for a moment and looked at each other in a rather strange way. But I couldn't see clearly in the crowd. People asserted, on the contrary, and entirely seriously, that Liza, on glimpsing Nikolay Vsevolodovich, quickly raised her hand to the level of his face and probably would have struck him if he hadn't contrived to move away. Perhaps she was displeased by the expression on his face or by something in the way he smiled [. . .] I confess that I myself saw nothing, yet everyone insisted they had seen it, although because of the con-

> fusion there was no way that absolutely everyone could have seen it, so only some could have seen it. Except at that point I didn't believe it. I remember, though, that Nikolay Vsevolodovich was rather pale all the way back. (*D*, 372; *PSS*, 10:260–61)

Over the course of this brief passage, G——v makes three different assertions, only to cast doubt on each one. First, he says he saw Stavrogin and Liza meet in a doorway. Or did he? In the next sentence, he admits that he could not see them very well after all. Then he recounts the testimony of other eyewitnesses, only to undermine it ("there was no way that absolutely everyone could have seen it"). Finally, he claims that he didn't believe the rumors, only to introduce evidence that seems to confirm them (Stavrogin's pallor). Through all the visual confusion, hazy memories, and conflicting accounts, G——v reveals enough about Liza and Stavrogin's encounter to pique readers' curiosity but conceals enough to keep them turning pages to find out more.[31]

PROBLEMS OF OMNISCIENCE IN *DEMONS*

For each fact G——v claims not to know, however, he reveals several more that he could not have learned about in any plausible way. He explains that he is telling his story with the benefit of hindsight, but some of his knowledge nevertheless seems positively supernatural. To give one famous example, G——v recounts, word for word and with complete certainty, a private conversation that takes place between Liza and Stavrogin on his estate during the early hours of the morning. G——v could not have been eavesdropping, because he spent the night first at Yulia Mikhailovna's gala and then gazing at the fire. He could not have learned about it secondhand either: both Liza and Stavrogin die soon after this scene and presumably neither tells G——v, or anyone else, the details of their tête-à-tête before their swift, violent ends.

There are several possible explanations for the scene's existence. Maybe G——v made up the entire thing; maybe he reconstructed it from the bits and pieces of information he *was* able to uncover; or maybe his ability to relate it is simply a literary convention that Dostoevsky hopes readers will accept. Scholars have experimented with all these possibilities. Some critics have declared G——v "objective, conscientious, and sincere," while others have labeled him "a gossip and a busybody" who cannot be trusted.[32] Adam Weiner reads him as a demonic parody of the Russian chronicler-monk, an inventor who, rather than impartially recording the facts, creates entire scenes at will.[33] By contrast, David Stromberg sees G——v as a "kind of fictional forebearer to the modern figure of the 'witness' of historical trauma" who tries to make sense of the novel's tragic events by supplementing documentary evidence with good-faith reconstruction.[34] According to Joseph Frank, *Demons* has not one but *two* narrators: the eyewitness chronicler and another, omniscient narrator who relates scenes like Stavrogin's early-morning conversation with Liza.[35]

It is worth pausing to consider why the narrative structure of *Demons* has caused so much controversy. *The Idiot* and *The Brothers Karamazov* are also characterized by what Wayne Booth has called a "highly unnatural mixture of omniscience and limitation."[36] Yet the narrators of those novels have not sparked anything like the critical debate that G——v has. In fact, moments when a character narrator relates more information than he should know—a device Gérard Genette dubbed paralepsis—are relatively common in nineteenth-century European fiction.[37] According to James Phelan, certain types of paralepsis are so conventional that most readers will not even notice them. If the "departure from the mimetic code" is very short, readers may overlook it. The same holds true if it is extremely long: a character narrator's bout of omniscience "can extend for such a long duration and be so compelling that readers (a) accept it as the new normal and (b) focus their attention on what is being disclosed rather than on the break that makes the disclosure possible."[38] Finally, there is what Phelan calls the "Rule of Self-Assurance": if the narrator "does not call attention to the break, it is less likely to be noticed."[39]

Three things make the paralepsis in *Demons* especially provocative, however. First, compared with the narrators of *The Idiot* and *The Brothers Karamazov*, G——v is the most fully embodied: he is the only one who is given a (partial) name and the only one who takes part in the novel's action. G——v seems more fully human and therefore more humanly limited than many of Dostoevsky's other narrators, and so his bouts of omniscience are more surprising. Second, he breaks Phelan's "Rule of Self-Assurance." Far from masking deviations from the mimetic code, he seems to *want* us to notice them. In one instance, he relates Pyotr Verkhovensky's thoughts and feelings at such length and in such depth that most readers, I suspect, will accept their access to Verkhovensky's mind as the "new normal," an admissible, if not entirely true-to-life, literary convention. Suddenly and unexpectedly, however, G——v casts doubt on everything he has written about Pyotr Verkhovensky's internal life so far. He concludes a long description of it with the words, "This is how Pyotr Stepanovich's thoughts must have run, or something like it" (*Tak ili pochti tak dolzhen byl zadumat'sia Petr Stepanovich*) (*D*, 428; *PSS*, 10:299). With this one short line, he cloaks in darkness and uncertainty what previously seemed clear and fully revealed.[40] Dorrit Cohn famously argued that fiction can make other minds transparent to us; it allows us to know what and how characters think with a certainty that we can never have about people in our day-to-day lives.[41] But Verkhovensky's mind is neither transparent nor opaque to readers of *Demons*, and even to say that it alternates between those two poles would be an oversimplification. This is a bewildering partial transparency and partial opacity: his mind first seems inaccessible, then accessible, until we start to suspect that we never knew it in the first place.

The third, and perhaps most important, reason why G——v's occasional omniscience disturbs is that *Demons* explicitly condemns the desire for totalizing knowledge, the desire to become a *man-god* who would usurp God's powers and God's place. A blasphemous inversion of Christ's designation as God-man, the term is introduced into the novel by Kirillov, who kills himself with the aim of becoming a kind of secular Jesus. (It is a self-defeating dream, however: Kirillov's suicide ends not with his transformation into a god but instead with his brain splattered against the wall.) Only the most misguided, deluded, or wicked characters in *Demons* try to attain absolute knowledge of the world around them, and G——v's occasional superhuman insight raises the possibility that he is one of them. Sometimes he expresses uncertainty about the trustworthiness of the information he relays, but at others he recounts events with such authority that he really does resemble the omniscient narrator Joseph Frank takes him to (sometimes) be—all-seeing and all-knowing. G——v morphs from human to superhuman narrator, from man to *man-god* and back again.[42]

In this novel, however, even the possibility of such transformations is extremely troubling. No one could have overheard Liza and Stavrogin's early-morning conversation, but there *is* someone who tries. Their tête-à-tête ends only when Pyotr Verkhovensky, who has been lurking outside the door, attempting to listen in on it, bursts into the room with "eyes looking as if they wanted to plumb the depths of Stavrogin's soul" (*D*, 582; *PSS*, 10:402). G——v's retrospective attempts to penetrate into Stavrogin's internal world are just as invasive. Although G——v sometimes admits that he cannot read Stavrogin's mind (*D*, 228; *PSS*, 10:166), at other points he relates his protagonist's internal thoughts and feelings confidently and without hesitation (*PSS*, 10:204, 219, 220, 398). Through the process of literary creation, G——v seems to have achieved something Stepan Trofimovich could only dream about: he has taken up God's spot on Olympus and gained a new, superhuman "insight" into his subject matter.

There is an important difference between G——v's and Verkhovensky's curiosity, however. Verkhovensky's is plainly pernicious: he wants to "plumb the depths of Stavrogin's soul" in order to manipulate him more effectively. G——v's interest in Stavrogin is more ambiguous. It is not clearly voyeuristic, but it is not clearly compassionate either. Nor does Dostoevsky provide unequivocal evidence either of G——v's deceitfulness or of his good faith. Instead, he keeps us wondering: should we accept G——v's version of events as his best effort to make sense of what has happened? Or should we second-guess everything he writes, knowing that it is riddled with rumor, speculation, and pretensions to omniscience? Ultimately, Dostoevsky leaves G——v's reliability, like his last name, half-concealed and curiosity-provoking.[43]

Thanks to an accident of fate, even the novel's publication history contributes to the reveal-conceal-reveal-conceal pattern of its overall design. Dostoevsky originally planned to conclude part 2 with "At Tikhon's," a chapter that would explain the psychological motivation underlying much of Stavrogin's otherwise inexplicable behavior. In the missing chapter, Stavrogin would visit a local monk and confess to raping a young girl, who hangs herself as a result. But the editor of the *Russian Herald* (*Russkii vestnik*), Mikhail Katkov, deemed the chapter too scandalous to publish. Although Dostoevsky tried to revise it (concealing the rape scene further and further from view), it was cut from the manuscript at the last minute.[44] Careful readers of *Demons* might still have noticed that something was missing, however. At the beginning of part 2 there is a reference to Tikhon that goes nowhere: Stavrogin promises to visit him but never does (*D* 284; *PSS*, 10:203).

Any readers who cried foul would have had to wait a long time for their curiosity to be satisfied. Dostoevsky did not reincorporate "At Tikhon's" into later versions of the text. Perhaps he worried it would never pass the censorship. Perhaps, as W. J. Leatherbarrow has suggested, he excluded it for artistic purposes, in order to keep Stavrogin "a half-grasped enigma."[45] Whatever the reason, the excised chapter was not published until long after Dostoevsky's death. Even today, most editions of *Demons* half reveal, half conceal the Tikhon chapter, including it as an appendix in the back of the novel, where many readers will fail to notice it altogether.[46] Indeed, the suspense that builds up over the course of the novel never fully dissipates. Even its last line poses a puzzle. In it, we learn that at Stavrogin's autopsy, doctors "rejected insanity completely and resolutely" (*D*, 748; *PSS*, 10:516). Stavrogin's sanity has long been in question, but the town doctors' pronouncement leaves the matter as murky as ever. Surely no autopsy can prove or disprove the presence of mental illness; not all psychological disorders leave a physical, visible trace. These provincial doctors have succumbed to the illusion of omniscience as well.

THE CURIOUS READER

Demons seems designed to provoke its reader's curiosity from page 1 to page 516. This is perhaps not surprising: after all, reading is an inherently curious activity. Peter Brooks defines narrative as a seduction and a subjugation, "the play of desire in time that makes us turn pages and strive toward narrative ends."[47] Although Brooks does not specifically use the word "curiosity" to describe this narrative drive, other critics have made the connection for him. Lorri Nandrea calls curiosity "isomorphic with the arc of plot in nineteenth-century novels, as read through the lens of psychoanalysis by theorists like Peter Brooks. Curiosity as a state of tension or agitation propels the forward movement of reader, and plot, toward closure."[48] In *Demons*, Dostoevsky reminds readers of this fact again and again. Through metaliterary allusions that drive home the parallel between reading *about* scenes of violence and scandal and *witnessing* them, Dostoevsky highlights his readers' own curious impulses, especially at those moments when they are most in danger of spiraling out of control.

In a passage that serves as one of the epigraphs to this chapter, Liputin sneers at Stepan Trofimovich: "It's all very well for you to shout about gossip and spying, but observe that it's after you've squeezed everything out of me, and with such an excess of curiosity besides" (*D*, 114; *PSS*, 10:84). His words apply not only to Stepan Trofimovich but to the novel's interested readers as well. And the more engaged we become in the novel's unfolding plot, the harder it becomes to escape Liputin's accusation. We may very well be consuming Liputin's tales—which serve as essential sources of plot information—with nearly the same degree of curiosity that his listeners do.[49]

The novel's chapter headings draw attention to readerly curiosity, too. Part 2, chapter 4 is titled "All Wait Expectantly"—an "all" that can be taken to include not just the novel's characters but also its engaged *readers*. The title of part 3, chapter 3—"A Finished Romance" ("Zakonchennyi roman")—is even more revealing. A play on words, it could be taken to mean either the "finished romance" between Liza and Stavrogin or a "finished *novel*." "Zakonchennyi roman" was the first chapter of *Demons*' final serial installment. So when Dostoevsky's original readers took up the long-awaited finale to this most "engaging" novel, the pun would have been the first thing that caught their eyes. It serves as a subtle reminder: this is the denouement they have been waiting for, and it will be a terrible one. The Lebiadkins, Liza, Kirillov, Shatov, Marie Shatova and her child, the convict Fedka, and Stavrogin all die violent deaths. If, like the gawkers at Yulia Mikhailovna's gala, readers have been "rubbing their hands in anticipation" of the denouement, then they have been rubbing them in anticipation of a bloodbath (*D*, 509; *PSS*, 10:354).

COMPASSIONATE INTEREST

My argument thus far raises an important question: why did Dostoevsky decide to write a violent, suspenseful novel like *Demons* in the first place? The answer, I believe, is that for Dostoevsky demonstrating too little curiosity about the suffering of others is an even greater moral failing than showing too much. Neil Kenny has noted the "extraordinary moral reversibility" of curiosity as a concept: it can have negative, neutral, or positive connotations, depending on context.[50] Dostoevsky felt this reversibility keenly. In his fictional world, the desire to know about another person can be a virtue *or* a vice, depending on one's emotional attitude toward the person in question. Even Liputin's rumormongering contains a hint of its moral flip side. As G——v puts it, "one had to marvel at the extent to which [Liputin] took to *heart* things that sometimes didn't concern him at all" (*D*, 93; *PSS*, 10:68; emphasis added). The malicious gossip takes intense interest in other people's trials and tribulations; but the compassionate person takes intense interest in them as well.[51]

"Curiosity is seeing your way out of your place. It is looking beyond," writes one critic, and Dostoevsky's most self-absorbed characters often demonstrate a *lack* of curiosity, failing to look beyond themselves.[52] The self-involved Stepan Trofimovich, for example, realizes too late that he has failed to "take to heart" Liza's suffering. When he meets her, muddied and tear-stained, on her way to see the bodies of the Lebiadkins, he is so immersed in his own troubles that he does not find out what is wrong. In the moments of moral lucidity before his death, Stepan Trofimovich realizes that he has committed a grave blunder: "I didn't ask, I didn't find out! I was thinking only of myself! Oh, what's become of her, do you know what's become of her? (*D*, 720; *PSS*, 10:496). His newfound interest in Liza's pain comes too late, however; she has been killed by the mob in front of the Lebiadkins' house, and he has missed his chance to help her.

The writer Karmazinov's squeamish refusal to look upon human suffering is even more negatively marked. A vicious caricature of Turgenev, Karmazinov writes an article about witnessing a shipwreck, which G——v paraphrases ironically: "Why are you looking at this drowned woman with the dead child in her dead arms? Look at me instead, and see how I endured this spectacle and turned away from it. You see, I stood with my back to it; you see, I am horrified and have not the strength to look back; I am shutting my eyes tight—that's so interesting, is it not?" (*D*, 95; *PSS*, 10:70). Instead of taking an interest in the dead woman and her child, Karmazinov tries to attract interest to himself. We know that Dostoevsky would have agreed with his narrator's criticism. This passage parodies both Turgenev's reputation for cowardice at sea and his aforementioned article "The Execution of Troppmann." In it, Turgenev remains the "quintessential observer" right up to the last second before the guillotine comes crashing down. At that moment he averts his gaze, looking back only after the execution is over. Dostoevsky had nothing but disdain for Turgenev's article. "Why is he continually acting embarrassed and insisting that he had no right to be [at the execution]?" Dostoevsky protested in a letter. "Yes, of course, if he came only to see a show; but a person living on the surface of the earth does not have the right to turn away and ignore what is happening on earth, and there are higher *moral* reasons for this" (*PSS*, 29.1:127–28). Here, more clearly than anywhere else in his writings, Dostoevsky reveals how he believes we should respond to the suffering of others, especially when we can do nothing to relieve it. We should not treat it as a show, but we should not look away from it either. It should always *interest* us.

The scene when Marie Shatova returns to her husband, only to go directly into labor with Stavrogin's child, shows why turning *toward* other people's pain is so important in Dostoevsky's world. As the labor becomes more difficult, the midwife chases Shatov out of the room, but he can still hear Marie's cries, "dreadful [*uzhasnye*], sheer animal cries, unbearable, impossible" (*D*, 654; *PSS*, 10:451). In a gesture akin to Karmazinov shutting his eyes, Shatov tries to cover his ears, but another, stronger impulse prevents him: "He thought of stopping up his ears, but couldn't do so, and fell on his knees, unconsciously repeating, 'Marie, Marie!'" (*D*, 654; *PSS*, 10:451). Like the novel's most curious characters, Shatov listens through a closed door to something he was not invited to hear. But unlike those spies, he does not eavesdrop on Marie's pain, listening to it as if from above, or as a bystander (*postoronnii*), someone who is standing to the side of it. Instead, he suffers along with her. An earlier moment in the same scene demonstrates just how much Marie's suffering hurts Shatov, too. When Marie "directed this tormented look at him, he suddenly understood that this being, so beloved, was suffering and perhaps had been wronged. His heart sank. He looked into her features with pain [*s bol'iu*]" (*D*, 630, translation modified; *PSS*, 10:435).

In "At Tikhon's," Stavrogin speculates that "we always find something pleasing in someone else's misfortune [*v chuzhoi bede*]," and Tikhon confirms the truth of his supposition (*D*, 782; *PSS*, 11:26). In Shatov's case the maxim no longer holds true, however, because his wife's suffering is no longer other to him. By opening himself up to her pain-filled and pain*ful* cries, he makes her suffering at least partly his own. Significantly, this experience of compassion propels Shatov toward his first spontaneous religious gesture in the novel. He has been trying (and failing) to believe in God for years. But when he hears his wife's screams, he unconsciously falls to his knees in prayer. And when he finally hears the newborn cry, he crosses himself without a second thought.[53]

FROM SPYING TO COSUFFERING AND BACK AGAIN

Compassion (*sostradanie*—literally, "suffering with") is a key moral emotion for Dostoevsky, but it is also a tricky one, a "messy, unhygienic" business that can easily go wrong.[54] Alina Wyman has shown just how far. Wyman argues that "active empathy"—a concept she develops with the help of Max Scheler and Mikhail Bakhtin—represents the challenging ideal of interpersonal understanding in Dostoevsky's fiction. But such empathetic acts are hard to achieve and even harder to maintain. They require a delicate balance of emotional distance and emotional proximity: the loving empathizer must "imagine [another's] consciousness from within" but without "peer[ing] *through* another's face."[55] She must attempt to understand how the other person feels but also recognize the limits of her own understanding, so that empathy does not become just another illusion of omniscience.[56] According to Wyman, even Dostoevsky's most compassionate characters—like Prince Myshkin—often get the balance wrong. Sometimes Myshkin assumes a godlike ability to predict his interlocutors' actions; at others, he becomes so overwhelmed by their suffering that it paralyzes him.[57]

The characters in *Demons* tend to get the balance wrong as well. They oscillate between the extremes of *curiositas* and *studiositas*, "greedy curiosity" on the one hand and compassionate interest on the other. G——v provides some of the best examples of this oscillation in action. As the plot builds toward Yulia Mikhailovna's scandalous gala, G——v runs frantically around town, now trying to warn the governor's wife of the impending catastrophe, now trying to dissociate himself from the entire affair: "Really and truly, what business is it of mine?" he asks himself (*D*, 525; *PSS*, 10:364). But he always stays to find out what will happen next. When he hears that Liza has ruined her reputation by running off to Stavrogin's, his first response is a purely compassionate one: "The disaster had struck me to the very heart. I was pained almost to the point of tears; yes, perhaps I was even crying. I had absolutely no idea what to do" (*D*, 554; *PSS*, 10:384). Yet G——v's initial fellow feeling of pain—already complicated by his own romantic interest in Liza—quickly morphs into the desire not to help her but to find out more: "That she was ruined, utterly ruined I had no doubt, but I had absolutely no understanding of the psychological aspect of the matter, especially after yesterday's scene between her and Stavrogin" (*D*, 554; *PSS*, 10:384).

G——v's fixation on the "psychological aspect" of Liza's catastrophe implies that his interest has begun to transform from the compassionate-empathic into the scientific-intellectual. As he scurries around town trying to gather more information, even he has to admit that his behavior bears an uncomfortable likeness to gossip: "To run around and make inquiries in the houses of gloating acquaintances, where of course the news would already have spread by now, struck me as disgusting, and demeaning to Liza besides. But strangely enough I ran to Darya Pavlovna's . . ." (*D*, 554; *PSS*, 10:384). When G——v breathlessly reports the news to Shatov, Shatov tells him to visit Liputin: "You'll learn everything there" (*D*, 555; *PSS*, 10:384). I read Shatov's words as a covert insult: if you are so anxious to learn all the dirty details, go see Liputin. If it is gossip you want, go visit the town rumor-monger himself. The pain and concern G——v first felt when he learned of Liza's disaster have become tainted by his desire to know more for the sake of knowing more, even at the expense of demeaning someone he loves.

The conspirators' reactions to Shatov's death are similarly unstable, fluctuating between an emotionally distant curiosity at the sight of his corpse and a horrified awareness of their own guilt. After Tolkachenko, Erkel, and Liputin pin Shatov to the ground, and Verkhovensky shoots him, the entire group gathers around the body:

> Liputin was standing in front, right by the corpse. Virginsky was behind him, peering over his shoulder with a peculiar, seemingly bystander's curiosity [*postoronnim liubopytstvom*], even standing on tiptoe to have a better look. And Liamshin had hidden behind Virginsky and would peer out from behind him occasionally and apprehensively, and then immediately hide himself again. (*D*, 669, translation modified; *PSS*, 10:461)

Although they were forewarned of the killing, allowed it to happen, and looked on as it did, Virginsky and Liamshin did not actively participate in the crime. Standing behind the more obvious murderer—who serves as both a literal and metaphorical barrier separating them from the bloodshed—they can indulge in a brief illusion of moral distance, of being mere bystanders to Shatov's death. The sight of his bloodied corpse quickly shatters the illusion, however. Virginsky cries, "This isn't right, it isn't right!" and Liamshin lets out a terrible, animal-like scream. But the horror Shatov's corpse arouses in them, and their awareness of the responsibility they bear for his death, does not last long either. Once they throw Shatov's body into the pond, "Pyotr Stepanovich raised his lantern, and they all leaned forward behind him, looking on with curiosity as the dead man disappeared under the water, but now nothing could be seen" (*D*, 671, translation modified; *PSS*, 10:462). Just as Liamshin and Virginsky had earlier hidden behind Liputin, now the entire group stands behind Verkhovensky—the most obviously guilty one of all. Once again, the shield he provides allows them to imagine themselves mere curious onlookers at, rather than participants in, a grisly murder. For a few short moments anyway.

In *Demons*, Dostoevsky suggests that nearly everyone wavers to some degree between feeling a participatory compassion for and a "bystander's curiosity" about other people's misfortunes. Even the saintly monk Tikhon acknowledges that he may, on some level, take "delight" in Stavrogin's suffering (*D*, 782; *PSS*, 11:27). Even he is not perfectly compassionate all the time.[58] Yet curiosity's moral reversibility is also the source of its ethical potential and what makes even the greediest curiosity preferable to none in Dostoevsky's eyes. Because the line separating insatiable curiosity from "insatiable compassion" is narrow, a change in emotional orientation can make one slide into the other. G——v notes that some "admirers" of town fires will nevertheless throw themselves into the flames in order to save an old woman or a child.[59] It is not clear what motivates these gawkers-turned-heroes—whether bravado, vanity, compassion, or some mixture of the three. What is clear, however, is that if the fire had not attracted them in the first place, they would not have saved the child either.

By comparison, the lack of interest is much more difficult to redeem. Stavrogin represents the demon of boredom and disengagement in the novel, and he is a more frightening figure than Liputin, the convict Fedka, and Pyotr Verkhovensky combined. In "At Tikhon's" this "indolent" nobleman describes himself with a quotation from the book of Revelation: "I know your works, you are neither cold nor hot! Would that you were cold or hot! Because you are lukewarm, and neither cold nor hot, I will spue you out of my mouth" (*D*, 759; *PSS*, 11:11).[60] Stavrogin calls this a reference to "the indifferent ones" (*dlia ravnodushnykh*), and "indifferent" may be the best adjective to describe him.

In fact, the "disease of indifference" is what *drives* Stavrogin to hurt other people in the first place (*D*, 765; *PSS*, 11:15). He is experiencing a particularly severe bout of this malaise when he decides to drum up some interest in life by raping his prepubescent neighbor, Matryosha. Horribly, Stavrogin derives the most excitement not from the rape or even from the expectation of punishment but from the young girl's suicide afterward.[61] When Matryosha disappears into a closet and he begins to suspect what has happened to her, he squeezes every ounce of suspense out of the situation that he possibly can. Twenty minutes pass, but he drags out his anticipation for yet another quarter hour. Heart pounding, he counts down the last three minutes before creeping up to the closet door. Even then, he continues to delay gratification. Instead of opening the closet and immediately finding out what has happened, he stands "on tiptoe" and peeks through a crack in the door, staring into the semidarkness until he is "absolutely sure" Matryosha is dead (*D*, 772; *PSS*, 11:19). Stavrogin's body language perfectly captures the unequal power dynamics of the scene: a wealthy nobleman peers voyeuristically at the corpse of his poor young victim (even standing on tiptoe, as if to exaggerate the height from which he looks *down* at her).[62] Neither this titillating event nor the increasing guilt that he feels over what he has done can cure Stavrogin of his "disease," however. In the letter that he writes to Dasha before hanging himself, Stavrogin admits that he is incapable of love, hate, or strong emotions of any kind. It is only fitting that he dreams of moving to a dark, cramped ravine in Switzerland, a place he calls "dull" or "boring" (*skuchno*) (*PSS*, 10:513).[63]

READING AS SPYING AND GOSSIP, OR EMPATHY, SYMPATHY, AND COMPASSION?

Dostoevsky's investigations into how we respond to the pain of others—including fictional others whose fictional sufferings we encounter on the pages of novels—remain relevant to debates in the study of narrative ethics today. Like Dostoevsky, contemporary scholars interested in the ethics of reading return repeatedly to several major questions: What drives us to read novels in the first place? Can reading be a morally formative experience? Can it make us more empathic or more attuned to the complexities of ethical judgment in our day-to-day lives? Some critics have tried to understand if and how novels engage readers' empathy, sympathy, and compassion for their characters, while others, taking a different tack, have emphasized the similarity between reading novels and gossip and spying. *Demons* reveals the link that binds these two strands of scholarly inquiry. It suggests that while novels *may* activate readers' compassion, they never do so reliably, and never in an uncomplicated way.

Martha Nussbaum set the terms of debate for the first camp. In her influential *Love's Knowledge*, she argues that reading novels, or at least certain classics, fine-tunes our moral awareness, attentiveness, and, ultimately, our capacity for love.[64] Ever since, scholars interested in the relationship between empathy and reading have taken her work as a point of departure, even when they vigorously challenge her conclusions. Suzanne Keen, for example, questions whether narrative empathy is a source of "altruism in the real world," insisting that the empathy we experience while reading novels does not necessarily translate into our daily lives, no matter how much professors of literature might like to think that it does.[65] Like Keen, Amy Coplan forwards a "pluralist account" of the way readers engage with works of fiction. Examining the many ways literary texts can trigger empathy (usually defined as "feeling with"), sympathy (usually defined as "feeling for"), and emotional contagion, Coplan concludes that empathic engagement is an important, but by no means the only, way in which readers interact with literary characters.[66] More recently, there has been a surge of interest among scholars of Victorian literature in how British novelists not only explore the virtues and pitfalls of sympathy but also try to train their readers in the "right" kind.[67]

At the head of the second camp stands Patricia Meyer Spacks, who argues that "reading novels establishes a tie resembling that of gossip, since what reader and narrator share is a set of responses to the private doings of richly imagined individuals."[68] Following Meyer Spacks is Blakey Vermeule, who posits that a love of gossip motivates reading practices to this day: "Why else do we allow ourselves to become absorbed in stories about people we have never met and never will meet if not to get large doses of the delicious social information we crave?" she asks.[69] Thomas Pavel has even speculated that writers who want to spark their readers' interest could use one of two tests for choosing a plot: the "gossip test" (would it make for a juicy piece of gossip?) or the "news test" (would it make newspaper headlines?).[70] Alongside the critics who trace the interconnections between novels and gossip (*hearing* about the exciting, intimate details of other people's lives) are those who trace the similarities between novels and spying (*peeking* at the same). Bakhtin famously called novels of private life the "literature of snooping about, of overhearing 'how others live,'" and recent scholars have expanded on his claim.[71] Jeremy Hawthorn, for example, suggests that we read novels in order to indulge our voyeuristic impulses, while circumventing the guilt and shame that we feel when we spy on our real-life neighbors.[72]

Demons implies that Nussbaum, Keene, Vermeule, and Hawthorn are all right, but only partly so. In this novel, compassionate interest and the impulse to gossip and spy are two sides of the same coin, two different ways in which our fascination with other people (including fictional people) can manifest itself. The difference between them lies in our willingness to suffer too. Will we love the sufferer as ourselves? Or will we treat his pain as a spectacle that we can watch from a safe distance, without any danger of suffering along with him? To make matters even more complicated, our emotional attitude toward other people is rarely stable, as Dostoevsky emphasizes time and again. Even his most positive characters sometimes respond to the sight, sound, or rumor of one another's pain and misfortune with alternating feelings of compassion and *curiositas*. The parallels that Dostoevsky builds between readers *of* the novel and the now voyeuristic, now compassionate observer characters *in* the novel hint that he expected readers to respond to its scenes of violence in a similarly fluctuating way. Novel reading can take the form of curious spying on characters' thoughts and feelings or an empathetic participation in them, or both or neither. Which it resembles more depends on the particular reader and her emotional relationship with each character, a relationship that is likely to shift and change over time.

Naturally, authors can encourage their readers to empathize with certain characters, whether by portraying them sympathetically or inflecting the narrative with their point of view. Dostoevsky, for one, has long had a reputation for doing just that. According to Vyacheslav Ivanov, Dostoevsky has a preternatural capacity for emotional "penetration," an almost otherworldly ability to represent the depths of another person's soul "not as an object but as another subject" with its own "distinctive, boundless, and sovereign" existence.[73] Like Ivanov, Bakhtin argues that Dostoevsky develops his poetics explicitly in *opposition* to the literature of "spying" and "overhearing." Rather than representing his characters as objects "that can be spied upon, defined, predicted apart from its own will, 'at second hand,'" Dostoevsky writes about them as if they were "*actually present*, someone who hears him (the author) and is *capable of answering him*" (*PDP*, 59, 63; *SS*, 70, 75). In Dostoevsky's novels, Bakhtin claims, "not a single element of the work is structured from the point of view of a nonparticipating 'third person' [*bezuchastnogo 'tret'ego'*]" (*PDP*, 18; *SS*, 24). As I have tried to show, however, the narrator of *Demons does* spy on his subjects, at least on occasion. Most of what he knows about them he has learned at second hand. And sometimes he even seems to transform into an omniscient narrator, a *man-god*–like "nonparticipating 'third person'" in relation to the story he tells.[74]

Moreover, an author's attitude toward his characters does not necessarily determine the *reader's*, which is subject to extratextual forces outside his control. Amy Coplan's account of the emotionally variable experience of reading maps especially well onto the imagery in *Demons*. Coplan posits that "the reader is neither fixed nor immobile; he is neither forced to mirror exactly the characters' experiences nor forced to observe the characters' experiences from the outside."[75] It is thanks to our emotional "mobility" as readers—our ability to become utterly absorbed in a character's thoughts and feelings but also to pause, to reflect on what we have read, and to consider what it might look like from another point of view—that we can both empathize with a character and maintain the necessary emotional distance in order to evaluate his actions as wise or foolish, moral or immoral, aesthetically satisfying or dissatisfying within the novel's larger structure. This mobility also means, however, that the author ultimately cannot control which characters readers empathize with, if they empathize with any.[76] In fact, readers may choose to disengage from the characters' emotions entirely, devoting themselves exclusively to careful literary analysis instead. Or they may go to the opposite extreme and identify with characters to a pathological degree—like Dostoevsky's Underground Man, who so loves to imagine himself a novelistic hero that he reads and daydreams his life away.

Stavrogin's lukewarm boredom maps onto a potential reader response as well. Some readers of *Demons* will find the characters' hysterical outbursts tediously long-winded. They will either close the book out of boredom or apathetically keep reading in spite of it, following the heroes' dramas with as little interest as the briefly appearing Petersburg prince, who turns his pince-nez toward a guffawing German, but "without the slightest curiosity"

(*D*, 500; *PSS*, 10:349). I suspect, however, that Dostoevsky would consider this the worst possible outcome, indicating an artistic failure on the author's part, an ethical failure on the reader's part, or both. If readers remain disengaged from the suffering that the novel depicts, then his project has missed its mark.

THE SECOND EPIGRAPH: AGAINST SCAPEGOATING

Dostoevsky writes *Demons* knowing that this bloody and suspenseful novel, based on a scandalous true crime, might provoke his readers' voyeuristic impulses. But for him the alternatives—writing a novel that either ignores or leaves readers indifferent to the human suffering around them—are much worse. His solution to the problem, albeit an uneasy one, is to use an entire arsenal of suspense-building techniques in order to engage reader interest in scenes of violence and pain. At the same time, he highlights the moments when that interest is most likely to morph from compassionate concern into a bystander's curiosity, thus helping keep readers on their guard against it.

Even before *Demons* begins, Dostoevsky draws our attention to the ethical task facing us as the interpreters of an extremely violent text. The novel's famous second epigraph is an excerpt from the story of the Gadarene swine in the Gospel according to Luke:[77]

> Now there on the hillside a large herd of swine was feeding; and the demons begged Jesus to let them enter these. So he gave them permission. Then the demons came out of the man and entered the swine, and the herd rushed down the steep bank into the lake and was drowned.
>
> When the swineherds saw what had happened, they ran off and told it in the city and in the country. Then people came out to see what had happened, and when they came to Jesus, they found the man from whom the demons had gone sitting at the feet of Jesus, clothed and in his right mind. And they were afraid [*uzhasnulis'*]. Those who had seen it told them how the one who had been possessed by demons had been healed. (Luke 8:32–36 [New Revised Standard Version])

The second epigraph is usually interpreted as an allegory for the novel's major events. On his deathbed, Stepan Trofimovich will read it as such: the demoniac, he explains, is Russia, the demons are the spiritual contagions that have "possessed" it, and the drowned herd of swine is Stepan Trofimovich and the rest of the radical intelligentsia, who will destroy themselves, leaving Russia healed by Christ's side. Most extended analyses of *Demons* include a discussion of the first half of the epigraph (which describes the drowning of the swine). None that I am aware of, however, examines the second, which recounts how the townsfolk react to hearing eyewitnesses tell the story of the violent healing. But it is just as significant. If the drowning of the swine parallels the bloody events *in* the novel, then the swineherd eyewitnesses parallel the novel's narrator, G——v, and the townsfolk parallel *us*, its readers. The second epigraph, thus, foreshadows not only the novel's gruesome subject matter but its manner of transmission and reception as well.

Dostoevsky cuts off his Gospel epigraph at a key moment in the text. In the very next line of Luke's story, the listeners expel Jesus from their town. By leaving out this conclusion, Dostoevsky also leaves open a door to the possibility that this time the townsfolk (stand-ins for the novel's readers) will react differently. Perhaps they will find the bloody story a little bit *too* entertaining; perhaps, like the Gospel listeners, they will feel so much horror that they will throw the book down halfway through; or perhaps they will respond in a more productive way. The excised chapter "At Tikhon's" hints at what that way might be. In it, Tikhon describes the ideal response to a written account of violence and pain. After he reads Stavrogin's confession—which the young man is planning to distribute around town—the monk warns him that he may not like the public's response. Most of Stavrogin's readers will laugh, taking malicious joy in Stavrogin's suffering and the suffering he has caused. (In a subsequent draft, Dostoevsky added an extra detail: "There will also be curiosity about the madman, because they will consider you a madman" [*PSS*, 12:118].) But a small, almost invisible minority—whom Tikhon calls "the pure souls"—will respond to Stavrogin's confession in a different way. They will "be horrified [*uzhasnutsia*] and will blame themselves" (*D*, 782; *PSS*, 11:26). They will not mentally close their eyes to this story of suffering or take voyeuristic pleasure from reading about it, but instead witness it simply, and then turn their gaze inward.

Most readers of *Demons* cannot count themselves among Tikhon's "pure souls." After all, even Tikhon does not include himself in their number. Yet Dostoevsky circuitously leads the novel's impure readers, receivers of a story not unlike Stavrogin's confession in its gruesomeness, toward Tikhon's ideal response: a feeling of shared guilt and personal responsibility for the chief sins that the novel depicts.[78] Readers may feel tempted to dismiss morally repulsive characters like Liputin and Pyotr Verkhovensky and distance themselves from their bad deeds. Yet by pushing us to consider what we have in common even with someone as evil as Verkhovensky (the impulses to power, control, and godlike totalizing knowledge), Dostoevsky discourages us from doing so. He takes curiosity—a famously outwardly oriented impulse that "fears and shudders at what lies within"—and turns it into a tool for self-reflection.

Perhaps the only unambiguous aspect of *Demons'* plot is how many different people share responsibility for its disasters. As Malcolm Jones puts it, "Who, indeed, is not in some measure responsible for the catastrophe which overtakes 'our town'?"[79] Yulia Mikhailovna for her gullibility and ambition? The drunken crowds for causing the ruckus at the gala? The townsfolk who come not in order to help maintain order but out of a gleeful desire to find out what will happen next? Pyotr Verkhovensky for planning everything? Stavrogin for inspiring Verkhovensky? Or Stepan Trofimovich, the only real father figure either of them has ever had, for how he helped shape their characters? In an 1873 entry of his *Writer's Diary*, Dostoevsky explained that his aim in *Demons* was not to tell the story of a single individual (Sergei Nechaev) but instead to investigate the broader social patterns that facilitated his unlikely rise to power: "How is it possible in our changing and astonishing society of today to have not a Nechaev but *Nechaevs*, and how does it happen that these *Nechaevs* eventually acquire their own Nechaevists?" (*WD1*, 279; *PSS*, 21:125). Dostoevsky does not set out to investigate the guilt of one person but the guilt of an entire nation.

Dostoevsky insisted that even *he* had something in common with Nechaev and his followers. Remembering his own youthful, quasi-revolutionary activities—which led to years of hard labor in Siberia—Dostoevsky wrote, "But let me say one thing about myself alone: a *Nechaev* I probably could never have become, but a *Nechaevist*—well, of that I can't be sure; perhaps I could have become one . . . in the days of my youth" (*WD1*, 284; *PSS*, 21:129). Indeed, Dostoevsky has more in common with the characters in this novel than a youthful weakness for political conspiracy. If they are a little bit *too* interested in scandal, murder, and suicide, then Dostoevsky himself is as much or more so. To quote Merezhkovsky once again, it is Dostoevsky's own "insatiable curiosity" about the "most frightening and shameful ulcers of the human soul" that prompted him to write this book in the first place.

In one of the key scenes in *Demons*, Shatov experiences a spontaneous outpouring of love for his enemies. "All are guilty, all are guilty and . . . if only everybody were convinced of that!" he murmurs to himself (*D*, 646; *PSS*, 10:446). *Demons* is designed to convince its readers, and perhaps even its author, of precisely that. Interestingly, the story of the Gadarene demoniac has been interpreted as a lesson about communal guilt by another thinker as well. René Girard reads the relationship between the townsfolk and the demoniac as a prototypical example of group violence. The possessed man serves as a scapegoat for the entire community: by expelling him from the town (an expulsion masked as voluntary withdrawal), the townsfolk reinforce their bond with one another. Their common social identity as the good, righteous, and sane is founded on their rejection of him, the wild, demon-possessed lunatic and convenient fall guy for their social anxieties. According to Girard, the townsfolk send Jesus away at the end of the story because they do not actually want the demoniac to be healed. Their social coherence depends on his remaining an outsider. Once he is cured and able to return to normal village life, they find themselves without a scapegoat and so with no one but themselves to blame for the social disorders that plague them.[80]

Girard's reading of the Gospel story resonates with both the plot and the narrative dynamics of *Demons*. Over the course of the novel, Dostoevsky shows the "scapegoat mechanism" in action more than once. The scene in which an angry mob attacks Liza, for example, has all the attributes of Girardian collective violence. A large group encircles a powerless victim, who symbolizes the undesirable traits of the community itself. The crowd accuses Liza of two crimes, murder and voyeurism: "It's not enough for them to commit murder, they have to come and look!" someone shouts (*D*, 597; *PSS*, 10:413). But, of course, every person in the mob is guilty of these same two crimes: they have *also* come to look at the dead bodies, and they are about to commit a group murder. They punish her with such righteous indignation, perhaps, in order to convince themselves that the labels "murderer" and "voyeur" do not apply to them too.

If we read the second epigraph through a Girardian lens, then Dostoevsky's decision to leave out the expulsion of Jesus acquires yet another shade of meaning. It raises the possibility that this time the townsfolk—and, by extension, the novel's readers—*may* stop scapegoating. They may form a new kind of community, one created not by expelling outsiders but through an awareness of the personal responsibility of each for all. As Dostoevsky's next two novels show, however, the building of such an ideal collective is an extraordinarily difficult task. *The Adolescent* demonstrates that the moral regeneration of just one person can be a seemingly endless project. And in *The Brothers Karamazov*, establishing a community in which "all will be holy and will love one another, and there will be neither rich nor poor, neither exalted nor humiliated" turns out to be nearly impossible (*BK*, 31; *PSS*, 14:29).

Chapter Two

The Endings of *The Adolescent*

(Atheism.) Here I never could come to a conclusion . . . [*Tut ia nikogda ne umel konchit'* . . .]
—Versilov, the notebooks to *The Adolescent*

IN 1989 WAYNE BOOTH took aim at what he called a "fashionable generalization about ethical effect": the assumption "that techniques or styles that 'close' questions are always inferior, the very mark of the nonliterary or nonaesthetic or didactic," while "techniques that raise questions, that leave the fiction open-ended and the reader unresolved are in general superior."[1] This assumption has long reigned in Dostoevsky studies as well, thanks in large part to Bakhtin's enormous influence. For Bakhtin, "rigorous unfinalizability [*nezavershennost'*] and dialogic openness [*otkrytost'*]" are what make a Dostoevsky novel a Dostoevsky novel (*PDP*, 272; *SS*, 6:300). According to him, Dostoevsky's works resist narrative closure on principle: participating in a "carnival sense of the world," which "knows no period, and is, in fact, hostile to any sort of *conclusive conclusion* [*okonchatel'nomu kontsu*]," they depict a universe that "is open and free," in which "*everything is still in the future and will always be in the future*" (*vse vperedi i vsegda budet vperedi*) (*PDP*, 165–66; *SS*, 6:186–87).[2]

Bakhtin's argument raises as many questions as it answers, however. If in Dostoevsky's literary universe everything is still in the future and will always be that way, why do characters reference, quote, or interpret the book of Revelation in all his late great novels? How can Bakhtin's position be reconciled with Dostoevsky's claim—recalled by a coworker—that his political foes "do not suspect that the end of everything is coming soon . . . to all their 'progress' and chatter! They have no idea that the Antichrist has already been born . . . and *is coming* [. . .] And the end of the world is close, closer than they think"?[3] Or with a story Dostoevsky liked to tell acquaintances: that he had met the Antichrist at a party and even touched his tail?[4]

Some of Dostoevsky's plots are as open-ended as Bakhtin would have them. (The conclusion to *Demons* leaves readers in a state of utter uncertainty: Pyotr Verkhovensky escapes to Europe, and we don't know how long his reign of terror will last.) But Bakhtin's model fits some of Dostoevsky's other works much less comfortably. As Bakhtin himself acknowledges, some Dostoevskian endings will not seem especially "open" or undetermined to most readers. In fact, he admits, there is a "unique conflict between the internal open-endedness [*nezavershennost'iu*] of the characters and dialogue, and the *external* (in most cases compositional and thematic) *completedness* [*zakonchennost'iu*] of every individual novel," although he declines to discuss this "difficult problem" any further (*PDP*, 39; *SS*, 6:50). And while Bakhtin concedes Dostoevsky's deep interest in eschatology, he denies that it functions as a governing principle of the author's aesthetics. Instead, it is just another "one of the embodied voices of an unfinalized and open dialogue" in his novels (*PDP*, 166; *SS*, 6:187).[5]

This chapter addresses some of the questions that Bakhtin left unanswered. Using *The Adolescent* as a test case, it asks the following: To what extent does Dostoevsky consider narrative open-endedness a virtue? How does Dostoevsky's eschatological thought shape his narratives, if at all? Frank Kermode has famously drawn a parallel between the endings of fictions—which he calls "models of the temporal world"—and fictions about the end of time.[6] According to Kermode, both types of endings serve a similar purpose: they help create sense, meaning, and "concordant structure," helping us understand how "the end is in harmony with the beginning, the middle with beginning and end."[7] Dostoevsky wrote extensively about the end of time in both his fiction and his journalism: do his novelistic endings correlate with these predictions in some way?

If in *Demons* Dostoevsky warns against the dangers of excessive certitude, in *The Adolescent* he shows that excessive doubt and irresolution can be just as perilous. To put the problem in narrative terms: highly open-ended stories leave their audience without ethical or intellectual guidance, uncertain of how to interpret them or what to do next. By contrast, stories about contemporary life that resolve their tensions too quickly and easily are both unrealistic and potentially dangerous, because they imply that harmony can be achieved without suffering or sacrifice. When he was composing the ending of *The Adolescent* itself, Dostoevsky tried to find a balance between these two extremes, combining references to continuing tensions, discords, and instabilities with hope for future resolution. The novel's conclusion, thus, is only incompletely "concordant": like Dostoevsky's predictions about the end of time, it points toward the possibility of future harmony and synthesis without fully realizing either.

A brief terminological aside: One of the challenges of writing about narrative closure is the multivalence of the term itself. As Peter Rabinowitz points out, it has multiple meanings. It can be used to refer to plot closure: are all the major characters accounted for and their stories rounded off?[8]

Has the novel achieved "the removal of the instability" that drives the story line forward?[9] Has it reached the new state of "equilibrium" that, according to Tzvetan Todorov, marks the conclusion of a "minimal complete plot"?[10] But the term can be used to refer to whether a text is *interpretatively* open or closed as well: does it lend itself to multiple interpretations, or not?[11] To make matters even more complex, these two types of closure are often interconnected: a story that does not tie up its characters' plotlines is usually open to multiple interpretations as well. In order to keep confusion to a minimum, I will try to distinguish these two types of closure—plot closure, on the one hand, and interpretative closure, on the other—as carefully as possible.

DOSTOEVSKY'S QUEST FOR "FORM, FORM!": THE NOTEBOOKS TO *THE ADOLESCENT*

Originally titled *Disorder* (*Besporiadok*), *The Adolescent* has a reputation for being a formal mess. Scholars like Edward Wasiolek and Nathan Rosen argue that the "ethical chaos" in the novel is bested only by the "structural chaos" of the work itself.[12] But the notebooks to *The Adolescent* show how frequently questions of novelistic form were on Dostoevsky's mind while he was writing it. When he began working on the novel he was still smarting from a string of negative reviews of *The Idiot* and *Demons*, which critics had panned for their tortured structures, dozens of digressive subplots, and endless parades of minor characters. Dostoevsky took this criticism very seriously. He devoted pages and pages of notes to thinking up ways of making *The Adolescent* more formally coherent and cohesive. If the youthful protagonist narrated his own story, would it have greater structural unity? Would devoting less attention to secondary characters and secondary plotlines make the novel easier to follow? "PLOT! PLOT!" (*FABULU! FABULU!*) and "Form, form!" (*Forma, forma!*) he reminds himself (*PSS*, 16:45, 122). At times his frustration with his recalcitrant subject matter is palpable. His notes are littered with "definitive" plot summaries that changed almost as soon as he put them down on paper. Headings such as "the final, certain composition," "Final Plan" or "FINAL DECISION" are generally succeeded by an "IMPORTANT CHANGE IN THE PLAN," only to be followed by a third, and sometimes very different "DEFINITIVE PLAN," which, of course, was subject to change as well (*PSS*, 16:295, 351, 310, 354, 357). In June 1874, Dostoevsky wrote to his wife, "My work is moving slowly, and I'm agonizing over the plan. An abundance of plans—that's the main flaw. When I looked it over as a whole I saw that four novels had merged together in it. Strakhov always saw this as my main flaw" (*PSS*, 29.1:338). A year later he still had not resolved the dilemma. As he wrote in another letter, "The main thing would be at least to work, then I would become absorbed [in my work]. But I can't even do that, because the plan hasn't come out and I see extraordinary difficulties" (*PSS*, 29.2:43).

The novel bears the traces of its difficult conception. It is narrated by Arkady Dolgoruky, the illegitimate son of the nobleman Versilov and his former serf, Sofia. Raised far away from his family, Arkady joins them for the first time soon after graduating from high school. He arrives in Saint Petersburg bearing two secrets: his beloved "idea" of becoming the next Rothschild and a damaging letter in which the society beauty Katerina Nikolaevna considers declaring her wealthy and eccentric father, the old Prince Sokolsky, mentally incompetent. The plot only gets more complicated from there, snowballing to include a group of young socialists, multiple suicides, several scandalous pregnancies, a scheme to counterfeit stock shares, Arkady's romantic rivalry with Versilov over Katerina Nikolaevna, a blackmailing ring led by his former schoolmate, Lambert, and the death of Arkady's legal father, a saintly wanderer named Makar Dolgoruky. An abundance of plans indeed.

There is, however, a central theme that ties all these motley subplots together: the quest for moral structure in a world in which "the definitions of and borders between good and evil have disappeared and *been worn away*" (*PSS*, 16:7). The Great Reforms of the 1860s had led to large-scale social disruption in Russia: the flight of newly freed peasants to the cities, a surge in suicides and violent crime, and, as it became clear that Alexander II's liberalizing policies would extend only so far, the rise of revolutionary terrorism.[13] As Dostoevsky once wrote, "the Petrine period of Russian history was truly ended by [the abolition of serfdom on] the 19th of February, so that long ago we entered into a period of complete uncertainty" (*WD1*, 169; *PSS*, 21:41). In *The Adolescent*, Dostoevsky depicts characters who are attempting to cope with this "complete uncertainty" in different ways. Katerina Nikolaevna clings to the outwardly beautiful but ultimately empty external "forms" (*formy*) of Russian noble life, dreaming of a fixed role in high society and a respectable marriage to Baron Bjoring (*A*, 514; *PSS*, 13:414). Versilov avoids "formulating" (*formulirovat'*) his beliefs altogether, since he knows he will only start mocking them if he does (*PSS*, 16:20). As for the novel's young hero, Arkady, he seeks moral form throughout the novel, finally finding it in Makar Dolgoruky's "seemliness" (*blagoobrazie*; literally, "blessedness of shape/image/form").

In short, Dostoevsky created a protagonist whose "quest for form" resembled his own.[14] One notebook entry makes the connection between these two quests especially clear. In it, Dostoevsky thinks through problems of order and disorder on several different levels of his text:

> Order [*Poriadok*]: First the letter with a proposal of marriage. Then Anna Andreevna calls the Adolescent and shows him the letter. (At the end of the conversation *ex abrupto*).
>
> Then Anna Andreevna lets him spy on the meeting. Later, when the Old Prince ran away, Anna Andreevna got scared: "I don't want it to be like that."
>
> Seemliness [*Blagoobrazie*] in Makar, disorder [*besporiadok*] in Versilov. The Adolescent wants to escape from disorder [*ot besporiadka*].
>
> *The order of psychology* [*Poriadok psikhologii*]. First the Adolescent, under the influence of a bad feeling (revenge), gets together with Lambert and even lets him know about his project. But after his meeting with her (alms) after the scene between her and Versilov, after the death of Makar and, finally, the breaking of the icons and the flight of the Old Prince—THE ADOLESCENT IS SUDDENLY STRUCK BY THE UGLINESS OF THIS ENVIRONMENT, and he gives himself over to her and swears to protect her honor, despite the fact that he has been insulted by Bjoring and at the station. But he sees *order* [*poriadok*] in this, that is, in responding to evil with good. (*PSS*, 16:394–95; underlining added)

Here, Dostoevsky meditates on multiple kinds of order and disorder simultaneously: the order of events in the plot, the order of Arkady's psychological development, and, finally, Arkady's perceptions of moral orderliness or disorderliness in the world around him. All three types of "order" were interconnected in Dostoevsky's mind and in his notes, each one echoing the others in a passage that reads like a series of identical rhymes.

Dostoevsky was not satisfied with this echoing effect, however. By making Arkady a first-person narrator, he did more: he brought the quests for moral and literary form into the purview of a single personality. Rather than keep the roles of author searching for aesthetic order and hero searching for moral order distinct, Dostoevsky invented a writer-protagonist who was looking for both.[15] And, indeed, Arkady's two searches often overlap. At novel's end, he claims that he has "re-educated" himself "precisely through the process of recalling and writing down" everything that happened to him (*A*, 554; *PSS*, 13:447). Arkady is reformed not only through his trials and tribulations but also through the process of describing and evaluating them, of ordering them into a narrative with a beginning, middle, and end.

ARKADY'S QUEST FOR BEGINNINGS

Constructing this narrative turns out to be an enormous challenge. Arkady opens his notes by trying to explain "who I am, where I was before then, and therefore also what might have been in my head, at least partly, on that morning of the nineteenth of September, so that it will be more understandable to the reader, and maybe to me as well" (*A*, 6; *PSS*, 13:6). His confusion is understandable. Everything about his identity is perplexing. The natural son of a nobleman, he nevertheless bears the surname of a former house serf (Dolgoruky). To make matters even more disorienting, a famous line of Russian princes *also* bears the last name Dolgoruky, a coincidence that never fails to remind Arkady of his social insignificance. Acquaintances keep on mixing up his patronymic, and no one understands his parents' relationship, not even, it would seem, his parents themselves.[16] Arkady repeatedly asks Versilov how he (a handsome young aristocrat) and Sofia (a married serf of unremarkable beauty) first fell in love, but he "never could find out or make a satisfactory surmise as to precisely how it started between him and my mother [*s chego imenno nachalos'*]" (*A*, 10; *PSS*, 13:9). This was not a typical, exploitative master-serf encounter, but it did not live up to Versilov's enlightened liberal ideals either. It stubbornly eludes all of Arkady's attempts to classify it: "What form [*V kakoi zhe forme*] could the beginning between this 'silly pup' and my mother have taken?" he asks himself in dismay (*A*, 10–11; *PSS*, 13:10). After Versilov starts dragging Sofia with him around Europe, their relationship becomes even more difficult to define: "But though it started in a landowner's way, it turned out that way and not that way [*tak, da ne tak*], and, essentially, it's still impossible to explain anything. There's even more darkness" (*A*, 12–13, translation modified; *PSS*, 13:12). Like so much else in this novel, the story of their relationship splits and doubles: it runs in two directions at once ("tak, da ne tak"), frustrating all of Arkady's attempts to understand it.

Just as Arkady has difficulty explaining his family beginnings, he has difficulty beginning his narrative (which, after all, is about *him*). He just cannot seem to get the story started. As he declares early on, "To business; though there's nothing trickier than getting down to some sort of business—maybe even any sort" (*A*, 5; *PSS*, 13:5). He tries multiple times, but with little success. His narrative includes a grand total of four "prefaces," which are scattered throughout all three parts of the novel. (The first appears on page 1, the second precedes the explanation of his "idea," a third follows it, and a fourth appears at the beginning of part 3). In this last "preface," Arkady finally acknowledges just how confused the structure of his tale has become: "You can't imagine how sick I am of all these apologies and prefaces that I'm forced to squeeze every minute even into the very middle of my notes!" (*A*, 347; *PSS*, 13:281).

Arkady's "idea" to become the next Rothschild can be read, in part, as his response to the difficulty of defining his identity, the challenge of putting his life story into a comprehensible narrative order. It allows him to sidestep the confusion of his murky past and uncertain future and instead to tell a clear story about himself, one with an ending that he calls "mathematically assured" (*A*, 78; *PSS*, 13:66). His plan is so simple that it could indeed be represented by the mathematical formula to which he compares it: 100 rubles starting capital plus strength of will plus constant accumulation minus close interpersonal relationships equals Rothschild's wealth. But Arkady's "idea" seems simple only on the surface. At heart, it is far more complicated, full of hidden tensions, the "doubleness of [his] plans and aims" regarding his family (*A*, 17; *PSS*, 13:16). His very choice of the Parisian banker James Rothschild as a role model hints at the contradictory impulses that underlie his plan. Arkady dreams of building his fortune by cutting himself off from friends and family and devoting himself to accumulation, but the man he has chosen to emulate was no loner or abandoned child. To the contrary, he was the legitimate son and heir to great wealth. Rothschild's father was a powerful banker who passed his name and legacy down to his five sons, all of whom he installed as representatives of the family business in different European cities. Arkady's "idea" may project an image of independence and self-sufficiency, but it is shot through with the covert desire to be supported, accepted, and loved. It reaches in two directions simultaneously, toward isolation on the one hand and social interdependence on the other.

ARKADY'S QUEST FOR ENDINGS

The Adolescent is dominated by the as-of-yet incomplete: its title refers to the age of its half-grown author-hero; Dostoevsky once called its characters "unfinished people" (*nedokonchennye liudi*) (*PSS*, 16:330); and it concludes with the fragments of a letter declaring nothing in it "artistically finished" (*A*, 563; *PSS*, 13:455). But precisely because this is a novel about process and development, it is an ideal medium for exploring *potential* endings—to the stories people tell about their lives, about Russia's national destiny, and about the end of the world as such.

As for Arkady, he is even more obsessed with endings than he is with his own beginnings. He spends hours scouring Russian newspapers with Katerina Nikolaevna, counting "up the murders and criminal cases, ma[king] comparisons with the good news . . . want[ing] to know where it was all going and what, finally [*nakonets*], would happen with us ourselves" (*A*, 254; *PSS*, 13:207). These questions haunt him, and he raises them more than once. Earlier in the novel, he tries to get Versilov to answer them as well, asking his father (1) "how the contemporary states and world would end and what would bring about a renewal of the social world" and (2) "precisely what I'm to do and how I'm to live" in the meantime (*A*, 210–11; *PSS*, 13:172).

It is no accident that Arkady poses these two questions together. For him, the answer to the first determines the answer to the second; how he imagines the world will end shapes the choices he makes today. Arkady accuses a group of young socialists of failing to understand the interrelationship. They demand that people sacrifice their peace and happiness not for any tangible benefit but for the good of some distant social utopia that their own atheistic materialism dooms to oblivion:

> And why should I necessarily love my neighbor or your future mankind, which I'll never see, which will not know about me, and which in its turn will rot without leaving any trace or remembrance (time means nothing here), when the earth in its turn will become an icy stone and fly through airless space together with an infinite multitude of identical icy stones, that is, more meaningless than anything one can possibly imagine! There's your teaching! Tell me, why should I necessarily be noble, especially if it all lasts no more than a minute? [. . .] What do I care what happens to this mankind of yours in a thousand years, if, by your code, I get no love for it, no future life, no recognition of my great deed? No, sir, in that case I shall live for myself in the most impolite fashion, and they can all go to blazes!" (*A*, 56–57; *PSS*, 13:49)[17]

If there is no God or eternal life, Arkady argues, "time means nothing." Because it is preceded and succeeded by oblivion, it lacks any frame of reference that might give it shape, size, and significance. And the meaninglessness of time on a cosmic scale makes the span of each individual life meaningless as well. How we spend our time on earth (wisely or unwisely, selfishly or altruistically) cannot alter the terrible fate awaiting everyone and everything in the world. Our actions, good or bad, have no lasting significance: they will fade into oblivion just as quickly as we ourselves—and the people we have helped or hurt—do.

Fortunately, however, Arkady has not accepted this catastrophic vision of the end of time or the ethics he associates with it. He keeps searching, trying to develop a more hopeful eschatology, one that will give meaning to his life and significance to the choices he makes. Three characters, spanning three generations and two social classes, help him on his way: his middle-aged biological father, Versilov; his elderly legal father, Makar Dolgoruky; and a friendly young blackmailer named Trishatov. Each one tells Arkady a different narrative about human destiny. Taken together, they give him the tools he needs to develop his own.

THE PROBLEM WITH RADICALLY OPEN ENDINGS

Versilov's narratives are perhaps the least satisfactory. Derived from the Latin *versus*, Versilov's name highlights the mutability of his personality: he is neither moral nor immoral, religious nor irreligious, Russian nor European.[18] He cannot commit to a single vision of human destiny, either. Instead, he tells *multiple*, conflicting narratives about the end of time, none of which he is willing to fully endorse. During his Catholic flirtation, he fixated on the Last Judgment (*A*, 37; *PSS*, 13:31). But by the time Arkady meets him in Saint Petersburg, he has developed a new theory. He tells his son that the beginning of the end will be marked by financial collapse: one day all of the world's governments will simultaneously declare bankruptcy. The wealthy will grab power, leading to the establishment of a "kingdom of the Yids." Then, in response, the poor will rebel, overthrowing the rich and taking their places. They will soon undergo bankruptcy themselves, sparking yet another social upheaval, which will spark another . . .[19] Characteristically, Versilov cuts off his story before reaching the end. "Beyond that, my friend," he concludes without concluding, "I can't predict anything in the destinies that will change the face of this world" (*A*, 210; *PSS*, 13:172).

Later, Versilov tells a second tale about the end of human history, which is utterly unlike the first. This time he imagines life on earth culminating not with universal bankruptcy and repetitive revolution but in a new golden age. In this future utopia people will no longer believe in God or immortality, but they will love one another all the more. Although they must die, the knowledge that their fellow men will remain after them "loving and trembling for each other in the same way" will "replace the thought of a meeting beyond the grave" in their minds (*A*, 471; *PSS*, 13:379). Yet Versilov refuses to commit to this atheistic vision of the future either. He admits that he always imagined this new golden age ending, unexpectedly, with the glorious second coming of Christ and "the great exultant hymn of the new and last resurrection" (*A*, 472; *PSS*, 13:379). Staying true to his name, however, he goes on to undercut this prediction as well, calling it a "fantasy" that he will never repeat to anyone else (*A*, 471–72; *PSS*, 13:379).

Versilov's stories about the end of time are open-ended in every sense of the word. They have undetermined plots (he describes multiple possible trajectories for human history without committing to any one) and they are open to so many different interpretations that Arkady can barely make sense of them. Students of narrative have long argued that the way a story ends crucially affects how we interpret it and what lessons we draw from it, if any. According to Barbara Herrnstein Smith, it is only when we reach the *end* of a text that we can see its "total pattern" and start to analyze the structural principles that govern the whole.[20] Caroline Levine connects "wholeness to the very possibility of conceptualization." Unless we set limits to our narratives—knowing what to exclude and where to stop—they will not make any sense; in fact, they may no longer be narratives at all.[21]

Versilov's stories, with their inconsistent or absent conclusions, resist coherent interpretation. Ethically confused themselves, they only confuse Arkady all the more. So it is no surprise that Versilov's answers to Arkady's second question—"what [he's] to do and how [he's] to live"—are just as contradictory as his answers to the first. Over the course of a single conversation Versilov alternately advises Arkady to follow the Ten Commandments, to love his neighbor (although he doubts if this is possible), and to do nothing at all: "Generally, it's best to do nothing; at least your conscience is at peace, since you haven't taken part in anything," he shrugs (*A*, 211; *PSS*, 13:172). When Arkady presses him for a more definite answer, Versilov recommends that his son aim for what he calls a "secondary" goal: turning stones into bread; that is, contributing to the purely material welfare of his fellow human beings. As for what Arkady's primary goal should be, Versilov cannot or will not say: "The question remains eternally open," he claims (*A*, 212; *PSS*, 13:173). Like his internally contradictory nonnarratives about the end of time, Versilov's ethics are destructively open-ended; they cannot provide his son with the moral structure that he craves. Versilov's lack of ethical commitment even betrays traces of the demonic. As W. J. Leatherbarrow explains, in the Russian Orthodox imagination, the devil's "only constant characteristics are those of inconstancy, adaptability, flexibility, lack of clear focus, and deceptiveness."[22] (Indeed, Ivan Karamazov's devil describes himself in much these terms, as "some sort of ghost of life who has lost all ends and beginnings [*vse kontsy i nachala*]" [*BK*, 642; *PSS*, 15:77].) Versilov's unstable personality, incoherent ethical norms, and end-less stories about human destiny are equally formless.

The inadequacy of Versilov's moral guidance becomes even more apparent when read in the context of one of the novel's main intertexts: a passage from chapter 19 of the Gospel according to Matthew.[23] In it, a wealthy young man asks Christ, "Teacher, what good deed must I do to have eternal life?" (Matthew 19:16 [NRSV]). Like Versilov, Christ first tells the youth to follow the Ten Commandments. But when the young man is unsatisfied with this response, Christ says something that Versilov will not: "If you wish to be perfect [*sovershennym*], go, sell your possessions, and give the money to the poor, and you will have treasure in heaven; then come, follow me" (Matthew 19:21 [NRSV]). At one point in the novel Arkady's mother compares Christ to a father, which implies the reverse should be true as well: the ideal father figure will be *like* Christ, teaching his children how to win eternal life. Versilov—who tells Arkady to despise his neighbors—does not even come close to the ideal.[24]

TRISHATOV'S PREMATURE ENDINGS (OR, WHY WE NEED MIDDLES)

Trishatov's narratives about the end of time suffer from the opposite problem of Versilov's. If Versilov's remain unfinished and inconclusive, then Trishatov's are clearly formulated but even more clearly deformed. Tales of salvation without suffering or sacrifice, they conclude prematurely, eliding difficult truths about life on earth and cutting off their protagonists' moral development just as it is getting started.

Trishatov conjures up two scenes that are endings in a double sense: both purport to be the conclusions to famous narratives (Dickens's *The Old Curiosity Shop* and Goethe's *Faust*) and both share attributes with the many other predictions for the end of time that appear throughout the novel. But both are revisions: they skip essential plot points, presenting a scene from the middle of a narrative as if it came at the end. While guzzling wine at a raucous blackmailer's dinner, Trishatov reminisces about "that place at the end" (*mesto v kontse*) of *The Old Curiosity Shop*, which he calls so moving that "you'll never forget it" (*A*, 438; *PSS*, 13:353). Ironically, however, Trishatov seems to have forgotten (or intentionally altered) most of the scene's details. In Trishatov's version, Little Nell stands on the porch of a medieval cathedral (*srednevekovogo sobora*; literally, "a cathedral of the middle ages"), staring at the sunset and pondering a "riddle—the sun as God's thought, and the cathedral as man's thought," while her grandfather looks on (*A*, 438; *PSS*, 13:353). Although not explicitly a depiction of the end of time, it resonates with several such depictions in the novel: like Versilov's vision of the end of European civilization, it includes a setting sun, and, like Makar Dolgoruky's description of the final harmony (discussed below), it is a scene of synthesis. In it, youth, old age, and the "middle ages" all come together as God's world and human creation stand face-to-face.

Trishatov's revised ending of *The Old Curiosity Shop* may be beautiful, but it is riddled with elisions. In order to create it he takes a scene from the middle of Dickens's novel and transforms it almost to the point of unrecognizability.[25] The original takes place not at sunset but in the morning, and not in a medieval cathedral but in a run-down country church, which Nell ominously calls a "quiet, happy place—a place to live and learn to die in!"[26] Like Trishatov, Dickens meditates on the relationship between the works of man and the works of God, but rather than considering their mutual greatness he stresses the common death and destruction to which all are bound:

> Here were the rotten beam, the sinking arch, the sapped and mouldering wall, the lowly trench of earth, the stately tomb on which no epitaph remained,—all,—marble, stone, iron, wood, and dust, one common monument of ruin.

> The best work and the worst, the plainest and the richest, the stateliest and the least imposing—both of Heaven's work and Man's—all found one common level here, and told one common tale.[27]

In the original, Nell stands alone (her grandfather is absent) and ponders human mortality, particularly her own. And this is perhaps the most important plot point that Trishatov's telling elides. By representing chapter 53 as a "place at the end" of a seventy-three-chapter novel, he erases the tragic final chapters, in which Nell and many of the other major characters die. Trishatov's version of *The Old Curiosity Shop* lies by omission: it is a vision of harmony and synthesis that ignores the tragic aspects of the novel and of human life itself, which, like Little Nell's story, involves suffering and death.[28]

Trishatov's version of *Faust*, part 1, foreshortens and distorts that narrative in an even more extreme way. Explaining how he would stage the play if he were to rewrite it as an opera, Trishatov once again ends the story in the *middle*. He takes an intermediate scene (when Gretchen is harassed by an evil spirit in the cathedral) and transforms it into the finale, which he imagines as a battle between a retributive Catholicism and a salvific Russian Orthodoxy. In his telling, strains of the Latin requiem "Dies irae, dies illa!" ("Day of Wrath, Day of Judgment!") harmonize with Mephistopheles's voice, which announces to Gretchen that her story is at an end: "It's all over, you are cursed!" (*Konets vsemu, prokliata!*) (*A*, 438; *PSS*, 13:353). But Gretchen refuses to give in to despair. When she falls to her knees in prayer, she is suddenly lifted up by a "thundering choir," which bursts into "an inspired chorus, victorious, overwhelming, something like our 'Up-borne-by-the-an-gel-ic-hosts.'" Then "everything's shaken to its foundations, and everything changes into an ecstatic, exultant, universal exclamation—'Hosanna!'—as if it were the cry of the whole universe" (*A*, 438; *PSS*, 13:353). After what sounds less like the salvation of one woman than like the salvation of the entire world, the curtain falls.

Trishatov has skipped an essential part of *Faust*'s plot, however: the part of the story when Gretchen actually earns her salvation. In Goethe's text, Gretchen's visit to the cathedral is just one step in her narrative, which ends with her in prison awaiting execution for murdering her infant child. Only *after* Mephistopheles and Faust offer to set her free and she refuses to go with them—thereby renouncing evil, dedicating herself to God, and willingly accepting punishment for her sins—does a voice from heaven declare her saved. By contrast, Trishatov's imagined opera obviates Gretchen's sacrifice entirely. In his version, redemption comes to her (and, it would seem, to the rest of the universe) quickly and painlessly, after one brief prayer.[29] It suggests that salvation can be won at little personal cost, and that has a significant downside. Trishatov's easy and assured redemption is the obverse of the inescapable icy doom that Arkady predicted earlier in the novel, but it leads to the same disturbing ethical consequences. In Arkady's scenario, no matter how kind and selfless we may be, we will still inevitably be destroyed. In Trishatov's, no matter how evil our actions or brief our repentance, we will invariably be saved. Either way, our behavior does not determine our ultimate fate, either as individuals or as a human community.

And that is, of course, precisely why Trishatov's version of *Faust* appeals to him. He does not want to take responsibility for his actions. Friendly but weak-willed, Trishatov is in many ways a typical representative of his generation.[30] The suicidal Kraft enumerates the younger generation's faults: "The present time is a time of the golden mean and insensibility, a passion for ignorance, idleness, an inability to act, and a need to have everything ready-made. No one ponders; rarely does anyone live his way into an idea" (*A*, 63; *PSS*, 13:54). Indeed, Trishatov calls himself "a nasty, lost little brat" who would like to leave his life of crime but lacks the strength to do so (*A*, 436; *PSS*, 13:352). He warns Arkady to stop drinking but keeps doing so himself, insisting that he "can't restrain [him]self in anything" (*A*, 437; *PSS*, 13:352). He has lost all capacity for work; even his idea for writing an operatic version of *Faust* never moves beyond the planning stages. As he tells Arkady, "No, you know, if I could, I'd have done something! Only I can't do anything now, but only keep dreaming" (*A*, 438; *PSS*, 13:353). If Trishatov could be saved like his Gretchen, instantly and painlessly, he would never have to do anything at all.

By this point in the novel, however, Dostoevsky has already hinted that "ready-made" redemption, which is not preceded by the hard work of atonement, is neither desirable nor, perhaps, even possible. A few chapters earlier, Makar Dolgoruky tells a story that resembles Trishatov's *Faust* but ends in a very different way. It is about a former soldier who takes to drinking, commits a robbery, and ends up standing trial for his crime. Even though there is no hard evidence against him, the soldier surprises everyone by silencing his lawyer and confessing his guilt "with tears and repentance." Impressed by the soldier's honesty, the jury triumphantly declares him not guilty. Yet their apparent act of mercy turns out to be anything but merciful. Instead of atoning for his crime with jail time or hard labor, the soldier is declared innocent before he *feels* innocent, and he hangs himself in confusion and despair. "That's how it is to live with a sin on your soul!" Makar Dolgoruky declares (*A*, 383; *PSS*, 13:310). Trishatov pardons Gretchen as easily as the jury pardons the former soldier. But it is not clear that a repentant Gretchen would want a salvation that she had not earned, or if it would even be salvation at all.

Father Zosima's meditations on hell and hellfire in *The Brothers Karamazov* can help explain what makes Trishatov's vision of effortless salvation so dangerous in Dostoevsky's eyes. Zosima speculates that there may be no such thing as hellfire in the material sense: God's arms are always open in love and forgiveness to all sinners, no matter how grievous their sins. Instead, hell resides within sinners themselves. Having forgone their chance to love on earth, in death they cannot learn to love again, and this eternal inability to love will torture them more than hot coals or iron hooks ever could. By granting Gretchen a precipitous and as-yet unearned ascension to heaven, Trishatov could well be condemning her to just such a fate: God would love and forgive her, but she might not feel worthy of loving God back. In Dostoevsky's literary universe, granting the semblance of redemption before it has been truly won forestalls the possibility of its full realization.[31]

MAKAR DOLGORUKY'S CLOSED-YET-OPEN NARRATIVE ABOUT THE END OF TIME

The novel's most morally authoritative character, Makar Dolgoruky, gives the most authoritative prediction about the end of time as well. A vision of harmony and synthesis, Makar's prediction of the end brings together all the novel's others, while correcting their mistakes. He begins by giving Arkady the instruction from Matthew 19 that Versilov does not: "Go and give away your riches and become the servant of all." Makar not only relates Christ's teaching, he also articulates why Arkady should follow it:

> You'll become inestimably richer than before; for not only in food, nor in costly clothing, nor in pride nor envy will you be happy, but in immeasurably multiplied love. Not little riches now, not a hundred thousand, not a million, but you'll acquire the whole world! Now we gather without satiety and squander senselessly, but then there will be no orphans or beggars, for all are mine, all are dear, I've acquired them all, bought them all to a man! Now it's not a rare thing that a very rich and noble man is indifferent to the number of his days, and doesn't know what amusement to think up; but then our days will multiply as if a thousandfold, for you won't want to lose a single minute, but will feel each one in your heart's mirth. And then you'll acquire wisdom, not from books only, but you'll be with God himself face to face; and the earth will shine brighter than the sun, and there will be neither sadness nor sighing, but only a priceless paradise . . . (*A*, 385; *PSS*, 13:311)

As in Arkady's prediction of the universe reduced to flying blocks of ice, in Makar's vision "time means nothing," not because each minute is as meaningless as the next, but because each moment has become so precious that our experience of time itself infinitely expands. Like Versilov's account of cyclical bankruptcy and revolution, Makar's relies on the language of financial exchange. But instead of a world dominated by endless rounds of senseless trade, where the poor change places with the rich again and again, he imagines a universe in which everyone and everything has become priceless.

Perhaps most telling of all is the way Makar's vision of mankind's ultimate destiny corrects Trishatov's. Like Trishatov, Makar imagines human history culminating in a state of unity and harmony, but he does not suggest that this harmony can be attained easily or painlessly. Far from an assured or predetermined salvation, what Makar foresees is one contingent on Arkady's own choices. In order for this paradise to come into being, Arkady must first become the servant of all—no simple task. Another one of Makar's stories emphasizes just how long, difficult, and complex the process of redemption can be. Makar tells of the wicked merchant Maksim Skotoboinikov and his worst sin: frightening his eight-year-old ward so badly that the child throws himself into the river and drowns. Thunderstruck by the event, Maksim commissions a painting to commemorate the boy's death. He wants the scene to appear exactly as it occurred in life, with one addition—a host of angels coming down from the sky to meet the child as he falls. Like the heavenly choir that carries Gretchen offstage in Trishatov's *Faust*, this host of angels will presumably lift the child directly to heaven. The artist objects to the idea, however, because the boy must "give at least some sort of answer" for his behavior: "How would angels come to meet him after such a sin?" (*A*, 395–96; *PSS*, 13:319). So they reach a compromise: the artist depicts, instead of a heavenly host, a single ray of light descending from the clouds, a symbol of hope for redemption to come.[32]

Makar's vision of human salvation as a work in progress, a story whose end has not yet been written, is also what allows for the possibility that the boy *may* eventually be redeemed. When Makar tells Arkady to pray for suicides, the young man wonders whether there is any use in praying for a soul that is "already condemned" (*A*, 384; *PSS*, 13:310). "But how do you know?" Makar responds. "A prayer from a still-living person for a condemned one truly gets through" (*A*, 384; *PSS*, 13:310). According to Makar, the stories of our salvation do not end when we die or even when God passes judgment on us. Long after our deaths the living can continue to intercede on our behalf and perhaps even change our ultimate fate. At one point in Makar's tale, a priest consoles Maksim by reminding him that "even the angels of God are not perfect [*nesovershenny*] but the only perfect [*sovershen*] and sinless one is Jesus Christ our God, whom the angels also serve" (*A*, 394; *PSS*, 13:318). In Russian, the word for perfection also implies *completion*—a significant correlation here. It suggests that until we finally become perfectly Christlike, we will not be complete, and the human story will not yet be over.

Since no one is perfect, that ending may still lie far in the future. Even the luminous Makar Dolgoruky is an "unfinished person," whose heart is only "almost sinless" (which is to say not completely so) (*A*, 382; *PSS*, 13:308).[33] As for Maksim, he is still further from achieving salvation. He tries to atone for his sins by marrying the dead boy's mother, building a church in his honor, and doing good deeds, but when his infant son dies, he becomes convinced that he has not yet been forgiven and sets off on a pilgrimage to save his soul. Makar's tale ends on an ellipsis: we learn that Maksim "performs his deeds of wandering and patience even to this day, and sends news to his dear wife every year . . ." (*A*, 399; *PSS*, 13:322). The story of Maksim's transformation is still ongoing. In fact, *The Adolescent* implies that *no* truthful narrative about human life can achieve total plot closure, because we and our world are still imperfect and unfinished. Even if the protagonist dies, his story does not really end (as Makar insists "there is love after death," and anyone who prays for the dead can help save them retroactively [*A*, 359; *PSS*, 13:290]). Narratives about life on earth cannot achieve total interpretative closure either, because until our stories are finished, we cannot pass final judgment on them. (A major sign of Arkady's moral growth is his newfound ability to condemn other people's bad behavior without judging them "ultimately" [*okonchatel'no*] [*PSS*, 13:293].) Instead, a truthful narrative about human life must end on an ellipsis, literally or figuratively speaking. To quote Diane Oenning Thompson: "There can be no absolute denouements in [Dostoevsky's] fictional worlds, because the final denouement is yet to come."[34]

Makar's ellipses should not be confused with the radical openendedness of Versilov's nonnarratives, however. Unlike Versilov, who cannot or will not choose between multiple internally contradictory accounts of human destiny, Makar draws a clear verbal picture of mankind moving toward a single, coherent goal. He explains where the human race is (or at least should be) headed and what it needs to do in order to get there, thereby giving Arkady a standard against which to measure his successes and failures in the present. Yet Makar's narrative includes a significant degree of plot and interpretative openness as well: he does not pretend to know when the final harmony will be reached or what twists and turns humanity will take on the way. (He reminds Arkady that only God can see the ultimate shape of human history: "He alone knows everything—every limit and every measure" [*A*, 383; *PSS*, 13:310].) Still, Arkady writes that throughout Makar's tales "there were always flashes of some sort of astonishing whole" (*udivitel'noe tseloe*) (*A*, 382, translation modified; *PSS*, 13:309). They finish on ellipses, but hints of wholeness flicker through them, illuminating everything he says with hope for the future.

THE END OF TIME ACCORDING TO DOSTOEVSKY

The debates about the end of time in *The Adolescent* represent just one small part of Dostoevsky's eschatological writings. During the 1870s, he meditated on the topic with increasing frequency, trying to discern in the "complete uncertainty" of the present moment signs of what or who would "resolve the final destiny of Russia" and, ultimately, the destiny of the entire world (*PSS*, 21:41, 34). Under the influence of the French utopian socialists he admired as a young man, he always envisioned human history concluding with the establishment of Christ's Kingdom on earth.[35] Like Makar Dolgoruky, he saw this kingdom as a world in which the old social, economic, and national barriers would finally break down and everyone would "never stop merging with everything" (*PSS*, 20:174). Moreover, he believed that Russia would play a pivotal role in establishing this new age. Thanks to her "*universality* [*vsemirnost'*], her capacity to respond, and the genuine, unquestioned, profound kinship of her genius with the geniuses of all ages and all peoples of the world," Russia was uniquely positioned to do so (*WD2*, 1068; *PSS*, 25:199). Revealed in and reinforced by Peter the Great's westernizing reforms—when Russia had come to know and love European culture better than Europe itself—this "universality" would allow her to become "the servant of all for the sake of universal reconciliation," "the ultimate unifying of humanity" (*WD1*, 527; *PSS*, 23:47) in the final "synthesis" (*PSS*, 20:174).

Panhuman as this dream may sound, it was intimately connected with the most disturbing aspects of Dostoevsky's thought: his anti-Catholic, antisemitic, and anti-Muslim sentiment. Although he loved to criticize his ideological foes for their lack of self-doubt, their conviction that human history must progress in one direction and one direction only (i.e., the way that *they* wanted it to), he sometimes succumbed to that same temptation in his journalism. According to Gary Saul Morson, Dostoevsky frequently takes on the role of the prophet, who "no longer seeks because he has already found the inner story of world and Russian history."[36] As Kate Holland points out, even Dostoevsky's grammar changes when he is writing in his prophetic voice, which "underline[s] its monopoly on a truth it demands we accept: future perfectives replace the conditional and subjunctive clauses we find in the novelistic narrator's discourse."[37] It is in his prophetic mode that Dostoevsky foresees the Russian conquest of Constantinople (a city that he insisted "must, sooner or later, be ours" [*WD1*, 527; *PSS*, 23:48] and "must remain ours forever" [*WD2*, 1208; *PSS*, 26:83]). It is likewise Dostoevsky-the-prophet who presages "the *inevitability* of a European war in the very near future," when the Catholic Church will finally breathe its last and "by the will of Providence a reborn Eastern Christianity will take its place" (*WD2*, 1123–24; *PSS*, 26:21–22). At times, he even starts to sound like the bloodthirsty revolutionaries he criticized so harshly in *Demons* (such as Shigalyov, who acts as if the apocalypse were "a fixed and definite thing" coming "the day after tomorrow, let's say, precisely at 10.25 in the morning" [*D*, 151; *PSS*, 10:109–10]).

The problem with Dostoevsky's prophecies is not only that they make him resemble his most dangerously deluded characters. The problem is that he wrote his most frightening racist and imperialistic tirades in his prophetic voice.[38] Russian chauvinism and the dream of building universal brotherhood on earth might seem incompatible, but for Dostoevsky they were not. Because he believed that Russia had been destined by God to lead the charge toward the new world harmony, anything that challenged his faith in Russian "universality" and political selflessness challenged his entire vision of the future. By resisting Russian political and cultural hegemony, the empire's Jewish, and Muslim populations did precisely that. If Russia could not establish peaceful relations with the peoples living in her own territories, how could she hope to establish peace and harmony throughout the entire world?

Dostoevsky dealt with this problem in the simplest way: by blaming the minority religious and ethnic groups. And the more categorically he insisted on Russia's soon-to-be-realized destiny as universal peacemaker, the more vociferously he blamed them. He suspected Polish rebels of participating in a nefarious global Catholic conspiracy.[39] He accused Jews of financially enslaving the Russian peasantry (if Jews have not yet been granted equal rights, he claimed, "then the Russian is much, much less to blame for it than the Jew himself" [*WD2*, 916; *PSS*, 25:86]).[40] As for the Muslim peoples living in the Caucasus—territory Russia had spent the first half of the nineteenth century trying to conquer—they had no legitimate claim to their lands: "The Russian land belongs to the Russians, to the Russians *alone*; it is a Russian land, and *there is not a bit of Tatar land in it*. The Tatars, the former oppressors of the Russian land, are outsiders here" (*WD1*, 628; *PSS*, 23:127). When Dostoevsky begins to believe too inflexibly in the accuracy of his own prophecies, this champion of brotherhood and "the universal reconciliation of nations" becomes a paranoid, racist war hawk (*WD1*, 530; *PSS*, 23:50).[41]

At their best, however, Dostoevsky's predictions are far more circumspect. Like Makar Dolgoruky's, they express a mixture of hope and uncertainty. At these moments, Dostoevsky writes about the triumphant end of human history (and how Russia can help bring it about) using the language of faith and presentiment rather than the language of knowledge—as something that may, but also may *not*, come to be. These predictions are full of expressions like "maybe" (*mozhet byt'*) (*PSS*, 22:75, 122, 25:100); "one can say almost with certainty" (*PSS*, 22:122); "it's difficult not to believe" (*PSS*, 23:28); "we have the good fortune to believe" (*PSS*, 25:100); and "[Russia's] mission is so lofty and her inner *presentiment* [*predchuvstvie*] of that mission so clear [. . .] that he who believes in this mission should [*dolzhen*] stand above all doubts and trepidation" (*WD2*, 1036, translation modified; *PSS*, 25:174–75).

At the height of his famous "Pushkin Speech"—which sums up his dreams for Russia and the entire world—Dostoevsky characterizes these dreams as beliefs (rather than as certainties), as possibilities (rather than as guarantees):

> I believe in this [*veriu v eto*], that we (I mean not we, of course, but Russian people to come) will realize to the very last man that to become a genuine Russian will mean specifically: to strive to bring an ultimate reconciliation to Europe's contradictions, to indicate that the solution to Europe's anguish is to be found in the panhuman and all-unifying Russian soul, to enfold all our brethren within it with brotherly love, and at last, perhaps [*mozhet byt'*], to utter the ultimate word of great, general harmony, ultimate brotherly accord of all tribes through the law of Christ's Gospel! (*WD2*, 1294, translation modified; *PSS*, 26:148)

Instead of saying what *will* be, and so claiming godlike omniscience for himself, Dostoevsky says what he believes *might* be. Instead of describing a future harmony that is already assured, he emphasizes the "striving" that would be required to bring it about.

Much striving would indeed be required. In order for Russia to fulfill its "destiny *in its ideal form*" (*WD1*, 527; *PSS*, 13:47), Dostoevsky believed, Russians first and foremost had to unify themselves, bridge the multicentury cultural gap that had opened up between the educated elite and the peasants, merchants, and urban poor. He had grandiose fantasies about what would happen if they did:

> And yet—what an awesome, constructive, blessed, and new—entirely new—force would appear in Holy Russia with the union of the educated classes and the People! I mean a spiritual union. Oh, gentlemen, you ministers of finance, you would then not be drawing up the kind of annual budgets you are drawing up today! Rivers of milk would flow in our kingdom; all your ideals would be realized at once! (*WD2*, 1353; *PSS*, 27:20)

But Dostoevsky was not sure how, when, or even if this would happen. His 1876 words on the topic are characteristically tentative: "We cannot utterly annihilate ourselves before [the People] and their truth, whatever that truth might be. Let that which is ours remain with us; we will not give it up for anything on earth, even, at the very worst, for the joy of unity with the People.

If such does not happen, then let us both perish on our separate ways. Yet certainly it will happen . . ." He ends on a note of anxious hesitation: "Nonetheless, I repeat once more: there is much ahead of us that is an enigma, so much that even the expectation is frightening" (*WD1*, 350; *PSS*, 22:45). He wavers from hope to doubt, referring to the possibility of future closure on the one hand and of continued uncertainty on the other.

CLOSURE BY NEGATION: THE DOUBLES DISAPPEAR

In the conclusion to *The Adolescent* itself, Dostoevsky revisits all the different types of endings I have discussed in this chapter. Some of the novel's plotlines do not conclude at all: Lambert and Trishatov disappear without a trace and neither Arkady nor the novel's readers ever learn what has happened to them. Other plotlines end on a note of strong closure, but at enormous expense to the characters who star in them. After much back-and-forthing, Versilov's story arc finally comes to an end, but only after he undergoes a kind of emotional lobotomy. George Eliot once wrote that the "very nature of a conclusion" is "at best a negation," and in Versilov's case her words hold true.[42] Only when he shoots himself in the chest, symbolically *negating* his love for Katerina Nikolaevna (and the sinful, earthly half of his personality that loves her), can he reach a state of equilibrium. The Versilov of the epilogue is "only half" (*tol'ko polovina*) his former self (*A*, 553; *PSS*, 13:446).

The ending of Versilov's plotline shares several features with the conclusion to Trishatov's *Faust* and is problematic for similar reasons. The first of many times that Versilov declares the end of his love for Katerina Nikolaevna, he talks about it as if it were the end of a play: "Today is the finale of the last act, and the curtain is coming down. This last act dragged on for a long time" (*A*, 464; *PSS*, 13:373). But like Trishatov, who ends his *Faust* on an intermediate scene, Versilov has dropped the curtain on his story of redemption too early, thereby threatening the foundations of the redemption itself. He, too, dreams of instantaneous salvation without sacrifice, without the piecemeal acts of self-control and self-denial that make long-lasting personal transformation possible. Versilov's many failures to transform himself affirm something Dostoevsky would write a few years later: "This is my view: one can, correctly and immediately, comprehend and feel something deeply; but one cannot, immediately, become a person; one must be formed into a person. It is a discipline" (*WD2*, 863; *PSS*, 25:47).[43]

In fact, from the very beginning of Versilov's "final act" there are hints that it may not be so final after all, and that his passionate nature has not been defeated just yet. Even he admits that the entire transformation "looks like a trick—really, like a most farcical trick" (*A*, 463; *PSS*, 13:372). Although not explicitly a conversion to religious belief, it has religious overtones: Versilov transforms under the influence of the saintly Makar Dolgoruky, and Katerina Nikolaevna uses the language of resurrection to describe the sudden change in his personality (*A*, 454; *PSS*, 13:366). But Versilov's conversion lacks what, according to William James, is the very essence of a successful one. James defines conversion as the attainment of spiritual unity, "the process, gradual or sudden, by which a self hitherto divided, and consciously wrong inferior and unhappy, becomes unified and consciously right superior and happy, in consequence of its firmer hold upon religious realities."[44] By contrast, Versilov's "conversion" brings neither harmony nor unity to his personality; it is instead a still more violent and aggressive division of self. Because he tries to eradicate his desires—rather than coming to terms with them—his "double" reasserts itself with an equal and opposite force. By trying to extinguish his love for Katerina Nikolaevna prematurely, he succeeds merely in reigniting it.

The full consequences of Versilov's attempts to split himself in half—like his breaking apart of the icon of two saints bequeathed to him by Makar Dolgoruky—become clear only in the epilogue. When he shoots himself, he finally kills his passionate side. He becomes gentle and sentimental, suffers from hysterical fits of tears, and spends his days discussing religion with Arkady's mother. There are hints, however, that the conclusion to Versilov's story is not as happy as it might at first seem. When he loses his "double," he also loses his vigor and emotional strength. Whereas before he devoted himself to ascetic penance (even, as rumor would have it, wearing penitential chains under his clothing), now he cannot even muster the fortitude to fast before the Eucharist. He promises Makar Dolgoruky that he will marry Arkady's mother, legitimizing their union and atoning for the sin that began it, but by novel's end he has no plans to do so. One even gets the impression that Versilov is no longer capable of becoming a husband, having passed into asexual old age. Or has he? He never resolves his highly sexualized feelings for Katerina Nikolaevna; he simply pushes them out of his mind. According to Arkady, it is "as if [*kak budto*] he has forgotten Katerina Nikolaevna completely, and has never once mentioned her name" (*A*, 554, translation modified; *PSS*, 13:447). But Arkady's hesitant "as if" raises questions: has Versilov really forgotten Katerina Nikolaevna, or does it only *seem* that way? How would he react if she suddenly reappeared? Would his "double" resurrect itself yet again? Because Versilov has not yet woven his personality into an integrated whole, the possibility cannot be ruled out. The equilibrium he has reached is partial and, perhaps, only temporary.

The splitting of the icon serves as an allegory not only for the conclusion of Versilov's plot but for the endings of several other story lines as well.

Old Prince Sokolsky has a dream about a man who holds up a broken icon and declares, "That's how your life will be split!" (*A*, 533; *PSS*, 13:430). Essentially, his dream comes true. Previously an uneasy mixture of solemnity and childish playfulness, the prince embraces his solemn side. Formerly torn between his love for two women—his daughter, Katerina Nikolaevna, and his young fiancée, Anna Andreevna—he makes his final choice: he devotes himself entirely to his daughter and "never once utter[s] a single word about Anna Andreevna" (*A*, 557; *PSS*, 13:449). Yet Old Prince Sokolsky's plot does not conclude at a point of true equilibrium either. Like Versilov, he attempts to rid his life of contradictions not by resolving them but by ignoring them (including his former friend and confidant Arkady, whom he refuses to see again).[45]

This type of closure—which quickly ends a two-sided conflict by negating half of it—is inherently violent. And the conclusion to Liza Dolgorukaya's plotline demonstrates just how destructive it can be. Right up until the epilogue, Liza is torn between the affection she feels for her cowardly criminal fiancé and her knowledge of his inadequacy. As Arkady puts it, "With the other, clear half of her mind [*iasnoi polovinoi svoego rassudka*], she must certainly have perceived all the worthlessness of her 'hero'; for who would not agree now that this unfortunate and even magnanimous man was at the same time in the highest degree a worthless man?" (*A*, 361–62; *PSS*, 13:292). Her ambivalent relationship with Prince Seryozha continues even after his death: she is pregnant with his child and so remains devoted to his memory. Finally, her predicament comes to an end when she falls down the stairs and suffers a miscarriage. But the quick, violent resolution to her internal conflict is much worse than the conflict itself. It not only destroys the life of Liza's unborn child, it also ruins her physical and mental health, leaving her future "a riddle" (*A*, 558; *PSS*, 13:451).

ARKADY'S ENDING AND A HOPE FOR SYNTHESIS

The conclusion to Arkady's plotline provides a stark contrast to the others. Simultaneously closed and open, it shows him *beginning* to reconcile the many strands of his identity into a single, synthetic whole. Earlier, Arkady, like Versilov, had imagined that he could simply reject his cruel side. In one scene, he assures Katerina Nikolaevna that all his malice toward her has completely disappeared:

> Everything's new now, and if anyone is resurrected, it's me first of all. I've been mean in my thoughts before you, Katerina Nikolaevna, and maybe no more than an hour ago I committed a meanness against you in deed as well,

> but you know, here I am sitting next to you, and I feel no remorse. Because everything has vanished now, and everything is new, and that man who was plotting a meanness against you an hour ago, I don't know and do not want to know! (*A*, 455; *PSS*, 13:366)

Here Arkady unwittingly reveals why disowning his past bad behavior will never help him overcome it. He is so disconnected from his former self that he does not even feel remorse, remorse that might keep him from doing something like this again. (And indeed, he enters into another plot against Katerina Nikolaevna almost immediately after this monologue.) By the time Arkady is finishing his notes, however, he has outgrown the desire to disavow his past misdeeds. As he is composing the final lines, he decides not to "cross out or correct a single word" of his story, even the parts he finds shameful (*A*, 554; *PSS*, 13:447). Arkady reforms himself not through a violent act of self-negation, not by rejecting the past iterations of his personality, but by carefully examining, judging, and coming to terms with them.

Arkady does not abandon his cherished "idea" either. Instead, he reworks it to fit his new life and new ideals. "Maybe some readers would like to know what became of my 'idea' and what this new life is that is beginning for me now and that I've announced so mysteriously," Arkady writes. "But this new life, this new path that has opened before me, is precisely my 'idea,' the same as before, but under a totally different guise, so that it's no longer recognizable" (*A*, 559; *PSS*, 13:451). He coyly avoids revealing the specifics of his new/old idea, but readers can imagine what traits it might share with the original. Before, Arkady dreamed of amassing capital in order to win personal power, a plan that necessitated immense self-control, sacrifice, and, in one fantasy, even giving away all his wealth as a proof of strength. If Arkady tweaked his idea slightly, keeping the emphasis on self-control and self-discipline but realigning the goal from service of self to service of others, he would arrive at Makar's—and Christ's—commandment: "Go and give away your riches and become the servant of all."[46]

Arkady's new/old idea is just one of many signs of unification and synthesis that mark the conclusion to his story line. At the end, he has finally come to terms with his familial origins. He carries on the legacies of *both* his fathers: he vows to live by Makar's spiritual teachings *and* he is planning to enroll in university, where he will be exposed to Versilov's beloved western-European culture. Whereas at the beginning of the novel Arkady insisted that he was writing his notes for himself alone, in the end he decides to share them with his former tutor, Nikolai Semyonovich. Even more surprisingly, Arkady includes Nikolai Semyonovich's response in the manuscript proper. What began as a hermetically sealed tale by a self-absorbed and socially isolated young man has become—in both form and content—a testament to his new social integration. As Lina Steiner has argued, Arkady's ending also augurs something bigger. It begins to achieve on a microscopic scale what Dostoevsky dreamed could be achieved on a macroscopic one—"the all-reconciliation of the classes," the healing of the social rift between the people (represented by Makar Dolgoruky) and the educated elite (represented by Versilov) (*PSS*, 23:176).[47] But it only *begins* to achieve this. Arkady's conclusion still contains many loose ends: he claims to have begun a "new life" but reveals few details about it; he says he has revised his "idea" but does not explain how; he says he has formed a new relationship with Katerina Nikolaevna but does not disclose its precise nature.

Dostoevsky constructed this balance between plot closure and openness carefully and self-consciously. While he was composing the novel, he drafted multiple variants of the ending, some of which resolved the tensions in Arkady's plot firmly and others hardly at all. Dostoevsky filled his notebooks with questions, such as: Should the story end with an enormous fire? With the death of the hero? Or with a hopeful gesture toward the future? In one variant, which ended on a note of strong closure and stability, Arkady declares that he has discovered *the* secret to living rightly. "Don't forget the last lines of the novel," Dostoevsky reminds himself: "'Now I know: I have found what I was looking for, what is good and what is evil, and I will never diverge from it.' *Finale*" (*PSS*, 16:63). Something like "And they lived happily ever after," this ending has a similar effect to those classic concluding lines. In fact, it pushes so aggressively toward plot closure that it may actually swing in the opposite direction and create interpretative openness instead. Will readers really believe that Arkady will *never* depart from his newfound moral principles? Isn't his very self-certainty an indication of his continued immaturity, a sign that he may stray after all?

Later in the notebooks, Dostoevsky experimented with a highly unresolved ending instead. In this open variant, Arkady has abandoned his Rothschild idea but has yet to replace it with any new set of convictions:

> The finale of the novel. Everyone is dead. The Adolescent remains alone. Hazy. He sat around for three days. He went out in the evening. The idea of accumulation has become dim. The sun is setting over the Neva. He wants to live. Every bit of grass prays. The Adolescent's prayer: "Save me, Lord, and I thank you that I want to live. And what will be, will be."
>
> The young generation, stepping into life. (*PSS*, 16:75)

With its theological language and natural imagery, this version gives readers hope for Arkady's future. But it gives almost no idea of what that future will look like, no hint of "what will be" other than it "will be."

Ultimately, Dostoevsky rejected both these extremes, opting instead for a middle course. Rather than leave Arkady's future entirely open-ended, he tells us where Arkady is headed next (university). And rather than have Arkady promise that he will never stray from his new ideals, Dostoevsky leaves the question—will Arkady lose his way in the future?—unanswered. The letter from Arkady's former tutor that closes the novel contributes to this open-yet-closed effect. Barbara Herrnstein Smith has argued that framing devices like Nikolai Semyonovich's letter can grant a degree of interpretative closure to even the most unresolved plot by "making a generalized or in some way stable comment on it from 'outside.'"[48] This letter only partly fits the bill, however. Arkady writes that it provides "a sort of general view and something explanatory, as it were" (*nekotoryi obshchii vzgliad i kak by nechto raz"iasnitel'noe*) on his life story (*A*, 559; *PSS*, 13:452). His hesitant descriptors—"sort of" and "as it were"—suggest that there could be other, possibly very different generalized views on his narrative as well. Moreover, the letter itself (or rather part of a letter, since Arkady provides only excerpts from it) is full of lacunae and references to the incomplete. Nikolai Semyonovich declares Arkady's notes lacking "beautiful finished forms" and anything even "somewhat completed" (*A*, 561; *PSS*, 13:453). He refuses to express an opinion about Arkady's idea either, hedging that he is still "not ready" to judge it (*A*, 560; *PSS*, 13:452).

Nikolai Semyonovich's letter, thus, is simultaneously stabilizing *and* destabilizing. On the one hand, it emphasizes the novel's provisional nature and so discourages readers from passing final judgment on what they have read. (Because Arkady does not yet have the distance necessary to see his subject matter clearly, Nikolai Semyonovich insists, "major mistakes are possible, exaggerations, oversights" [*A*, 563; *PSS*, 13:455].) On the other hand, the letter has proven itself to be an essential interpretative tool, which gives us the language that we use to talk about the novel to this day. Like Nikolai Semyonovich, scholars continue to describe *The Adolescent* as an artistically "unfinished" story about an "accidental family" trying to find its way through the "disorder and chaos" of postreform Russia (*A*, 563–64; *PSS*, 13:455). The letter sets the groundwork for any interpretation of the novel but also reminds us that other interpretations will always be possible.

Nikolai Semyonovich cautions that narratives about the contemporary moment like *The Adolescent* are rarely aesthetically pleasing. He would never attempt to write such a narrative himself, because such present-day tales lack even "the appearance of a beautiful order and a beautiful impression, so necessary in a novel if it is to have a graceful impact on the reader" (*A*, 561, translation modified; *PSS*, 13:453). And here is where Nikolai Semyonovich's point of view diverges from his creator's. Unlike Arkady's tutor, Dostoevsky was not interested in making "a graceful impact" on his readers. He was aiming to make an *ethical* impact on them, one that could influence their future behavior. His strategy for doing so is twofold. First (through Makar's vision of the harmonious end of time), he introduces his readers to the ultimate goal of life on earth as he understood it. Then (through the conclusion to Arkady's story line) he hints at how he believes they can get there: by healing the cultural rift between Russia's upper and lower classes first and foremost.

DOSTOEVSKY'S INCOMPLETE CONCORDANCES

The conclusion to *The Adolescent* is incompletely concordant: it points toward a future harmony in the life of the hero (and the nation he represents) that has not yet been realized. In fact, one could argue that all of Dostoevsky's optimistic endings are structured similarly. They partake in the way that Dostoevsky, at his best, writes about the future *as such*, combining hope and uncertainty, references to the possibility of future closure on the one hand and of continuing open-endedness on the other.[49]

Of Dostoevsky's major novels, two besides *The Adolescent* end on an optimistic note—*Crime and Punishment* and *The Brothers Karamazov*. The conclusions to *Crime and Punishment* and *The Adolescent* have the most in common.[50] Both feature protagonists whose enigmatic identities can be read (to quote Ilya Kliger) as "a fictional, biographical recasting of the question, What is Russia?" and both conclude with allusions to their protagonist's moral resurrection, his rebirth to a great but undefined and yet-to-be-realized new life.[51] Like so many characters in *The Adolescent*, Raskolnikov has a split personality: his last name is built on the Russian word for "schism," and he spends most of the novel swinging back and forth between his impulses toward pride and solitude on the one hand and those toward faith and human community on the other, "as if two contrasting characters were taking turns inside him" (*CP*, 200; *PSS*, 6:165). Then, in the epilogue, he undergoes a notoriously sudden change of heart. After nine unrepentant months in prison, he falls weeping at Sonya's feet: he "was resurrected and he knew it. He felt it fully with his whole renewed being" (*CP*, 517, translation modified; *PSS*, 6:421).

Even after his "resurrection," however, several of Raskolnikov's former, negative personality traits remain. He is still far from a believer: he "mechanically" picks up the copy of the New Testament that Sonya has given him but never actually opens it. Worse, he continues to express little remorse for his crime. Like Versilov, or an immature Arkady Dolgoruky, Raskolnikov mentally disowns his past. As the narrator informs us, "Everything, even his crime, even his sentence and exile, now seemed, in this *first surge*, somehow alien and strange, as if it were not even him they had happened to"

(*CP*, 517; *PSS*, 6:422; emphasis added). But Dostoevsky makes it clear that Raskolnikov cannot evade his past as easily as he thinks. Raskolnikov is the one who committed his crimes, and he is the one who will have to atone for them, sooner or later: "Raskolnikov didn't even know that his new life was not being given to him for free, that it would still cost him dear, that it would have to be paid for with a great, future deed . . ." (*CP*, 518; *PSS*, 6:422).

There are other signs that Raskolnikov's conversion is still in its incipient stages as well. His and Sonya's "sick and pale faces" are described as shining only with "the *dawn* of a renewed future, of full resurrection into new life" (*CP*, 517; *PSS*, 6:421; emphasis added). When Raskolnikov looks across the river, he sees yurts that seem to hail from the time of Abraham—an image that suggests a return to history's beginnings rather than the achievement of its ends. And just as there is much that Raskolnikov still does not understand at the end of *Crime and Punishment*, the reader's knowledge of his future remains only partial. The novel's famous last lines read, "But here a new story begins: the story of a man's gradual renewal and gradual rebirth, of his gradual crossing from one world to another, of his acquaintance with a new, as yet unknown reality. That could be a subject for another tale—our present one has ended" (*CP*, 518; *PSS*, 6:422). One way or another, Raskolnikov *will* eventually atone for his crimes. But what precise steps he will take on his "gradual crossing" and what sort of "unknown reality" he will find when he gets there remain unclear. This description of Raskolnikov's future resembles two points connected by a perforated line: we know where it begins and (at least theoretically) where it will end, but the middle is full of blank spaces.

The conclusion to *The Brothers Karamazov* provides its own set of interpretative challenges. Because the novel was meant to have a sequel (never written because of Dostoevsky's death), its major plotlines remain largely unresolved. At the end, the fates of all three legitimate Karamazov brothers still hang in the balance. We do not know if Dmitry will run away to America or accept his punishment and serve out his sentence in Siberia. We do not know if Ivan will recover from his brain fever or whether he will marry Katerina Ivanovna if he does. We know that Alyosha is planning to leave his hometown, but we do not know where he is going or what he will do next. Nevertheless, the novel's final scene resonates with Dostoevsky's vision of the end of time more closely than any of the others I have discussed so far. In what Robert Louis Jackson calls "a premonition of the harmonious family in heaven," it depicts a chorus of formerly wicked, stone-throwing schoolboys crowding around their mentor, Alyosha, and shouting, "Hurrah for Karamazov!" in unison.[52] But, as I argue in chapter 3, this is still only a *premonition* of harmony. Dostoevsky's final descriptions of the schoolboys alternate between images of social accord and hints of continuing dissension within the group. They suggest that the schoolboys could one day become a loving brotherhood but also reiterate how difficult it will be for them to do so.

In his late novels, Dostoevsky describes a world that, far from being "hostile to any sort of conclusive conclusion," is searching, hoping, and waiting for one. In this world, everything may still be in the future, but it will not be that way forever, and maybe not even for long. Dostoevsky envisioned the finale to human history as the harmonizing of all of life's contradictions in a final "synthesis," and the endings of *Crime and Punishment*, *The Adolescent*, and *The Brothers Karamazov* gesture toward that grand conclusion. But they only gesture toward it.[53] Like major chords missing notes and marred by several dissonant ones, Dostoevsky's optimistic endings hint at the coming harmony but leave readers to resolve the chord.

Chapter Three

From the Corners of *The Brothers Karamazov*: Minor Characters in Dostoevsky's Last Novel

> The little things, the little things are the main thing! . . . [*Melochi, melochi glavnoe!* . . .] It's the little things that always ruin everything . . .
> —Raskolnikov, *Crime and Punishment*

AS ANYONE WHO HAS READ Dostoevsky's novels can tell you, they contain *a lot* of characters. His characters are both famously numerous and famously vital: they are unconventional, unpredictable, and psychologically complex. E. M. Forster—who categorized literary characters into two types, the "round" (who are "capable of surprising in a convincing way") and the "flat" (who "can be expressed in one sentence")—thought Dostoevsky wrote hardly any flat characters at all.[1] Bakhtin made an even bolder claim. According to him, Dostoevsky's characters are capable of surprising not only their readers but even their *author*, who was never entirely sure what they would do next. They resemble "*free* people, capable of standing *alongside* their creator, capable of not agreeing with him and even of rebelling against him" (*PDP*, 6; *SS*, 6:10). Because Dostoevsky "reserved idealistic consciousness not for himself but for his characters, and not only for one of them but for them all," they can always do the unexpected (*PDP*, 99; *SS*, 6:114).

Writing a novel with a great number of "rebellious" characters can pose serious formal challenges, however. Flat, conventional characters serve important structural purposes. According to David Galef, "they carry out much of the mechanics of the fiction": they function as symbols and allegories, plot pushers, foils, contrasts and doubles that help readers better understand the protagonist and his social milieu.[2] In a similar vein, Boris Uspensky has argued that the "extras" or "background" characters organize and hierarchize our reading experience. They serve as a frame for the world of the novel: "Represented through compositional devices which are in opposition to those used to describe the main characters," depicted as "objects" or "puppets" rather than seeing subjects in their own right, they mark the boundaries of the artistic text. They help direct the reader's mental focus (generally toward the main characters and away from themselves).[3]

When background figures sneak into the foreground and flat characters take on dimension, it can be considered an artistic *failing*.[4] And in Dostoevsky's lifetime, it was. Dostoevsky's contemporaries criticized him for squeezing too many characters, too many scenes, too much of everything into his works. One reviewer of *The Idiot* called it a "compilation" consisting of "a multitude of absurd characters and events, without even the slightest concern for any artistic aim."[5] A few years later, the parodic journal *The Spark* published a mock recipe for a novel like *Demons*: "There is no need for a plot or a well-shaped plan as such [. . .] A million characters and their wholesale extermination at the end of the novel, which should have an epigraph from Pushkin's 'Scene from Faust': Faust: Drown everyone! Mephistopheles: Right away!"[6] Even Dostoevsky's admirers complained that his works were oversaturated. In 1871, his sometime friend the philosopher Nikolai Strakhov warned him that readers were having a hard time following the plot of *Demons*: "The impression on the public up to this point has been very vague; the public does not see the point of the story, and is getting lost in the multiplicity of characters and episodes, whose connection isn't clear [. . .] you overload, overcomplicate your works. If the fabric of your stories was simpler, they would have a more powerful effect."[7]

Dostoevsky took Strakhov's criticism to heart. In his response, he conceded that Strakhov had "pointed to the main flaw terribly accurately. Yes, I suffered from this and still suffer [. . .] Many separate novels and stories crowd their way into one simultaneously, so there's neither measure nor harmony" (*PSS*, 29.1:208). Dostoevsky had been suffering from this problem for a long time. When he was working on *The Idiot*, he bemoaned how populous the work had become:

> And imagine the horrors that have come about of their own accord: it turns out that besides the hero there is also a heroine, which means there are *TWO HEROES!!* And besides these heroes there are two more characters that are entirely major [*glavnykh*], which is to say *almost heroes*. (There are countless numbers of minor characters [*pobochnykh kharakterov*], for whom I'm very much responsible, and the novel has 8 parts). (*PSS*, 28.2:241)

Dostoevsky's words are playfully self-deprecating, but his anxiety is not misplaced. *The Idiot* ended up being one of his most formally unconventional works. Minor characters like the buffoons Ferdyshchenko and Keller appear and disappear from the novel seemingly without rhyme or reason, only to waltz back into the action just as inexplicably hundreds of pages later. They hijack the story line at will, "scatter[ing] novelistic focus and tension" (to quote Olga Matich).[8]

When Dostoevsky started working on *The Adolescent*, he decided to try a different compositional approach. Alongside reminders to "know the main point [*glavnuiu tochku*] in each chapter and [write] only about it" (*PSS*, 16:96), Dostoevsky set himself the following set of principles:

> Over the course of the novel follow two rules *without fail*:
>
> *1st rule*. Avoid the mistake in "The Idiot" and in "Demons" of describing (many) secondary events [*vtorostepennye proisshestviia*] in an unfinished, insinuated, romantic manner, spreading them out over a long space [. . .] As secondary episodes they were not worth such capital attention from the reader, and thus, to the contrary, the main aim was even obscured rather than clarified, precisely because the reader, knocked to a by-road [*proselok*], lost the main road and became confused in his attention.
>
> Try to avoid this and divert secondary things to a less-significant place, [treat them] much more briefly, and concentrate the action exclusively around the hero.
>
> The 2nd rule is that the hero is the Adolescent. And the rest is all secondary [*vtorostepennost'*], even HE [Versilov] is secondary. (*PSS*, 16:175)[9]

Dostoevsky worried that if he did not adequately distinguish major from minor characters, primary from secondary plotlines, readers might miss the point of his story entirely. They would be so busy trying to keep track of the "multitude of characters and plotlines" that his message would get lost in the noise (*PSS*, 16:87).

But such strict structural hierarchy can be achieved only at a cost. A novel that concentrates the action exclusively around the hero and keeps secondary characters *secondary* may be easier to follow, but it is also less egalitarian. The oversized protagonist will necessarily be depicted in greater depth and with more psychological nuance than the briefly appearing minor characters, who may seem like "partial constructs" by comparison, "a function of the action in which they are found and not beings who can be envisioned by themselves in their wholeness."[10] In *The One vs. the Many: Minor Characters and the Space of the Protagonist in the Novel*, Alex Woloch argues that Dostoevsky was far from being the only nineteenth-century novelist who struggled with this compositional dilemma. Because realist literary characters are meant to seem *real* (they are "implied" persons with an "implied humanness"), Woloch contends, exalting some at the expense of others is always problematic. It rankles against the nineteenth century's powerful democratic impulses, against "a specific notion of human right." This does not stop writers like Jane Austen and Charles Dickens from making "allegorical (or functional) use of subordinate characters," but it does lead them to "ferociously problematize such allegory."[11] With the help of one-eyed, one-legged minor characters who move in jerky and mechanical ways, they highlight what's missing: the potentially full-fledged personalities that have been sacrificed for the sake of novelistic structure.

Dostoevsky thought seriously about the ethics of narrative asymmetry as well. In the notebooks to *The Adolescent*, his initially *pragmatic* decision to center the action on the hero quickly takes on *moral* overtones. In one sketch, Arkady admits that his "idea" is founded on the egotistical desire to be "in the foreground [*na pervom plane*], always first" (*PSS*, 16:219). Then, a little later, Dostoevsky applies precisely these same words to the novel's structure: "The major character of the 2nd Part is that the Adolescent always puts *himself in the foreground* [*stavit sebia na pervyi plan*]. He doesn't so much describe the adventures of the other characters but precisely *his own adventures, only his own*, and other people's only insofar as they touch on his own" (*PSS*, 16:300). Arkady's narrative centrality has come to reflect his desire for *social* centrality; it has become another indication of his adolescent self-absorption.

Dostoevsky's work on *The Adolescent* sparked his interest in the ethics of narrative asymmetry, but his most significant meditation on the topic would come a few years later, with *The Brothers Karamazov*. In that novel, Dostoevsky suggests that narrative hierarchies—like all human hierarchies—are inevitable and unavoidable. In literature, as in life, we must choose where to direct our focus: we must concentrate our attention more on some people and things and less on others, or we risk spreading it so thin that we see nothing and no one properly. But Dostoevsky also emphasizes that such choices are ethically fraught. Attending to one person means turning away from others, vision in one direction means blindness in another, and our social stereotypes can warp our judgment, leading us to consider entire categories of people as minor or of lesser importance *by definition*. Dostoevsky worried that in his earlier novels the "secondary things" had confused readers and diverted their attention to a "by-road." In *The Brothers Karamazov*, however, it is precisely those characters who stand on the novel's by-roads (both literally and figuratively speaking) who in fact require the protagonists', the narrator's, and the *reader's* "capital attention."

CONFUSING THE PRIMARY AND THE SECONDARY IN *THE BROTHERS KARAMAZOV*

Starting in the novel's preface, we are asked to consider what and who deserves our time and attention. When faced with the information overload typical of modern life, where should we direct our eyes and ears? What, by contrast, can we safely ignore? "The author" (Dostoevsky's alter ego) worries that Alyosha Karamazov is not a "great" enough hero to command our interest. "Why should I, the reader, spend my time studying the facts of his life?" he imagines a skeptical public asking (*BK*, 3; *PSS*, 14:5). To make matters worse, he admits that *The Brothers Karamazov* is only the first part of a projected two-part series, and the second, "main novel" (*glavnyi roman*), is still to come (*BK*, 3; *PSS*, 4:6). In short, this is a nonmajor novel about a not-so-great hero: why should we bother reading it at all? "The author" spends the rest of his preface trying to convince us we should. Even in these first pages, he raises the possibility that someone like Alyosha who seems to be of only secondary importance can in fact be primary, that "it is precisely he, perhaps, who bears within himself the heart of the whole" (*BK*, 3; *PSS*, 4:5).

"The author" first introduces the difficulty of distinguishing the primary from the secondary, but the narrator is the one who dramatizes it. An unnamed resident of Skotoprigonyevsk, he has undertaken an enormous task: describing the complex series of events leading up to Fyodor Pavlovich Karamazov's murder, and Dmitry Karamazov's arrest, trial, and wrongful conviction for his father's death. This enormous, sprawling work embraces several inserted narratives as well, including Ivan Karamazov's poem "The Grand Inquisitor," Alyosha's hagiography of his spiritual father, the elder Zosima, not to mention the *long* speeches from the prosecution and defense at Dmitry's trial. At times the narrator even seems to be losing his grip on his material. In the first chapter of part 4, for example, he gets so carried away describing the adventures of the thirteen-year-old Kolya Krasotkin that he forgets to mention Kolya's relevance to the rest of the novel's plot for five full pages.

Faced with telling such a complex story, the narrator struggles to decide what to emphasize and what to downplay, what to make central and what to leave on the margins of his tale. Before launching on his description of Dmitry's trial, he acknowledges his fallibility:

> I will say beforehand, and say emphatically, that I am far from considering myself capable of recounting all that took place in court, not only with the proper fullness, but even in the proper order. I keep thinking that if one were to recall everything and explain everything as one ought, it would fill a whole book, even quite a large one. Therefore let no one grumble if I tell only that which struck me personally and which I have especially remembered. I may have taken secondary things for the most important [*vtorostepennoe za glavneishee*], and even overlooked the most prominent and necessary features." (*BK*, 656; *PSS*, 15:89)

If describing just the trial "as one ought" would mean filling "a whole book, even quite a large one," how much *else* has he left out? The narrator may "have taken secondary things for the most important" more than once.[12]

The novel's readers are just as overwhelmed by the complexity of the tale as he is. Robin Feuer Miller notes that, as we make our way through the novel, "it becomes increasingly difficult to determine what is primary and what is variation, what is a main theme and what is a digression."[13] But the more difficult sorting the primary from the secondary becomes, the more *important* it becomes as well, because we cannot trust the narrator to do it for us. For the narrator is not only a fallible storyteller, he is also a manifestly biased one. As V. E. Vetlovskaia has argued, he is Alyosha's would-be hagiographer and has the hagiographer's tendency to moral judgment, turning his tone "either reverent and sympathetic (when speaking about the positive characters [. . .]), or clearly negative."[14] He makes judgments that Dostoevsky would not have agreed with and that cast doubt, if not on his honesty then at least on his impartiality. The narrator is a snob: when characterizing the members of Dmitry's jury, he dismisses the nonnoble members of the group as hardly worth describing: "There is nothing much to say about the tradesmen and peasants. Our Skotoprigonyevsk tradesmen are almost peasants themselves, they even handle the plow [. . .] So that indeed the thought might well enter one's head, as it entered mine, for example, as soon as I took a look at them: 'What can such people possibly grasp of such a case?'" (*BK*, 660; *PSS*, 15:93). It soon becomes clear how seriously he has underestimated them, however. A member of the public voices a very different opinion about a merchant on the jury: "Palatial mind [. . .] Never says a word, but so much the better. Your man from Petersburg has nothing to teach him; he could teach the whole of Petersburg himself" (*BK*, 751; *PSS*, 15:176). Ultimately, these jurors have a deciding impact on the fate of the novel's protagonists: they "stand up for themselves," ignoring the lawyer's and prosecutor's high-flown speeches and convicting Dmitry according to their own understanding of the facts of the case (almost all of which point to his guilt).

The narrator's social prejudices surface in other parts of the text as well, especially when he is discussing Fyodor Pavlovich's servants Grigory, Marfa, and Smerdyakov (who is probably Fyodor Pavlovich's illegitimate son).[15] After describing Grigory and Marfa, the narrator interrupts his discussion of Smerdyakov: "I ought to say a little more about him in particular, but I am ashamed to distract my reader's attention for such a long time [*mne sovestno stol' dolgo otvlekat' vnimanie moego chitatelia*] to such ordinary lackeys, and therefore I shall go back to my narrative, hoping that with regard to Smerdyakov things will somehow work themselves out in the further course of the story" (*BK*, 100; *PSS*, 14:93). Here, he suggests not only that "ordinary lackeys" do not merit attention as a general principle but also that these particular lackeys will play a secondary role in his story. Discussing them "distracts" the reader's attention from "his narrative," which can resume only when he stops talking about *them*.

Although the narrator never explicitly calls Grigory, Marfa, and Smerdyakov secondary characters, his (perhaps unconscious) allusion to Gogol's *Dead Souls* makes it clear that this is precisely how he sees them. In this passage he echoes, almost verbatim, something the narrator of *Dead Souls* says when apologizing for devoting too much time to the servants Petrushka and Selifan: "But the author has serious scruples [*ves'ma sovestitsia*] about taking up so much of the readers' time [*zanimat' tak dolgo chitatelei*] with people of low class, knowing from experience how reluctantly they meet with the lower estates."[16] In any case, he explains, Petrushka and Selifan "are not such noticeable figures, what is called secondary or even tertiary" characters.[17] The readers of *The Brothers Karamazov* who recall this (memorable) passage from *Dead Souls* will realize that Dostoevsky's narrator considers Marfa, Grigory, and Smerdyakov "secondary or even tertiary" characters as well.[18] Ultimately his judgment of Smerdyakov coincides with Ivan and Fyodor Pavlovich's: "And furthermore to hell with him, really, is he worth talking about?" asks Fyodor Pavlovich. "Of course not," answers Ivan (*BK*, 132; *PSS*, 14:122). They have confused the primary and the secondary as well.

The narrator's dismissal of Smerdyakov as an "ordinary lackey" and secondary character may seem surprising. After all, he turns out to be the murderer, who kills Fyodor Pavlovich and frames Dmitry for the crime. As Olga Meerson has argued, however, the entire novel is constructed to draw attention away from Smerdyakov's subjectivity, to place the characters in and readers of *The Brothers Karamazov* in a similar moral quandary: will we recognize Smerdyakov as the fourth brother Karamazov and the spiritual equal of the other three, or will we, like Grigory, dismiss him as little more than "bathhouse slime," something not quite human? This is, of course, a narrative dilemma as well. Will we see him as one of the brothers and thus a titular protagonist of the novel? Or will we mentally relegate him to the role of Ivan's villainous disciple, if not quite a minor character then at least one of secondary interest compared with Dmitry, Ivan, and Alyosha?[19] Russian fairy tales often feature precisely three brothers, the youngest of whom, "Ivan the Fool" or "Ivan the Prince," is always the unexpected hero. Is there enough room in this story for a fourth?[20]

THE CORNER

While the readers *of* the novel try to figure out which characters they must keep in the forefront of their minds, which they can relegate to the background, and which ignore altogether, the characters *in* the novel face an analogous dilemma: how should they split their attention, energy, and affection between the many, many people around them? The kind and generous

Alyosha tries to love and care for everyone, but even he quickly comes up against the physical impossibility of attending to all who need him.

Early in the novel, Zosima tells Alyosha that in order to prevent catastrophe in his family, he must stay by not one but *both* of his brothers. This turns out to be a nearly superhuman task. Alyosha runs now to Dmitry, now to Ivan, now back to his dying elder (whom he cannot help but love most, "in some moments even to the forgetting of 'all and all'" [*BK*, 339; *PSS*, 14:306]). Again and again, he becomes so engrossed in conversation with one that he momentarily forgets about the others. When he is on the road to see Katerina Ivanovna, he bumps instead into Dmitry (who, despite Alyosha's admonitions to speak "quickly," proceeds to tell his entire life story [*BK*, 105; *PSS*, 14:97]). Later, when Alyosha really *is* looking for Dmitry, he happens across Ivan instead, who monopolizes him for so long that he forgets what he set out to do in the first place. As we learn, "later in his life, in great perplexity," Alyosha would wonder "how he could suddenly, after parting with his brother Ivan, so completely forget about his brother Dmitry, when he had resolved that morning, only a few hours earlier, that he must find him, and would not leave until he did, even if it meant not returning to the monastery that night" (*BK*, 264; *PSS*, 14:241).[21] Diane Oenning Thompson has argued that in *The Brothers Karamazov* "all forgetting is set within the novel's encompassing context of the collective Christian memories," and when characters forget one another, even temporarily, they fail to live up to the novel's Christian ideals.[22] But how can we remember all the people we are responsible for, when according to Father Zosima's teachings we are ultimately responsible for *everyone*?

The Brothers Karamazov is a novel about limited resources. Characters fight over money, power, prestige, attention, love, fishing rights, and even physical space. The novel's events play out in a series of small and crowded interior living rooms, carriages, and monastery cells that are rarely big enough for everyone who would fit themselves inside. When Zosima takes to his bed, space around the elder becomes limited and precious. The monks file in a few at a time to say their goodbyes, but on the night of Zosima's death, his "very small" bedroom has "barely enough room" to fit a privileged few, and unequally at that: four monks sit in chairs around the bed, the novice Porfiry stands, and as soon as Alyosha walks in, Zosima summons him directly to his side (*BK*, 284; *PSS*, 14:258). Having shown his preference for the youngest Karamazov by pulling him closest, Zosima explains what underlies it: Alyosha reminds him of his dead older brother, who first taught him that all are guilty for all. "Many times I have seen you look distressed, as it were, that I should love Aleksei more than you," Zosima tells Porfiry. "Now you know why it was so, but I love you, too, know that, and I have grieved many times at your distress" (*BK*, 286; *PSS*, 14:259). Zosima may love both young men, but in his heart, as in his cell, there are those who sit in the middle and those who stand by the door.

The good Porfiry seems to accept this explanation, and we last see him sleeping peacefully in an adjacent room. Other characters, however, do not accede to their secondary positions so gracefully. In his youth, Zosima was visited by a "secret guest" who knows firsthand how hard it is to share: he murdered the woman he loved in order to keep her from marrying another man. He warns Zosima: "Until one has indeed become the brother of all, there will be no brotherhood. No science or self-interest will ever enable people to share their property and their rights among themselves without offense. Each will always think his share too small, and they will keep murmuring, they will envy and destroy one another" (*BK*, 303; *PSS*, 14:275).[23] Much of the novel's plot revolves around just this kind of hatred and envy.

The most envious, and most dangerous, characters in *The Brothers Karamazov* occupy marginal spaces, both in the social world that they inhabit and in the structure of the novel that describes it. One of Father Zosima's foremost "haters and enviers," the poor monk Father Ferapont, lives apart from the rest of the brothers on the far edge of the monastery, "beyond the hermitage apiary, in a corner of the wall [*v uglu steny*], in an old, half-ruined wooden cell" (*BK*, 166; *PSS*, 14:151). Rakitin—"an insignificant person" (*litso melkoe*) in the monastery who must stand in the "corner" of Zosima's cell (*BK*, 85, 38; *PSS*, 14:36, 79)—finds himself on the edges of other social spaces as well. Grushenka silences and relegates him to a "corner" of her living room (*BK*, 353; *PSS*, 14:320). And he skulks in alleyways, both literal and metaphorical. After Rakitin storms off down a side street, Alyosha muses, "As long as Rakitin thinks about his grudges, he will always walk off into some alley [*v pereulok*]" (*BK*, 360; *PSS*, 14:326).

Of all the characters in the novel, however, Smerdyakov is the one most insistently associated with peripheral spaces. He was conceived in a back-alley ditch and born in the bathhouse on the edge of Fyodor Karamazov's garden. When he was a child he used to hide in a corner after his adoptive father, Grigory, beat him. And his perpetual place on the edge has permanently changed his perspective on the world. Even when Smerdyakov is not physically standing in the corner, he brings the mentality of the corner with him. Grigory complains that "the boy grew up 'without any gratitude' [. . .] solitary, and looking at the world from a corner [*smotria na svet iz ugla*]" (*BK*, 124, translation modified; *PSS*, 14:114). The word that Dmitry uses to describe Smerdyakov's relationship to Fyodor Pavlovich—"illegitimate son" (*pobochnyi syn*; literally, "son on the side")—drives home his marginal status (*PSS*, 14:428, 15:126). It is not a coincidence, I think, that Dostoevsky uses this very same adjective to describe the minor characters in *The Idiot*: "pobochnye kharaktery" (literally, "characters on the side") (*PSS*, 28.2:241).

Dostoevsky drew on the symbolism of corners throughout his career. A sign of social marginalization and self-marginalization, Dostoevsky's corners are also liminal spaces where demonic and heavenly forces meet: devils lurk in his corners, but icons hang there as well, a reminder that even the most desperate sinners can be redeemed. The Underground Man hides away in what he refers to as "his own corner" (*PSS*, 5:101); Raskolnikov's coffinlike room is described as a "corner" (*PSS*, 6:206); and Arkady Dolgoruky plans to realize his idea by retreating into a "corner" as well (*PSS*, 13:48). Even Pyotr Verkhovensky is associated with corners. He claims to have developed his plan for world domination while looking at Stavrogin from an oblique angle. "Oh, I've made a close study of you!" Verkhovensky tells his idol. "I often look at you from the side, from a corner [*iz ugla*]!" (*D*, 464, translation modified; *PSS*, 10:323).

What makes *The Brothers Karamazov* unique in Dostoevsky's oeuvre is that whereas in his earlier works the protagonists lurked in corners, in this novel the corner-dwelling characters (Ferapont, Rakitin, and Smerdyakov) occupy marginal positions in the structure of the narrative as well. But they refuse to stay in place. They hurl themselves toward a more socially central position in Skotoprigonyevsk and, by extension, toward a more central position in the the novel's discourse. In one scene, Ivan mentally compares Smerdyakov to something not in its proper *place*. Walking back to his father's house, Ivan experiences an inexplicable feeling of ennui:

> Somewhere some being or object was standing and sticking up just as when something sometimes sticks up in front of one's eye and one doesn't notice it for a long time, being busy or in heated conversation, and meanwhile one is clearly annoyed, almost suffering, and at last it dawns on one to remove the offending object, often quite trifling and ridiculous, something left in the wrong place [*ne na svoem meste*], a handkerchief dropped on the floor, a book not put back in the bookcase, or whatever. (*BK*, 265–66; *PSS*, 14:242)

When Ivan catches sight of the squint-eyed servant waiting for him by the gate, he suddenly realizes that the "offending object" is Smerdyakov himself. The passage reveals Ivan's subconscious feelings about his father's servant: Ivan sees him not only as a *thing* (comparable to a misplaced book or a handkerchief) but also as a *trifling* thing. It serves as a premonition and a warning as well. Smerdyakov will not stay in his proper place for long.

FROM FERAPONT'S CELL

The outsider status of Ferapont, Rakitin, and Smerdyakov is what *makes* them such dangerous adversaries: for them, the corner turns out to be a source of strength. By allowing Father Ferapont to skip communal meals and prayer, the head monks inadvertently help him construct his reputation for holiness and moral independence, thereby reinforcing his mystique as a righteous objector to the system of eldership and to the monastery leadership as a whole. When Ferapont bursts out of his corner and into the middle of Zosima's wake, his supporters start shouting, "It is he who is holy! It is he who is righteous!" and "He would not be made an elder . . . he would refuse . . . he would not serve a cursed innovation . . . he would not ape their foolery" (*BK*, 336; *PSS*, 14:304). In their minds, Ferapont ("he") is starkly divided from the monastery leaders ("they"). By permitting Ferapont to isolate himself from their community, the leadership has helped him establish that very distinction.

Of course, Ferapont's outburst is motivated less by theological principle than by personal envy. Almost every word he utters reiterates how deeply he resents Zosima's elevated position and his own lowliness by comparison. "You learned ones! In great wisdom you exalt yourselves above my nothingness," he cries. "I came here illiterate, and here forgot what I did know, the Lord himself has protected me, his little one [*malen'kogo*], from your wisdom" (*BK*, 336; *PSS*, 14:303). Ferapont resents not only Zosima's education but even the exalted funeral service to which his rank entitles him: "Tomorrow they will sing 'My Helper and Defender' over him—a glorious canon—and over me when I croak just 'What Earthly Joy'—a little song [*stikhirchik malyi*]" (*BK*, 336; *PSS*, 14:303–4). Ferapont's words rile up the angry monks (who are probably motivated by envy as well), and they gather behind him, threatening to erupt into full-scale rebellion. Only the timely chiming of the church bells calling the monks to mass prevents it.

While Ferapont is a dangerous enemy, he turns out to be more pitiful than frightening. The songlike intonations of his protest associate it with the self-flagellating "people's" grief described earlier in the novel (*BK*, 48; *PSS*, 14:45). A peasant woman lamenting the death of her young son provides the initial example. As she recalls her dead child, she "spoke in a singsong voice [*naraspev*], rocking her head gently from side to side with her cheek resting in her hand [*podpiraia shcheku ladon'iu*]" (*BK*, 48; *PSS*, 14:45). Ferapont's lamentation over Zosima's prominence (and his own insignificance) takes almost the exact same form: "He put his right hand to his cheek and spoke in a singsong" (*prilozhiv pravuiu ladon' k shcheke, proiznes naraspev*) (*BK*, 336; *PSS*, 14:303). Ferapont's sorrow may be unjustified, but it is painfully real and its similarity to the grieving mother's suggests how deeply he feels it. In his final gesture in the novel, Ferapont throws himself down on the ground and sobs "like a little child" (*kak maloe ditia*) (*BK*, 336; *PSS*, 14:304). The comparison emphasizes Ferapont's emotional immaturity, but it also underscores the universality of his experience. Who hasn't, at one time or another, envied someone else's success? Moreover, the comparison reminds us that even angry, envious old men need love and care. (According to Zosima, "most people need to be looked after like children, and some like the sick in hospitals" [*BK*, 217; *PSS*, 14:197].) In spite of his great age, Ferapont resembles the cold, hungry, crying "wee one" (*ditë*) that Dmitry sees in a dream, calling out for warmth, sustenance, and love. Because, as Dmitry puts it, "there are little children and big children. All people are 'wee ones'" (*BK*, 591; *PSS*, 15:31).

RAKITIN'S REVENGE

Rakitin shares many of Ferapont's attributes. Like the monk, Rakitin capitalizes on his reputation as an outsider, especially an outsider to the Karamazov family. And just as the monastery elders mishandle Ferapont—thereby increasing his power rather than defusing it—Dmitry, Ivan, Grushenka, and even occasionally Alyosha all inadvertently contribute to Rakitin's increase in social clout. By rejecting and belittling him, they stoke his resentment and solidify his outsider status at one and the same time. Thanks to his reputation as an external (and thus seemingly objective) observer of the Karamazov drama, Rakitin becomes an important witness for the prosecution, with the power to do the Karamazov brothers great harm (*BK*, 666; *PSS*, 15:99).

Rakitin's hatred of the Karamazovs could be explained as a simple case of class envy. "No, you gentlemen Karamazovs pose as some sort of great and ancient nobility," he snaps at Alyosha in one scene. "Granted I'm only a priest's son and a worm next to you noblemen, but still don't go offending me so gaily and easily" (*BK*, 83; *PSS*, 14:77). But Dmitry and Ivan repeatedly remind Rakitin of their social and moral superiority, which damages his relationship with them still further. Ivan predicts Rakitin's future: he foresees Rakitin's career as a journalist with socialist leanings (whose principles will not, however, keep him from getting rich) down to the exact street on which he will build his town house. As Rakitin complains to Alyosha, "[Ivan] was trouncing me right and left" (*BK*, 82; *PSS*, 14:76). The verb Pevear and Volokhonsky translate as "trouncing" (*otdelyvat'*) means literally "to finish something off." And indeed, Ivan's prediction utterly "finishes" Rakitin off, putting the final touches on the story of who he is and who he can become. To use Bakhtin's terminology, it "finalizes" him. Then Alyosha confirms it and finishes off Rakitin, too: "Ah, Misha, maybe it will all be just as he says, to the last word!" he laughs (*BK*, 83; *PSS*, 14:77).

If Ivan says "the last word" on Rakitin, then Dmitry goes a step further: he defines himself and his brothers in *opposition* to the seminarian, who becomes the embodiment of all things non-Karamazovian in his eyes. Dmitry treats Rakitin as a foil for Alyosha: "Rakitin wouldn't understand this," he says to his brother, "but you, you will understand everything" (*BK*, 591; *PSS*, 15:30). A few sentences later he juxtaposes Rakitin with Ivan as well: "Brother Ivan is not Rakitin, he is hiding an idea" (*BK*, 592, translation modified; *PSS*, 15:32). Dmitry even accuses Rakitin of being a false Russian: "The Karamazovs are not scoundrels, but philosophers, because all real Russians are philosophers, and you, even though you've studied, are not a philosopher, you're a stinking churl [*smerd*]" (*BK*, 588; *PSS*, 15:28). The insult he applies to Rakitin here—*smerd*—is a symbolically significant one. It suggests not only a person of low social class but also someone who literally *stinks*. The nickname of Smerdyakov's mother, "Stinking Lizaveta" (*Lizaveta Smerdiashchaia*), is built on the same root, and it forms the basis of Smerdyakov's offensive and despised last name. Unsurprisingly, Rakitin finds the label deeply offensive as well.

By dubbing Rakitin a nonphilosopher, a false Russian, and someone who does not understand, Dmitry stakes out his own (and Alyosha's and Ivan's) identity as philosophers, real Russians, and people who *do* understand. And some critics, seduced by Dmitry's arguments, have taken his judgment to be the last word on Rakitin's role in the novel. V. S. Dorovatovskaia-Liubimova calls Rakitin "a negation sign" who "acquires meaning only insofar as he is the inverse side of the Karamazovs."[24] She reads him as a conventional minor character, a "partial construct" who exists only to the extent that he serves as a foil and contrast for the heroes.[25] What she misses, however, is how Dmitry helps *turn* Rakitin into a "minus sign" of himself and his legitimate brothers by thinking and speaking about him in those terms. Grushenka does something similar. When she and Alyosha form an ecstatic emotional connection, she not only orders Rakitin to "sit in the corner like my lackey," she also contrasts him with her hero: "Rakitka, you're a mushroom, but he is a prince!" (*BK*, 353, 349; *PSS*, 14:320, 316).[26] Rakitin seems like a conventional minor character, a "foil" to the Karamazov brothers, at least in part because the other characters *treat* him like one.

Rakitin spends much of the novel trying to remake himself as something more and to take revenge on the family that sees him as less. He brings Alyosha to Grushenka's in the hopes that she will seduce him, thereby soiling the youngest Karamazov's reputation for goodness and chastity: "Your dear brother Vanechka once pronounced me a 'giftless liberal windbag,'" he mutters under his breath. "And you, too, could not help letting me know once that I was 'dishonest' . . . Very well! Now we'll see how gifted and honest you are" (*BK*, 342; *PSS*, 14:309). When Grushenka changes her mind about the seduction and starts insulting Rakitin instead, he decides to take revenge on her as well. His reductive description of Grushenka's personality, which the prosecutor reads aloud at the trial, pays her back in kind: "Anger was buried far too early in a young heart, which perhaps contained much good. What formed was a calculating, money-hoarding character. What formed was a derisive and vengeful attitude towards society" (*BK*, 702; *PSS*, 15:132). Rakitin's description emphatically denies Grushenka personal agency; it rarely even makes her the grammatical subject of a sentence. And although his objectifying narrative style reflects his personal beliefs (especially his adherence to a fashionable social determinism), it may serve another purpose as well. In her living room Grushenka silenced him, sent him to a corner, called him a lackey and a mushroom, and at the trial he evens the score. He treats her not as the active subject of her life story but as the passive victim of circumstance, not as a person with free will but, as it were, as a mushroom.

When the defense lawyer reveals that Grushenka and Rakitin are related—a fact he has been trying very hard to hide—his testimony is "destroyed in the general opinion" (*BK*, 684; *PSS*, 15:115). But he nevertheless continues to pose a threat, both to the Karamazov brothers themselves and, as a representative of atheism, materialism, and socialism, to Alyosha's system of belief. If his life path follows that of Grigory Eliseev, the left-wing journalist on whom Dostoevsky based Rakitin's character, then he will overcome his embarrassment in the courtroom, move to Saint Petersburg, and become an influential journalist, spreading his ideas throughout all of Russia.[27]

"MY HUT IS ON THE EDGE OF TOWN": SMERDYAKOV'S NARRATIVES FROM THE SIDE

Smerdyakov is the most dangerous of all. Only he fully understands that (as Gary Saul Morson puts it) "his power is the power of margins"—that his reputation as a lackey, an idiot, and an outsider to the Karamazov family is in fact his greatest strength.[28] Whereas Ferapont and Rakitin cannot resist self-display, taking center stage at public events like Zosima's wake and Dmitry's trial, Smerdyakov presses himself further into the corner, where, unnoticed and overlooked, he works his influence. His trick for hiding Fyodor Pavlovich's three thousand rubles from Dmitry and saving them for himself shows just how well he has learned the lessons of his childhood. He convinces his master "to transfer that same package with the money to the corner behind the icons [*v ugol za obraza*], because no one would ever think of looking there, especially if he was in a hurry" (*BK*, 626; *PSS*, 15:62). At the trial, the prosecutor unwittingly describes Smerdyakov's criminal strategy to perfection. He briefly entertains a scenario in which Dmitry and Smerdyakov collude to kill Fyodor Pavlovich: Dmitry carries out the murder while Smerdyakov lies in bed thinking, "and you can go and kill him any way you like, it's none of my apples [*moia izba s kraiu*]" (*BK*, 711; *PSS*, 15:140). The expression that the prosecutor attributes to Smerdyakov, *moia izba s kraiu*, means literally "my hut is on the edge of town." The scenario may be invented, but the saying fits the speaker. Smerdyakov asserts himself by effacing himself; he becomes the central plot-driving force in *The Brothers Karamazov* by making himself appear ever more peripheral to its main events.

First, Smerdyakov physically *removes* himself from the scene of the crime. He fakes an epileptic fit so that his bed will be moved from the front hall in the main house over to the servants' wing. After the murder, he is carried even farther away—to the hospital. Finally, upon recovery, he moves to his fiancée's new house, which is located, appropriately enough, on the edge of town (*na kraiu goroda*) (*PSS*, 15:126). More important, Smerdyakov hides behind his marginal social status. People believe Smerdyakov to be stupid, sickly, and cowardly, so he acts even more so in order to convince them of his innocence. When he speaks, he exaggerates his lowliness, adopting servile grammatical forms and expressions like the *slovoers* (*-s*)—the shortened form of *sudar'* (sir) and the linguistic marking of someone speaking to a social superior.[29]

Smerdyakov's self-effacement does more than just deflect suspicion; it gives him the means to actively shape the narrative that the prosecution will tell at Dmitry's trial. Socially and politically disenfranchised, not to mention a potential murder suspect, Smerdyakov knows that his opinion will not carry much weight in the courtroom. So he manipulates the police and medical authorities into speaking on his behalf. He suggests to his doctors the fabricated theory that he had an epileptic fit because he feared he would have one, and they, not suspecting him capable of tricking them, immediately seize on the idea. By the time of the trial, Smerdyakov's theory about epilepsy has morphed from a lie into a scientific fact, from what Smerdyakov says into—as the prosecutor proclaims—what "medical science tells us" (*BK*, 708; *PSS*, 15:137). By speaking indirectly, through hints and suggestions rather than open declarations, Smerdyakov gives his ideas infinitely more weight than they would have had if he had uttered them himself.

Much as Smerdyakov uses his social inferiority to convince the investigators of his innocence, he uses Dmitry's nobility to push suspicion his way. He deeply envies Dmitry his noble status, complaining that he is

> worse than any lackey, in his behavior, and in his intelligence, and in his poverty, miss, and he's not fit for anything, but, on the contrary, he gets honor

> from everybody [. . .] Dmitri Fyodorovich is a ragamuffin, but if he were to challenge the biggest count's son to a duel, he would accept, miss, and how is he any better than me? Because he's a lot stupider than me. (*BK*, 225; *PSS*, 14:205)

So Smerdyakov turns Dmitry's noble status against him. He feeds the prosecutor the idea that Dmitry must have committed the murder, because no one but Dmitry would have left the envelope that contained the three thousand rubles lying on the floor: "Because he's an unaccustomed thief, sir, and before that never stole anything obviously, because he's a born nobleman, sir, and even if he did decide to steal this time, it was not precisely to steal, as it were, but only to get his own back" (*BK*, 630; *PSS*, 15:66). Smerdyakov rewrites Dmitry's social advantage into a detriment, a sign of his guilt.

Smerdyakov even plays the game of self-marginalization with his own conscience. For a long time, he believes that Ivan consciously gave him permission to kill Fyodor Pavlovich. Thanks to this psychologically convenient fiction, Smerdyakov can consider himself only *secondarily* guilty of the crime. He says as much to Ivan during their final conversation: "I want to prove it to your face tonight that in all this the main murderer [*glavnyi ubivets*] is you alone, sir, and I'm just the most not main one [*samyi ne glavnyi*], though I did kill him. It's you who are the most lawful murderer [*samyi zakonnyi ubivets*]" (*BK*, 627, translation modified; *PSS*, 15:63). Once again, Smerdyakov turns his outsider status to his own advantage, in a monologue that plays on the Russian words for "centrality," "legality," and "legitimacy." The adjective he uses to describe Ivan here (*zakonnyi*, or "lawful") can also mean "legitimate" in the sense of a legitimate child. He hints that because Ivan is the *legitimate* (*zakonnyi*), "main" son, he is also the *lawful* (*zakonnyi*) parricide. The *illegitimate* (*nezakonnyi*), "not main" son is not. In a radical reversal of Zosima's belief that all are guilty before all, Smerdyakov insists that his low social status makes him less guilty than the rest.

Smerdyakov's final and most extreme act of self-effacing aggression is his suicide. At the trial, the defense lawyer explains that Smerdyakov did not necessarily kill himself out of any sense of remorse: "Despair can be malicious and implacable, and the suicide, as he was taking his life, may at that moment have felt twice as much hatred for those whom he had envied all his life" (*BK*, 740; *PSS*, 15:166). Indeed, Smerdyakov's suicide can be read as his ultimate act of revenge against the family that rejected him. By hanging himself on the eve of the trial, he virtually assures that his own narrative will win the day in court. It means that he does not have to face the questions of the defense lawyer (who suspects him) or Ivan (who plans publicly to accuse him of the murder). Smerdyakov even turns his suicide note into a weapon. As Gary Saul Morson points out, by *not* confessing in it, Smerdyakov upends the genre, thereby convincing the public of his innocence and making Dmitry's conviction almost inevitable.[30]

THE DANGERS OF MARGINALIZATION AND EXCLUSION

By failing to recognize Smerdyakov as a potential family member, by making him into a servant who stands at the edge of their table but cannot sit down with the rest, the Karamazovs not only inspire his deep envy and hatred. They also exponentially increase his ability to do them harm. As the novel shows again and again, marginalizing, isolating, or even killing harmful and destructive people does not neutralize the social danger they pose. To the contrary, it can make them *stronger*.

Dostoevsky makes this point on multiple levels of his text. Just as envious, socially marginalized characters like Rakitin and Smerdyakov tend to reappear unexpectedly and unpleasantly in the lives of the people who ignored and rejected them, they also have a tendency to reappear in the discourse of the novel itself, long after readers might think they have disappeared for good. Robert Belknap has argued that by the end of *The Brothers Karamazov*, "Fëdor, Smerdjakov, and the Pole are eliminated by death or derision [. . .] as the history presented in the novel develops toward a conclusion and stability."[31] While granting Belknap's point about the novel's overall structure, I would counter that socially disruptive characters like Fyodor Pavlovich, Smerdyakov, and Grushenka's former Polish lover are not eliminated from the novel as cleanly or as completely as it might seem. Smerdyakov does die, but his suicide ensures his revenge, and even after death he continues to speak through the prosecutor, who swallows his mendacious hints and repeats them at the trial wholesale. Rakitin is humiliated in court, but that does not silence him: the prosecutor quotes his dehumanizing characterization of Grushenka *after* the seminarian walks off the novel's stage. When Dmitry pushes Grushenka's former Polish lover and his companion into a side room at Mokroe, they do not vanish from the novel; in fact, they don't even leave town. Instead they start begging Grushenka for money, provoking Dmitry's jealousy and causing serious strains in his relationship with her.

Even the murdered Fyodor Pavlovich comes back into the novel metaphorically speaking in the figure of his minor double—the lecherous, sponging, nonlandowner Maksimov. Scholars have long noted the extraordinary number of similarities between the two men: both are close to sixty years old; both love sweets, liqueurs, and much younger women; both were married twice and had a wife desert them; both babble, mention the French epigrammatist Alexis Piron, and brag about being beaten. Fyodor Pavlovich compares Maksimov to the elderly murder victim von Sohn (a real person who was ignominiously killed by prostitutes in a Petersburg brothel) and so, in the words of Maxim Shrayer, "inevitably has converted Maksimov into his own double," since Fyodor Pavlovich resembles von Sohn himself. Not only will the Karamazov patriarch be murdered, but he will also die while trying to pay a young woman for sex.[32] When, just a few hours after Fyodor Pavlovich's death, Maksimov suddenly reappears, he "seems to be Fëdor himself resurrected"—as Robert Belknap puts it.[33]

Why might Dostoevsky have decided to reintroduce Maksimov—who has been absent from the novel for nearly three hundred pages—at precisely this moment in the text? A quote from Father Zosima may provide the answer. In it, Zosima insists that secular judicial punishments like death, exile, and imprisonment are singularly ineffective means of protecting the public from criminals and crime: "And it turns out that society, thus, is not protected at all, for although the harmful member is mechanically cut off and sent far away out of sight, another criminal appears at once to take his place, perhaps even two others" (*BK*, 64; *PSS*, 14:59–60). Fyodor Pavlovich does not break the law (at least not egregiously), but it would be no exaggeration to call him a "harmful member" of his social world. Zosima and Alyosha notwithstanding, nearly everyone in the novel wants the greedy, buffoonish Fyodor Pavlovich out of the way: Dmitry threatens to kill him, Ivan runs off to Moscow, thereby allowing the murder to take place, and Smerdyakov commits the act itself. But just as, according to Zosima, "mechanically" exiling or executing criminals only leaves a space in which more criminals will soon appear, so destroying the "harmful member" that is Fyodor Pavlovich does nothing to remedy the dysfunctional social dynamics that help *create* personalities like his. When Maksimov reappears immediately after Fyodor's murder—drinking liqueurs, gobbling sweets, and telling salacious anecdotes Fyodor Pavlovich–style—it proves Zosima's point.

Dostoevsky hints that there is another, more productive way to deal with sinful people besides exile or execution: bring them *closer*. In *Crime and Punishment*, Razumikhin explains his friendship with the bribe-taking Zametov: "Zametov's just a kid and I can still pull him up by his hair, because, you see, he needs to be kept close. Keep a man at arm's length and you'll never fix him, especially a kid" (*CP*, 125; *PSS*, 6:104). Ivan Karamazov tells the story of yet another unlovable person who nevertheless needs to be held close. In Ivan's tale, Saint John the Merciful happens upon a sick, shivering stranger and "began breathing into his mouth, which was foul-smelling and festering with some terrible disease" (*BK*, 236–37, translation modified; *PSS*, 14:215). Like this sick man, the most envious, unlikable characters in *The Brothers Karamazov* are associated with foul smells. Smerdyakov's last name literally means "stinker" (although he wears perfume, as if to hide the smell of his unclean origins), and Ivan calls him a "stinking lackey" (*voniuchii lakei*), a word with the same root as the adjective "foul-smelling" (*zlovonnyi*) that he uses to describe the sick man's mouth (*PSS*, 14:205). Dmitry calls Rakitin a "stinking churl" (*smerd*), and as for Ferapont, he claims to kill devils who then rot and stink in corners ("He must be rotten and stinking [*smerdit*] in that corner now, and they don't see, they don't smell a thing," he says [*BK*, 169; *PSS*, 14:154]). *The Brothers Karamazov* suggests that embracing even these most "stinking," repellent people is more than a virtue: it is a necessity. When we push them away, ignore or marginalize them, we only make them more dangerous.[34]

Yet the novel also demonstrates that embracing morally and physically repugnant people is extraordinarily difficult. (Ivan tells the story of Saint John's act of mercy only to question its authenticity.) Reintegrating envious, disruptive, and violent people into the communities they have harmed, and that have harmed them, is even harder. Zosima fervently believes that under the influence of Christian love and compassion one day even the most desperate criminals will be able to be brought back into the social whole. But not quite yet.[35] Because it is not just hardened criminals who are difficult to integrate into communal life: it is also the excessively garrulous, the drunks and the lechers, the self-asserting and socially inept who make it nearly impossible to live with them.

"WHERE IS MAKSIMOV?"

Once again Dostoevsky uses a secondary character to make his point. Fyodor Pavlovich's parodic double Maksimov is less offensive than the original in every way: he is less aggressive, less self-promoting, less financially successful, and he wields less social and economic power. Yet as the two characters (Kalganov and Grushenka) who make a concerted effort to include Maksimov in their lives discover, learning to love even this relatively harmless variant of Fyodor Pavlovich is an enormous challenge. In Maksimov's character, problems of social and narrative exclusion are tightly intertwined: in him, the question of how to incorporate a socially disruptive person into the community becomes, simultaneously, the question of how to incorporate a narratively disruptive minor character into a novel. Neither turns out to be easy.

From Maksimov's first appearance in the novel, Dostoevsky emphasizes his marginality. He is minor in every sense of the word: he is physically small and often described in diminutives. He has no family or friends, and he is mostly irrelevant to everyone and everything else in the plot. A "landowner" in name alone, he has been effectively homeless for years. When he chances to meet the Karamazov party at the monastery, he begins "not so much walking but, more precisely, almost running alongside, staring at them all with contorted, almost impossible curiosity" (*BK*, 35; *PSS*, 14:33). After Maksimov shows them the way to Zosima's cell, Miusov pointedly excludes him from the group: "You see, we have come to this elder on a private matter [. . .] and therefore, though we thank you for showing us the way, we cannot invite you to go in with us" (*BK*, 35–36; *PSS*, 14:33). No one will even allow the minuscule "landowner" to speak. He is interrupted by characters still more peripheral than he is: "his disjointed talk" is "cut short by a little monk in a cowl" who disappears from the novel almost as soon as he enters it (*BK*, 36; *PSS*, 14:34). After the scandal at the luncheon, Fyodor Pavlovich invites Maksimov to come drinking, but there is only enough room in the carriage for two (Fyodor and Ivan). Fyodor Pavlovich jokes, "Let him in, Vanya, it will be fun. We'll find room for him somewhere at our feet. Will you lie at our feet, von Sohn? Or shall we stick him in the box with the coachman . . . ?" (*BK*, 91; *PSS*, 14:84). But Ivan, in a displaced act of filial aggression, shoves his father's double off the step, out of the carriage, and out of the novel for hundreds of pages.

Maksimov is self-aware: he not only understands his peripheral position in Skotoprigonyevsk and in the Karamazovs' story, he plays it up. He claims to be the Maksimov from Gogol's *Dead Souls*, mentioned once as having taken a beating from Nozdryov but who never appears in the novel in person—a character so minor, he may not be a character at all. Tellingly, however, the character that Maksimov claims for himself plays an important role in the novel's plot. Thanks to this beaten, never-to-be-seen Maksimov, a police captain shows up on Nozdryov's estate just in time to save the hero, Chichikov, from getting beaten up himself. True to his name (which suggests something *maximal*, oversized, too big for the position it occupies), when Maksimov identifies with a minor character, he identifies with one who makes a splash.

By the time Maksimov reappears in the novel during Dmitry's spree at Mokroe, however, his fortunes have already begun to change. The kind and good-looking Kalganov—himself a minor character, who has attracted the interest of scholars for the surprising amount of narrative attention Dostoevsky devotes to him—has taken Maksimov under his wing.[36] Kalganov explains to Dmitry that he decided to adopt Maksimov precisely *because* the homeless sponger has been mistreated and excluded: "Ever since the day your brother pushed him out of the carriage and sent him flying, remember? That made me very interested in him then, and I took him to the village with me" (*BK*, 420; *PSS*, 14:379). Kalganov pulls Maksimov into his carriage, allowing the man who had been silenced to speak. But when Maksimov opens his mouth, Kalganov does not like what he has to say. He is taking the old man back to town, he explains, because Maksimov "keeps telling such lies that I'm ashamed to be with him" (*BK*, 420; *PSS*, 14:379).

Kalganov's irritation is understandable. Maksimov does not so much speak as babble: he has a habit of repeating himself, and one word from him quickly multiplies into four (as when he prattles on about the "elder, the splendid elder, the elder . . . The honor and glory of the monastery, Zosima. Such an elder . . . !" [*BK*, 36; *PSS*, 14:33]). He tells long and halting stories, full of giggles, inappropriate pauses, and sexual innuendos. A single paragraph of his tale about the exploits of pretty little Polish misses contains a total of *nine* ellipses. And the more he is encouraged to speak, the less coherent his tales become. He concludes one incomprehensible story, which references Sappho, various characters from *Dead Souls* and "pretty legs in tights," with the logically dissonant lines, "Then they up and thrashed me [. . .] For my education. A man can be thrashed for all sorts of reasons" (*BK*, 423; *PSS*, 14:382). Finally, Grushenka cuts him off in disgust: "Eh, enough, it's all bad, I don't want to listen, I thought there would be some fun in it" (*BK*, 423; *PSS*, 14:382). Maksimov's ever-expanding tales amuse for an instant but then quickly tire his listeners, not to mention the novel's readers, who may even feel tempted to flip a page ahead.

Kalganov makes conscious, repeated efforts to justify Maksimov's buffoonish behavior. When Maksimov tells the (perhaps partly true, but highly exaggerated) story about his lame wife, Kalganov turns to Dmitry: "Even if he's lying—and he lies all the time—he's lying so as to give pleasure to us all: that's not mean, is it? You know, sometimes I love him. He's awfully mean, but naturally so, eh?" (*BK*, 422; *PSS*, 14:381). It turns out, however, that telling long, blathering tall tales is not Maksimov's only vice. As Dmitry gets the party started at Mokroe in earnest, with girls, champagne, and song, another one of Maksimov's Karamazovian characteristics—his sexual appetite—rears its head. He starts kissing Grushenka's fingers and hovers around the women that Dmitry has hired to sing and dance, only leaving their side long enough to stuff himself with liqueurs and sweets, until his "little face had turned red, his nose was purple, his eyes were moist and sweet" (*BK*, 435–36; *PSS*, 14:393). Eventually, he asks Dmitry for money to procure one of the young women: "This girl Mariushka—hee, hee—could I possibly make her acquaintance, would you be so kind . . . ?" (*BK*, 436; *PSS*, 14:394).

Up until this moment, Kalganov has been worrying about Maksimov, following him around the party, trying to keep his new friend from getting into too much trouble. When Kalganov wakes up from a nap, the first question he asks "with a most worried look" is, "Where is Maximov?" (*BK*, 435; *PSS*, 14:393). But after Maksimov starts chasing after Mariushka, Kalganov stops mentioning him. Indeed, the raw sensuality of the entire party repulses him. When girls in bear costumes fall on the floor "quite indecently," Kalganov "looked as if he had soiled himself with something" (*BK*, 434; *PSS*, 14:392). And after Dmitry is arrested, Kalganov begins to despair of humanity as a whole: "'What are these people, what sort of people can there be after this!' he kept exclaiming incoherently, in bitter dejection, almost in despair. At that moment he did not even want to live in the world" (*BK*, 512; *PSS*, 14:461). Having lost his faith in human goodness, Kalganov loses interest in Maksimov as well. He gives the old man five rubles and tells him never to come to see him again (*BK*, 564; *PSS*, 15:6).[37]

After Kalganov sends Maksimov away, Grushenka attempts to adopt him next, consciously or subconsciously atoning for her mistreatment of Fyodor Pavlovich by taking in his pathetic double. When she finds out that Kalganov has abandoned Maksimov and that he truly has nowhere else to go, she sets up a bed for him on her couch. Initially, it seems that the homeless Maksimov has finally found his place. He refuses to budge: "All that day he sat in the same place almost without stirring" (*BK*, 564; *PSS*, 15:6). As if afraid to lose his new home, he will not even step beyond the perimeters of Grushenka's property: "Even during her illness he did not leave" (*BK*, 564; *PSS*, 15:6). One gets the sense that Maksimov has found his place in a metaphorical sense as well. Not just a sponger anymore, the affectionately dubbed "Maksimushka" plays cards with Grushenka to help her pass the time and forget her grief over Dmitry's imprisonment: "It turned out that the old man could occasionally come up with some story or other, so that finally he even became necessary to her" (*BK*, 564; *PSS*, 15:6). The old man's babbling stories turn out to be good for something after all.

The text also contains hints, however, that Maksimov is not as fully integrated into Grushenka's life as it might appear. When Alyosha comes to visit, the hidden tensions between Grushenka and her new housemate quickly rise to the surface. Dmitry has become terribly jealous thanks to another act of inclusion that Grushenka has undertaken: giving money and food to her impoverished Polish ex-lover. It is not at all clear that she will be able to continue her charity toward him without doing serious injury to her relationship with Dmitry, however. "What a fool!" she complains to Alyosha. "Well, there's no fear he'll get jealous of Maksimushka here" (*BK*, 566; *PSS*, 15:7). Grushenka's very *denial* that Dmitry could become jealous of Maksimov, however, reminds the reader that this is a real possibility. After all, Dmitry has an irrationally jealous personality, and the lascivious, albeit ridiculous, Maksimov resembles Fyodor Pavlovich too closely for comfort. If Dmitry were to become jealous of Maksimov, or even just excessively irritated by him, would Maksimov be able to keep his spot on Grushenka's couch?

This is precisely the moment when Grushenka and Maksimov's relationship begins to founder, and against the same shoals that his relationship with Kalganov did: Maksimov's verbal and sexual incontinence. Grushenka's words are actually an insult, and Maksimov responds to them by asserting himself, reminding her of his sexual potency: "'My spouse was also very jealous of me, ma'am,' Maksimov put in his own little word [*svoe slovtso*] [. . .] 'Of the chambermaids, ma'am'" (*BK*, 566, translation modified; *PSS*, 15:7–8). But even one *little* word from Maksimov is a word too many. Not only does Grushenka silence him, turning him from a minor participant in the conversation into no participant at all, she also cruelly reminds him of his dependent status: "'Eh, be quiet, Maksimushka, it's no time for laughing now, I even feel angry. Don't ogle the pirozhki, I won't give you any, they're bad for you; and I won't give you any liqueur either. Must I bother with him, too? Really, it's like running an almshouse,' she laughed" (*BK*, 566, translation modified; *PSS*, 15:8). Grushenka responds to Maksimov's sexual joke angrily, in part because she "doesn't feel like laughing," but perhaps even more because Maksimov will not remain within the confines of the role she has designated for him, that of a harmless little old man, who tells stories that amuse her but most certainly does *not* make inappropriate comments about maidservants. Her refusal to give Maksimov sweets can be read as yet another attempt to control his errant sexual impulses: sex and sweets go hand in hand for Maksimov as they did for Fyodor Pavlovich. (Right before he asks to make Mariushka's "acquaintance," Maksimov requests a special kind of chocolate: "I'd like one with vanilla . . . they're for old folks, sir . . . Hee, hee!" [*BK*, 436; *PSS*, 14:394].)

Only when Maksimov repents of his "own little word," retreating back into his assigned place, does Grushenka soften toward him. "I am unworthy of your benefactions, ma'am, I am nothing, ma'am [*ia nichtozhen-s*],' Maksimov said in a tearful little voice [*goloskom*]. 'You'd do better to lavish your benefactions on those who are more useful [*nuzhnee*] than I am, ma'am.'" (*BK*, 566; *PSS*, 15:8). Grushenka quickly retreats as well: "Ahh, everyone is necessary [*nuzhen*], Maksimushka, and how can anyone say who is more necessary?" (*BK*, 566, translation modified; *PSS*, 15:8). Ironically, however, Maksimov disappears from the novel at the very moment Grushenka utters these words.[38] He is not mentioned again during this scene, which lasts for several more pages and centers on Grushenka's highly plot-relevant discussion with Alyosha about her relationship with Dmitry (Maksimov's "own little word" is an interruption and a digression). In fact, the narrator never refers to Maksimov again except to say that he is *absent* from the trial because of illness. The last time readers hear of him is from the defense lawyer, who makes light of Maksimov's tendency to exaggerate, part and parcel of his oversized personality.

Alex Woloch has argued that the "strange significance of minor characters [. . .] resides largely in the way that the character disappears, and in the tension or relief that results from this vanishing."[39] I suggest that Maksimov's sudden disappearance from the scene at Grushenka's house creates tension—a tension between her claim that Maksimov may be a more "necessary" person than he thinks and his superfluity to both Grushenka's life and her story line, which ultimately revolves around her relationship with Dmitry. She may find him entertaining for the moment, as long as he keeps his stories within certain bounds (something he seems utterly incapable of doing). But how "necessary" will he be to her after Dmitry's conviction, when the couple either heads to Siberia or runs away to America? Where will Maksimov go then?

Neither Kalganov nor Grushenka manages to fully integrate Maksimov into their lives. Nor does the narrator, who drops the little old man in the middle of a chapter, manage to fully integrate Maksimov into his tale. It is no wonder the narrator turns away from him and does not look back: Maksimov is not merely peripheral to the history of the brothers Karamazov, he also says or does something irrelevant or inappropriate every time he walks into the room. He never forwards the plot, only retards it. But if both the characters and the narrator seem to have forgotten about Maksimov by novel's end, I do not believe that Dostoevsky has. When Maksimov suddenly disappears, at the precise moment that Grushenka insists that he may be *necessary*, the careful reader may be prompted to repeat Kalganov's question—"Where is Maksimov?"—and realize that neither the narrator, nor any of the characters, has quite figured out how to include him. Maksimov's disappearance reinforces on the level of the novel's narrative structure what has already become apparent in the story: it is hard to find a place for Maksimov. The social conundrum he poses for other characters and the narrative conundrum he poses for the narrator remain unresolved.

INTO ILYUSHA'S CORNER

Alyosha is the only character in the novel who unequivocally surmounts the distance between people who have been marginalized and the community that rejected them, reintegrating them into the social fold. By building a friendship with the humiliated Captain Snegiryov and his young son Ilyusha, Alyosha brings two characters who had been peripheral—both in the life of the town and in the structure of the novel—to the center of his attention. In so doing, he provides *The Brothers Karamazov*'s best lesson on how to prevent envy and resentment, to stop long-standing hatreds before they start.

Alyosha is horrified when he discovers that Dmitry dragged Captain Snegiryov down the street by his beard, deaf to the pleadings of Ilyusha, who watched it all happen. Unable to challenge Dmitry to a duel and thus restore his broken honor (Snegiryov is the impoverished sole provider of a large family, and his death would mean his children's ruin), the captain starts to suffer Smerdyakov-like attacks of wounded pride. Like Smerdyakov, he self-consciously adds the servile *slovoers* to the end of his words, introducing himself to Alyosha as "Captain Yessirov [*Slovoersov*] instead of Snegiryov, because it's only in the second half of my life that I've started saying 'Yessir.' 'Yessir' is acquired in humiliation" (*BK*, 199; *PSS*, 14:182). And like Smerdyakov, who has a demonic "slightly squinting left eye" (*prishchurennyi levyi glazok*) (*BK*, 267; *PSS*, 14:244), Snegiryov starts screwing up his left eye. When Alyosha tries to give Snegiryov a gift of two hundred rubles from Dmitry's fiancée, Katerina Ivanovna, the captain initially reaches for the money. Then, suddenly, "his mouth became twisted to the left side, his left eye squinted [*levyi glaz prishchurilsia*]," and he tramples the bills under foot (*BK*, 211; *PSS*, 14:193).

Snegiryov has good reasons to refuse the two hundred rubles; accepting money from Dmitry's relations would amount to selling his honor.[40] Nevertheless, the consequences of his refusal could be disastrous. If Alyosha had left things there, Snegiryov would have become more and more isolated from the rest of the community, and his left eye, like Smerdyakov's, might have distorted itself into a permanent squint, the embodiment of his envy and resentment. Instead, however, Alyosha empathizes with Snegiryov, immediately understands why he could not accept, and returns a few days later with a renewed offer of money and, more important, of friendship. Having proven that he cannot be bought, Snegiryov is now able to accept both, and he stops squinting.

Although Ilyusha is much younger, he has gone even further down Smerdyakov's path than his father has. Anne Hruska has pointed to the similarities between Ilyusha and Smerdyakov, whom she identifies as simultaneous victims and tormentors. Both are beaten (Smerdyakov by Grigory, Ilyusha by his classmates), both are cruel to animals (Smerdyakov hangs cats and teaches Ilyusha to torture dogs), and both draw human blood (Ilyusha stabs Kolya Krasotkin with a penknife and bites Alyosha's finger).[41] But the likeness does not stop there. Both suffer from seeing a parent publicly dishonored, and both express the desire to challenge the guilty party to a duel. Ilyusha swears that when he gets older he will fight Dmitry, thereby erasing Snegiryov's shame. Just a few pages later, Smerdyakov says he would "have killed a man in a duel with a pistol for calling me low-born, because I came from Stinking Lizaveta without a father" (*BK*, 224; *PSS*, 14:204).

Unlike Smerdyakov, however, Ilyusha always remains generous. He dreams of fighting a duel with Dmitry in order to restore his *father's* honor; Smerdyakov wants to fight anyone who calls *him* "low-born." When Snegiryov reminds his son that to kill is a sin, Ilyusha revises his plan: "I'll rush at him, throw him down, hold my sword over him and say: I could kill you now, but I forgive you, so there!" (*BK*, 207; *PSS*, 14:188–89). Smerdyakov will show no such mercy to Fyodor Pavlovich. Nevertheless, the similarities between the humiliated boy and the illegitimate son are striking. The day after Dmitry drags Snegiryov down the street, Ilyusha retreats (where else?) into the *corner* of his family house. As Snegiryov recalls, "All that day he hardly spoke to me, he was even quite silent, only I noticed him looking, looking at me from the corner [*iz ugla*]" (*BK*, 206; *PSS*, 14:188).

It is hard to imagine Ilyusha growing up to become a murderer and a thief, but his disturbing, Smerdyakov-like behavior suggests that he is at the very least in danger of becoming isolated, angry, and vengeful. From the moment Alyosha first visits the boy's corner, however, and the curtain that separates him from the rest of his family is pulled back, it becomes clear that Ilyusha can and will be redeemed. Because the sick child is resting not just in any corner but in the so-called red or beautiful corner, where Russian Orthodox families traditionally hang their icons. The icon corner has enormous symbolic importance in Russian culture. It is the place toward which one directs one's eyes and prayers immediately upon entering a room. Generally oriented toward the south or the east, it is also the corner that gets the most natural light. In the icon corner, periphery and center meet: it serves as the emotional and spiritual heart of the entire house.[42] When Alyosha brings Ilyusha's former enemies, the other schoolboys, into this corner, it becomes the spiritual center of their group as well.

HARMONY (AND DISSONANCE) BY THE STONE

When Alyosha leads the schoolboys into Ilyusha's corner, he has two aims, one more and one less explicit: he is not only trying to reincorporate a shunned child back into the schoolboy collective, he also dreams of transforming that collective into a harmonious brotherhood, a microcosm of the universal brotherhood that he hopes will one day encompass all the earth. But Alyosha encounters the same obstacles to creating a peaceful and inclusive community that have arisen again and again over the course of the novel. Like so many other interior spaces in *The Brothers Karamazov*, Snegiryov's hut is not big enough to fit everyone comfortably inside. When Alyosha first visits, it is described as "rather spacious but extremely cluttered both with people and with all kinds of domestic chattels" (*BK*, 197; *PSS*, 14:180). I count only six people in the room (Alyosha, Snegiryov, his wife, two daughters, and Ilyusha), but nevertheless the atmosphere is close and oppressive, the windows shut and the air unclean. When the boys pile in to visit, it becomes even more overfull, "stuffy and crowded with a numerous gathering of visitors" (*BK*, 538; *PSS*, 14:484). Ilyusha's half-mad mother accuses the boys of barging into the hut one on top of the other: "One sits on another's shoulders in the entryway, and they come riding in like that, to see respectable people" (*BK*, 542; *PSS*, 14:488). She has imagined the entire scenario, but the comic image reinforces the crowded atmosphere of the scene.

There is simply not enough room for everyone, and tension within the group is both literally heightened and metaphorically reinforced by the lack of interior space. The young Kolya Krasotkin, dominator of boys, dogs, and dialogue, stands in the center of the hut and talks without ceasing, while other children find themselves pushed to the edges of the room. One of the sidelined boys—Kartashov—"was sitting just next to the door" and "had said almost nothing till then, was silent and obviously shy" (*BK*, 550; *PSS*, 14:496–97). Suddenly he speaks up, challenging Kolya's authority by insisting that he knows who founded Troy, too (the secret knowledge Kolya has been using to assert himself over everyone, even his teachers). Immediately, "what is known as a dissonance [*dissonans*] came into the general mood" (*BK*, 550; *PSS*, 14:497). By challenging Kolya's dominance, Kartashov threatens to destroy the social harmony of the schoolboy collective, which relaxes into laughter only after Kolya shames Kartashov and reasserts his power. In short, this large group, in its tiny space, *depends* on some members dominating others in order to maintain its imperfect, and necessarily temporary, harmony. It has major characters (Kolya) and minor characters (Kartashov) who must stay in place if the group is not to collapse into internal fighting and chaos. And since Kartashov will not stay in place, "dissonance" is never far away.

Ilyusha's death has a transformative effect on everything and everyone around him, however. It not only unites his family and friends together in grief, it even seems to make Snegiryov's hut *expand*, creating enough room for all those who were previously pushed to its edges. If, when Alyosha first visited, the hut seemed crowded with only six people inside, I count eighteen people standing around Ilyusha's coffin, and there is no mention of tightness or crowding. At the very least, the group has learned how to share space: nobody steps on anyone else's toes or envies anyone else's place, if only for a short time.[43] The transformations do not stop there, however. Snegiryov's landladies emerge from their closed-off, isolated space to participate in mourning the child's death as well. When Alyosha first visited, the landlady and her elderly daughter are described as "apparently deaf" and perhaps even mute: "In reply to his question about the captain, repeated several times, one of them finally understood that he was asking for the tenants and jabbed with her finger across the hall" (*BK*, 197; *PSS*, 14:179). After Ilyusha's death, however, the landlady has miraculously acquired the power of communication. She stands by Ilyusha's coffin and impresses on Snegiryov the importance of burying his son not in unconsecrated ground by his favorite stone but in the church cemetery. And this formerly deaf woman actually describes the *sound* of the prayers that will float over Ilyusha's grave: "You can hear singing from the church there, and the deacon is so clean-spoken and literal when he reads, it will all reach him every time, as if they were reading right over his grave" (*BK*, 770; *PSS*, 15:191).

I do not mean to suggest that Dostoevsky intentionally transformed these landladies from deaf-mutes into lovers of the sounds of church prayer. The first time the narrator mentions them, he calls them mother and daughter; the second time, several hundred pages later, he refers to them as sisters. This is most likely a mistake; over the years Dostoevsky spent writing the novel, even he seems to have forgotten details about these (very) minor characters. And yet the inconsistencies concerning the landladies are utterly *consistent* with the rest of the scene. The landladies' transformation from mother and daughter to sisters reinforces the neutralization of familial hierarchy that characterizes Ilyusha's funeral (when Snegiryov hugs his son's coffin with cries of "Batiushka!" [Father!]—his favorite nickname for the boy). These reversals foretell an end to the time when fathers rule over sons, as Fyodor Pavlovich did, and the beginning of a time when everyone will truly be brothers, or, as in the case of Snegiryov's landladies, sisters.[44]

The inconsistency concerning the landladies is just one of many examples of the sweeping transformative power of Ilyusha's death. It ushers in a brief period of social communion into which even the most marginal people in Ilyusha's life, and many of the most marginal characters in *The Brothers Karamazov*, are drawn. The new community that gathers around Ilyusha's coffin requires a new type of narrative, with a new type of minor character, to describe it. Consciously or not, Dostoevsky transforms the landlady to fulfill her new function: no longer deaf, silent, and physically isolated, nor excessively garrulous like Maksimov, she speaks her mind without interrupting anyone else or being silenced herself. She both allows herself to be drawn into community and brings others along with her: by insisting that Ilyusha be buried in the cemetery and not by an isolated stone, she brings him, even in death, back into human society.

Yet just when the social and narrative questions that dominate the novel seem to have finally been resolved, Dostoevsky hints that this new unity will not, in fact *cannot*, last. Ilyusha's death, like Christ's, enacts miracles: a deaf-mute suddenly regains her sense of hearing and the power of speech; eighteen people fit into one hut, and no one feels crowded. In contrast with Zosima's body, Ilyusha's is wondrously preserved ("strangely, there was almost no smell from the corpse" [*BK*, 769; *PSS*, 15:190]). The scene provides a brief glimpse of the Kingdom of Christ on earth as Dostoevsky imagined it, when those with squinted eyes, like Smerdyakov, will see clearly, the deaf will hear the sounds of prayer, everyone will share his love and attention with everyone else, and all will be brother and sister. But that day has not come yet, and, for now anyway, the scene in the hut both stretches the limits of physical possibility and the limits of literary realism.

The spell is broken as soon as the boys venture out into the open air, where there truly is enough room for everyone. "Suddenly in a loud voice" Kartashov blurts out a tactless remark about the salmon to be served at the funeral reception and Kolya cruelly silences him: "I ask you seriously, Kartashov, not to interrupt anymore with your foolishness, especially when no one is talking to you or even cares to know of your existence" (*BK*, 773; *PSS*, 15:194). Dostoevsky emphasizes the continuing tensions within the group through a series of repeating images. Snegiryov sprinkles bread crumbs on Ilyusha's grave so that birds will gather at his tomb (a symbol of unity), but as they are leaving the cemetery, the boy Smurov throws a piece of brick at a flock of sparrows (replacing the symbol of unity with one of disorder and dispersion).[45] When Alyosha compares the boys to little doves, he only strengthens the reader's sense that this group will soon fly away in many different directions. In his speech by the stone, Alyosha attempts to reinforce this moment of communal brotherhood and love so that the boys remember it when it passes, as he knows it must. Yet Alyosha finds composing a harmonious, inclusive speech almost as difficult as building a harmonious, inclusive brotherly community, one that does not marginalize anyone or leave anyone out.

Alyosha does his best. He makes inclusive grammatical choices. Robert Louis Jackson argues that Alyosha tries to connect himself with his audience, and his audience members to one another, by using "the plural 'we' and its variants ('us,' 'our') thirty-seven times" over the course of his speech.[46] Alyosha promises that he will keep each and every one of them in mind: "I give you my word, gentlemen, that for my part I will never forget any one of you; each face that is looking at me now, at this moment, I will remember, be it even after thirty years" (*BK*, 775; *PSS*, 15:196). Yet just as the narrator has introduced the reader to some, but not all, of the boys in his history (only Kolya, Kartashov, and Smurov are named; the other boys remain anonymous), so Alyosha cannot help but elevate some children over others in his speech. He chastises Kolya for his cruelty to Kartashov, calling on all the boys to be "brave" like the former and "clever" like the latter. And then suddenly, Alyosha catches himself: as if realizing that by singling out Kolya and Kartashov he might be perceived as favoring them and thus create even more friction in the group, he qualifies his words: "But why am I talking about these two? You are all dear to me, gentlemen" (*BK*, 775; *PSS*, 15:196). Alyosha *has* to catch himself, however. No matter how hard he tries to compose an inclusive speech that touches on each boy equally, he cannot help but make some of them more central and others more peripheral. Just to defend the maligned Kartashov, Alyosha must afford him more attention than, say, Smurov or the nine other boys who remain unnamed.

Even when the boys shout "Hurrah for Karamazov!" in unison—the height of their brotherly harmony—there are hints of potentially destabilizing inequalities within the group. Not all their voices resound with equal strength. Kolya cries out by himself five times; the other boys only ever cry in unison, except for one voice "which seemed to be Kartashov's" (*BK*, 776; *PSS*, 15:196). (No surprise there: Kartashov is always trying to make himself heard.) For the moment, Kartashov does not seem to mind playing second fiddle and repeating Kolya's words, but how long will that last? Even these famously harmonious cries contain the fractures that could lead to future dissonance.

Critics have often read the final scene as the epitome of brotherly love in the novel.[47] But a growing contingent of scholars has begun to draw attention to the cracks that run below its surface. Carol Apollonio points out that this brotherhood has no room for women, calling it "a stunted version of the world," and Joe Andrew objects to it for similar reasons.[48] Indeed, it is hard to imagine the harmony of the brotherhood remaining intact in the presence of an attractive young woman. What would have happened to this loving group if the flirtatious Lise had decided to attend Ilyusha's funeral instead of just sending flowers? Or if the beautiful Katerina Ivanovna had showed up to pay her respects in person? Sex is the source of much of the novel's conflict: the rape of Stinking Lizaveta leads to Smerdyakov's illegitimate birth; Fyodor Pavlovich's fight with Dmitry is spurred on by their mutual love for Grushenka; Grushenka argues with Maksimov over his raunchy jokes about maidservants. The problems of sexual violence, sexual jealousy, and sexual incontinence—which cause so much disharmony in this narrative—remain in full force at its end.

Other problems remain as well. An even more all-encompassing one is the difficulty of sharing resources—wealth, prestige, and power. Father Zosima acknowledges that in human society there will always be masters and servants, bishops and novices, the richer and the poorer, the more and the less talented. "Equality is only in a man's spiritual dignity, and only among us will that be understood," he explains. Zosima believes that one day men will recognize this universal spiritual equality, and "it will come to pass that even the most corrupt of our rich men will finally be ashamed of his riches before the poor man, and the poor man, seeing his humility, will understand and yield to him in joy" (*BK*, 316; *PSS*, 14:286). Until that day, however, the unequal distribution of power and privilege will make for a chronically unstable social world, in which those on top will be tempted to abuse their power and those below will threaten to rebel against them.

Dostoevsky ultimately comes to a conclusion about narrative structures analogous to the one Zosima comes to about social structures: all narratives, even the most inclusive, will have protagonists and secondary characters, focus on some stories and exclude others. For Dostoevsky, the problem is not narrative inequality as such. Rather, problems arise because narratives are composed—and consumed—by fallible human beings. And whether we are writing a narrative or reading one, we are prone to error, to taking "secondary things for the most important, and even overlook[ing] the most prominent and necessary features" in ways that reflect our social prejudices.[49] In both form and content, *The Brothers Karamazov* affirms this point. The novel's characters tend to neglect and underestimate precisely those people whom it is most dangerous to neglect and underestimate (whether Rakitin, Smerdyakov, or the members of Dmitry's jury). The narrator underestimates them as well, tempting readers to do the same. We may or may not take the bait. To quote Olga Meerson, "the reader can take Smerdyakov's consciousness into account or brush it aside like the protagonists do"; it's our choice.[50]

DOSTOEVSKY'S MINOR CHARACTERS AND BAKHTIN

I conclude this chapter where I began it: with *Problems of Dostoevsky's Poetics*. A close reading of Bakhtin's text reveals an unresolved tension in his argument. He does not seem to have finally decided whether each and every character in Dostoevsky's novels has "a fully valid" and autonomous voice, or if some characters are more "autonomous" than others (*PDP*, 6; *SS*, 6:10). In some places Bakhtin suggests that *all* of Dostoevsky's characters resemble free people (*PDP*, 99; *SS*, 6:114). But in others he states his case with greater reserve, allotting this status only to the *major* characters (as when he writes that "Dostoevsky's major characters [*glavnye geroi*] are, by the very nature of his creative design, *not only objects of authorial discourse but also subjects of their own directly signifying discourse*" [*PDP*, 7; *SS*, 6:10–11]). So which is it? Are all Dostoevsky's characters created equal? Or are some, belonging to the category of "major" characters—as opposed to the "minor" ones—more equal than the rest?

When he was in the process of revising the Dostoevsky book, Bakhtin apparently considered the second possibility. His 1961 notes for the revision include two references to the "secondary objectified personages" (*vtorostepennye ob"ektnye personazhi*) in Dostoevsky's works. In one note, he describes these "object" characters as the ones "who are depicted essentially beyond the boundaries of dialogue, depicted as extras who do not have their own word with which to enrich or change the meaning of the dialogue."[51] In another, he calls them "the ones who do not take part in the great dialogue (the ones who merely serve as the material or the paradigm for dialogue)."[52]

But Bakhtin chose not to include either reference in the final version of his text. In *Problems of Dostoevsky's Poetics*, it remains unclear where, or if, Dostoevsky's minor characters fit into the argument.[53]

Perhaps Bakhtin avoids discussing Dostoevsky's "objectified personages" for practical reasons. Doing so would put significant strain on his more provocative claims (such as, "In Dostoevsky's world generally there is nothing merely thing-like, no mere matter, no object—there are only subjects" [*PDP*, 237; *SS*, 6:264]). Yet there may be another reason for Bakhtin's reticence as well. Maybe he could never quite decide how much "freedom" Dostoevsky grants his minor characters because Dostoevsky *himself* wobbled on this point. The tension in Bakhtin's argument reflects a tension in Dostoevsky's fiction, a formal problem that Dostoevsky struggled with throughout the 1870s: how much narrative attention to grant secondary characters and secondary plotlines. How many stories can you tell in one novel? How many voices can sound in one narrative before it collapses into cacophony? Some voices must be dampened, and others muted entirely, but which ones? How does the author decide, and what are the ethical consequences of making this decision?

Conclusion

IN "MR. ——BOV AND THE QUESTION OF ART," Dostoevsky wrote, "How do we recognize artistic merit in a work of art? When we see a harmony, as full as possible, between the artistic idea and the form in which it is realized" (*PSS*, 18:80). Dostoevsky's late novels achieve just such a harmony between form and content. Not between *ideal* form and *ideal* content but between their warped, dissonant narrative structures and the warped, dissonant social worlds they represent. Mikhail Bakhtin famously argued that the form of Dostoevsky's novels reflects the author's ethical worldview. According to Bakhtin, Dostoevsky's "fundamental principle—the affirmation of someone's else's 'I' not as an object but as another subject" becomes, simultaneously, "the principle behind Dostoevsky's *artistic* visualization of the world" (*PDP*, 11; *SS*, 6:15). As I have tried to show, however, the narrators of *Demons*, *The Adolescent*, and *The Brothers Karamazov* reject that "fundamental principle" almost as often as they respect it. They gossip and spy, make precipitous moral judgments, and sometimes even dehumanize the people they describe.

Dostoevsky firmly believed in the redemptive power of narrative art, but he was also fascinated by narrative dysfunction—how stories can hurt the people who hear, read, and tell them. In his late novels, Dostoevsky asks (of his narrators, his readers, and himself) the following: Why do tales of suffering and scandal interest us so much, and is the interest they inspire compassionate, voyeuristic, or both? How do the endings we project onto our stories, our lives, and human history as a whole shape their ethical content? When constructing a narrative about contemporary life, how do we decide what (or whom) to make central and what to push to the margins? And what are the consequences of making the wrong choice?

In chapter 1, I explored the ethics of curiosity in *Demons*, Dostoevsky's most violent and suspenseful novel. I argued that, when faced with the sight, sound, or story of other people's suffering, both the narrator of and the characters in *Demons* express fluctuating emotions, from compassionate interest at one end of the spectrum to "greedy curiosity" at the other. Indeed, Dostoevsky suggests that these responses are two sides of the same coin, two different ways in which we manifest our intense interest in other people, and especially in their pain. The difference between the two inheres in the degree to which we are willing to suffer ourselves: Will we love these others as ourselves and suffer along with them? Or will we treat them as a spectacle that we can watch from an emotionally safe distance? Because our attitudes toward other people are unstable, even the best of us respond to suffering—whether we encounter it in life or on the pages of a book—with alternating feelings of compassion and *curiositas*.

Chapter 2 examined Dostoevsky's experiments with endings and closure in *The Adolescent*. In that novel, Dostoevsky explores the many ways in which narrative closure (and open-endedness) can go wrong. *The Adolescent* suggests that stories about human destiny that are excessively open-ended simply confuse their audience, leaving them without ethical or intellectual guidance. When such narratives resolve their tensions too quickly and easily, however, they can be even more dangerous, because then they imply that redemption can be achieved easily as well. In the ending of *The Adolescent* itself, Dostoevsky strives for a middle ground between these two extremes. Like the conclusions to *Crime and Punishment* and *The Brothers Karamazov*, the ending of *The Adolescent* combines plot and interpretative open-endedness with closure. It hints at the triumphant end of human history as Dostoevsky envisioned it—but only hints. It leaves the details (what precisely this renewed world will look like and what twists and turns humanity will take on the road toward it) open to interpretation.

The third chapter investigated the problem of primary and secondary characters in *The Brothers Karamazov*. Overwhelmed by the complexity of his tale, the novel's narrator finds it difficult to sort the major from the minor, the essential from the trivial elements of his story. The characters wrestle with a similar set of questions, struggling to decide where to focus their attention, and what (and whom) to put off thinking about until later. As the novel demonstrates, however, such choices are always subject to error, and grievous error at that. Nearly everyone in *The Brothers Karamazov* underestimates or dismisses as secondary precisely those people they should be paying the *most* attention to. All narratives, even the most inclusive, will necessarily focus on some subjects and marginalize or exclude others; the real danger, Dostoevsky implies, is that we will allow our social prejudices to determine how we allocate our limited time, space, and attention.

In each of his last three novels, Dostoevsky uses a different aspect of novelistic form to engage readers in a distinct moral dilemma. In *Demons*, he deploys every trick in the serialized-novelist's trade to create suspense and provoke curiosity. Then he prompts readers to ask themselves what emotional impulses underlie that curiosity, and if they are something we should be proud of. In *The Adolescent*, he presents multiple narratives about the end of time—some more, some less open-ended—and invites readers to consider the ethical ramifications of each. In *The Brothers Karamazov*, both the narrator and the characters deem the socially marginal Smerdyakov, Rakitin, and Ferapont figures of secondary importance, tempting the novel's readers to do the same. If we fall into this pattern of thinking, however, we simply re-create their mistakes.

The famous epigraph to Gogol's comedy *The Government Inspector* reads, "Don't blame the mirror if your mug is crooked."[1] Dostoevsky's early works bear the clear imprint of Gogol's influence. (When Nikolai Nekrasov first read *Poor Folk*, he is supposed to have declared, "A new Gogol has appeared!" [*WD2*, 842; *PSS*, 25:30].) Dostoevsky's late works are less Gogolian in style, but they nevertheless carry on an important aspect of Gogol's project. Like his predecessor, Dostoevsky attempts to reflect his readers' moral mugs back at them, with the crookedness in full relief. How readers respond to his novelistic mirrors, however, is up to them. Nikolai Mikhailovsky was not wrong when he wrote that readers find the violence and cruelty in Dostoevsky's novels "pleasant, without the slightest partaking of other feelings or thoughts."[2] Some undoubtedly do. As I have tried to show, however, Dostoevsky designs his scenes of violence *both* to attract readers *and* to evoke other feelings and thoughts as well—specifically, an awareness of how demonically attractive violence can be. But not every reader will play along. In fact, some will respond in the opposite way: they will find Dostoevsky's "revolting spectacles" so horrifying they will put the book down halfway through. (Like my father, who could never make it through more than twenty pages of *Crime and Punishment*, and still shudders every time I mention the novel.)

Dostoevsky felt keenly the limitations of his ability to control reader response. In the preface to *The Brothers Karamazov*, he meditates on this very topic. After fretting that readers will not recognize the "noteworthiness" of his hero ("But suppose they read the novel and do not see, do not agree with the noteworthiness of my Alexei Fyodorovich? I say this because, to my sorrow, I foresee it" [*BK*, 3; *PSS*, 14:5]), "the author" considers the possibility that they will not read the novel at all. "Of course, no one is bound by anything," he acknowledges. Readers "can also drop the book after two pages of the first story and never pick it up again" (*BK*, 4; *PSS*, 14:6). The tone of the preface may be humorous and playful, but it raises questions that Dostoevsky asked himself again and again. How would his novels affect their readers? Would they have a positive moral impact, a deleterious one, or none whatsoever? In *Demons*, *The Adolescent*, and *The Brothers Karamazov*, Dostoevsky undertook a variety of formal experiments (with suspense, closure, and shifts in narrative focus) to make their impact as powerful as he could. But he knew that the depth of that impact would depend on readers themselves.

Notes

INTRODUCTION

1. Leonid Grossman, *Poetika Dostoevskogo* (Moscow: Gosudarstvennaia akademiia khudozhestvennykh nauk, 1925), 57.

2. As one critic puts it, "Dostoevsky loves to agitate the reader with the mysterious, to make him impatiently turn pages in expectation of the resolution of their secrets" (M. G. Davidovich, "Problema zanimatel'nosti v romanakh Dostoevskogo," in *Tvorcheskii put' Dostoevskogo: Sbornik statei*, ed. N. L. Brodskii [Leningrad: "Seiatel'" E. V. Vysotskogo, 1924], 112).

3. A. M. Skabichevskii, "Mysli po povodu tekushchei literatury: Nechto o romanakh g. F. Dostoeskogo voobshche; 'Podrostok,' roman g. F. Dostoevskogo, chast' pervaia," *Birzhevye vedomosti*, no. 35, February 6, 1875, quoted in A. S. Dolinin, *Poslednie romany Dostoevskogo: Kak sozdavalis' "Podrostok" i "Brat'ia Karamazovy"* (Moscow: Sovetskii pisatel', 1963), 199.

4. N. K. Mikhailovskii, *Literaturno-kriticheskie stat'i* (Moscow: Gosudarstvennoe izdatel'stvo khudozhestvennoi literatury, 1957), 211. Mikhailovsky compares reading "cruel" novels like Dostoevsky's to attending a bullfight or a gladiatorial game.

5. Lev Tolstoy said something similar. In response to Nikolai Strakhov's accusation that Dostoevsky's characters are little more than reflections of the author's own warped psychology, Tolstoy retorted, "And so what! As a result, not only people who are akin to him like us, but even foreigners recognize themselves, their souls, in these exceptional characters" (L. N. Tolstoi, *Polnoe sobranie sochinenii*, iubileinoe izdanie, vol. 66 [Moscow: Gosudarstvennoe izdatel'stvo khudozhestvennoi literatury, 1953], 253–54).

6. V. N. Maikov, *Literaturnaia kritika: Stat'i, retsenzii* (Leningrad: "Khudozhestvennaia literatura," 1985), 182.

7. Robert L. Belknap, *Plots* (New York: Columbia University Press, 2016), 101–7. In a fascinating aside, Belknap suggests that "manipulat[ing] readers into experiencing for themselves what the characters in the novel are feeling and arguing" is not just Dostoevsky's forte but a characteristic of the nineteenth-century Russian novel more broadly (88).

8. Robin Feuer Miller, *Dostoevsky and "The Idiot": Author, Narrator, and Reader* (Cambridge, Mass.: Harvard University Press, 1981), 6, 156.

9. Alexander Spektor, "From Violence to Silence: Vicissitudes of Reading (in) *The Idiot*," *Slavic Review* 72, no. 3 (Fall 2013): 561, 556. (Spektor puts Dostoevsky in dialogue with Nabokov in his forthcoming book, *Reader as Accomplice: Narrative Ethics in Dostoevsky and Nabokov*). Alyson Tapp interprets the ethical potential of reading *The Idiot* more optimistically. She argues that the many scenes of embarrassment and empathy in the novel provide readers with a "sentimental education": "In being implicated in the novel's own circuits of embarrassment, the reader of *The Idiot* is herself instructed in the exercise of tact, delicacy and empathy." Tapp also suggests, however, that this readerly education is generally indirect and provided via negative example (through Myshkin's failure to adequately respect particularity and difference) ("Embarrassment in *The Idiot*," *Slavic and East European Journal* 60, no. 3 [Fall 2016]: 441).

10. Both Olga Meerson and Deborah Martinsen have studied this problem as well. See Olga Meerson, *Dostoevsky's Taboos* (Dresden: Dresden University Press, 1998), 203–7; "Chetvertyi brat ili kozel otpushcheniia ex machina?," in *Roman F. M. Dostoevskogo "Brat'ia Karamazovy": Sovremennoe sostoianie izucheniia*, ed. T. A. Kasatkina (Moscow: Nauka, 2007), 565–604; *Personalizm kak poetika: Literaturnyi mir glazami ego obitatelei* (Saint Petersburg: Izdatel'stvo "Pushkinskii dom," 2009), 31–41. See also Deborah A. Martinsen, *Surprised by Shame: Dostoevsky's Liars and Narrative Exposure* (Columbus: Ohio State University Press, 2003).

11. For a brief but thorough state of the field, see James Phelan, "Narrative Ethics," in *The Living Handbook of Narratology*, ed. Peter Hühn et al. (Hamburg: Universität Hamburg), last modified December 9, 2014, http://www.lhn.uni-hamburg.de/article/narrative-ethics. I adapt Phelan's expression "the ethical dimensions of the narrative's techniques" here.

12. Kate Holland has written the authoritative study of Dostoevsky's experiments with genre during the 1870s: *The Novel in the Age of Disintegration: Dostoevsky and the Problem of Genre in the 1870s* (Evanston, Ill.: Northwestern University Press, 2013).

13. James Phelan and Peter J. Rabinowitz, "Narrative as Rhetoric," in *Narrative Theory: Core Concepts and Critical Debates*, ed. David Herman et al. (Columbus: Ohio State University Press, 2012), 3–8.

14. Phelan and Rabinowitz, "Narrative as Rhetoric," 5. As James Phelan elaborates elsewhere, "narrative is not just a story, but also an action, *the telling of a story by someone to someone on some occasion for some purpose*" (*Narrative as Rhetoric: Technique, Audiences, Ethics, Ideology* [Columbus: Ohio State University Press, 1996], 8).

15. Adam Zachary Newton has argued that, because narrators engage readers in ways that mimic how speakers engage listeners in general, fictional narrative "places claims upon us, not exactly as life and persons do, but similarly, and

with similar ethical consequences" (*Narrative Ethics* [Cambridge, Mass.: Harvard University Press, 1995], 26). If Newton is right, then Dostoevsky's novels—which so often blur the boundaries between fiction and nonfiction—would have "placed claims" on their original readers in an especially visceral and immediate way. Dostoevsky insisted that even his explicitly fictional characters had real-life counterparts. As he writes at the beginning of *Notes from Underground*, "Both the author of these notes and the 'Notes' themselves are, of course, invented. Nevertheless, personalities like the author of these notes not only may, but even must exist in our society" (*PSS*, 5:99).

16. Andrzej Wajda was especially attuned to the continuing relevance of Dostoevsky's fiction. Alexander Burry argues that, when Wajda staged *Demons* as a play, he blurred the boundaries between audience and actors, thereby "indirectly suggest[ing] his audience's complicity with the political machinery of his era" (i.e., communist Poland) (*Multi-Mediated Dostoevsky: Transposing Novels into Opera, Film, and Drama* [Evanston, Ill.: Northwestern University Press, 2011], 168).

17. Some important works of Dostoevsky criticism that have been influenced by Bakhtin include Malcolm V. Jones, *Dostoyevsky after Bakhtin: Readings in Dostoyevsky's Fantastic Realism* (Cambridge: Cambridge University Press, 1990); Gary Saul Morson, *Narrative and Freedom: The Shadows of Time* (New Haven, Conn.: Yale University Press, 1994); Meerson, *Dostoevsky's Taboos*; Sarah J. Young, *Dostoevsky's "The Idiot" and the Ethical Foundations of Narrative: Reading, Narrating, Scripting* (London: Anthem Press, 2004); and Alina Wyman, *The Gift of Active Empathy: Scheler, Bakhtin, and Dostoevsky* (Evanston, Ill.: Northwestern University Press, 2016).

18. Sergey Bocharov, "Conversations with Bakhtin," trans. Stephen Blackwell and Vadim Liapunov, *PMLA* 109, no. 5 (October 1994): 1012.

19. Bakhtin explains, "Artistic form, correctly understood, does not shape already prepared and found content, but rather permits content to be found and seen for the first time" (*PDP*, 43; *SS*, 6:54).

20. Bakhtin makes the religious dimension of Dostoevsky's aesthetics, as he understands it, most explicit in his 1961 notes for revising the Dostoevsky book. There he compares Dostoevsky's relationship with his characters to "the activity of God in His relation to man, a relation allowing man to reveal himself utterly (in his immanent development), to judge himself, to refute himself" ("Toward a Reworking of the Dostoevsky Book," in *PDP*, 285; *SS*, 5:342). Robert Louis Jackson elucidates the connection between Bakhtin's theory and Dostoevsky's "ethical-religious point of view" in *Dialogues with Dostoevsky: The Overwhelming Questions* (Stanford, Calif.: Stanford University Press, 1993), 269–92. For a recent study that reads both Dostoevsky's fiction and his religious thought in light of Bakhtin's work, see Rowan Williams, *Dostoevsky: Language, Faith, and Fiction* (Waco, Tex.: Baylor University Press, 2011).

21. V. E. Vetlovskaia, *Roman F. M. Dostoevskogo "Brat'ia Karamazovy"*

(Saint Petersburg: Izdatel'stvo "Pushkinskii dom," 2007), 393–408; Jones, *Dostoyevsky after Bakhtin*, 196; Natalia Reed, "The Philosophical Roots of Polyphony: A Dostoevskian Reading," in *Critical Essays on Mikhail Bakhtin*, ed. Caryl Emerson (New York: Hall, 1999), 140. For a summary of the critiques of Bakhtin's work on Dostoevsky (along with a compelling defense of it), see Caryl Emerson, *The First Hundred Years of Mikhail Bakhtin* (Princeton, N.J.: Princeton University Press, 1997), 73–91, 127–61. Some of the best critiques include Galin Tihanov's analysis of the (only partial, and thus inconsistent) shifts in emphasis from the 1929 to the 1963 versions of the book (*The Master and the Slave: Lukács, Bakhtin, and the Ideas of Their Time* [Oxford: Oxford University Press, 2000], 187–215) and Ruth Coates's *Christianity in Bakhtin: God and the Exiled Author* (Cambridge: Cambridge University Press, 2004), 84–102.

22. Caryl Emerson discusses this "benevolence" in "Problems with Baxtin's Poetics," *Slavic and East European Journal* 32, no. 4 (Winter 1988): 514–17.

23. Robert Louis Jackson has written the classic study of the "unity of moral and aesthetic categories, of the good and the beautiful" in Dostoevsky's aesthetic thought; *Dostoevsky's Quest for Form: A Study of His Philosophy of Art* (New Haven, Conn.: Yale University Press, 1966), 44. Much has been written on Dostoevsky's debt to Schiller. See, for example, Jackson, *Dostoevsky's Quest for Form*, 197–203; Alexandra H. Lyngstad, *Dostoevskij and Schiller* (The Hague: Mouton, 1975), and, more recently, Larisa Poluboyarinova, "Impello–Impuli–Impulsum: Dostoevsky and Schiller between Logos and Pathos," *Dostoevsky Studies* 20 (2016): 31–46 (which includes an extensive bibliography of works on the topic).

24. Jackson, *Dostoevsky's Quest for Form*, 65.

25. Ani Kokobobo notes that grotesquery is universal in *The Brothers Karamazov*. To one degree or another, *everyone* is ugly (or promises to become so in old age), and so "no one's ugliness should be deemed alien, since it is ultimately not their pristine beauty but precisely their blemishes that unite individuals" (*Russian Grotesque Realism: The Great Reforms and the Gentry Decline* [Columbus: Ohio State University Press, 2018], 128).

CHAPTER ONE

1. Caroline Levine, *The Serious Pleasures of Suspense: Victorian Realism and Narrative Doubt* (Charlottesville: University of Virginia Press, 2003), 1–2.

2. E. M. Forster, *Aspects of the Novel* (London: Harcourt, 1927), 26, 86. Meir Sternberg distinguishes between two readerly impulses: "curiosity" (the desire to know or understand something that has already taken place but remains hidden or unclear) and "suspense" (the desire to find out what will happen next) (*Expositional Modes and Temporal Ordering in Fiction* [Bloomington: Indiana University Press, 1978], 65). Dostoevsky, however, uses the word "curios-

ity" to describe both the desire to acquire knowledge broadly speaking *and* states of anticipation.

3. Grossman, *Poetika Dostoevskogo*, 11, 13, 17. Other scholars who have written about the centrality of suspense in Dostoevsky's fiction include Konstantin Mochulsky, who claims that Dostoevsky's novels excite our "curiosity," "demand[ing] our participation and collaboration" (*Dostoevsky: His Life and Work*, trans. Michael A. Minihan [Princeton, N.J.: Princeton University Press, 1967], 439); Robin Feuer Miller (*Dostoevsky and "The Idiot,"* 23–33); and Gary Saul Morson ("Return to Process: The Unfolding of *The Idiot*," *New Literary History* 40, no. 4 [Autumn 2009]: 858–59).

4. For more on the difficulties of writing serially published fiction in Russia during the nineteenth century (and the difficulties Dostoevsky faced in particular), see William Mills Todd III, "'To Be Continued': Dostoevsky's Evolving Poetics of Serialized Publication," *Dostoevsky Studies* 18 (2014): 23–33. Todd hypothesizes that Dostoevsky slowly perfected his poetics of serialization, making "less and less use of the sensational devices of European serialized fiction, such as plotting with abrupt surprises and melodramatic suspense" (24). Todd's analysis is compelling, but I disagree with him on one point: I would argue that in late novels such as *Demons* and *The Adolescent* Dostoevsky relies on melodramatic suspense just as heavily as he had in his earlier ones.

5. A few years later, Dostoevsky talked up *The Gambler* by insisting that it would attract just as much "attention" as *Notes from the House of the Dead* had. As he explained, the Russian public would read about the sordid underbelly of the life in glittering European gambling houses "with extreme curiosity" (*s chrezvychainym liubopytstvom*) (*PSS*, 28.2:51).

6. D. S. Merezhkovskii, *L. Tolstoi i Dostoevskii*, ed. E. A. Andrushchenko (Moscow: Nauka, 2000), 151.

7. Merezhkovskii, *L. Tolstoi i Dostoevskii*, 437.

8. Merezhkovskii, *L. Tolstoi i Dostoevskii*, 437.

9. Gary Saul Morson, "Misanthropology," *New Literary History* 27, no. 1 (Winter 1996): 63.

10. M. E. Saltykov-Shchedrin, *Sobranie sochinenii v dvadtsati tomakh*, ed. S. A. Makashin et al., vol. 9 (Moscow: Izdatel'stvo "Khudozhestvennaia literatura," 1970), 191.

11. For more information on how Dostoevsky incorporated aspects of the press reports into his novel, see *PSS*, 12:197–211.

12. Plutarch, *Selected Essays and Dialogues*, trans. Donald Russell (Oxford: Oxford University Press, 1993), 195.

13. Tikhon Zadonskii, *Uchenie Sviatitelia Tikhona ob istinakh very i tserkvi* (Saint Petersburg, 1864), 137.

14. Robert Alter, *The Five Books of Moses* (New York: Norton, 2004), 24–25.

15. Vladimir Lossky, *Orthodox Theology: An Introduction*, trans. Ian and

Ihita Kesarcodi-Watson (Crestwood, N.Y.: Saint Vladimir's Seminary Press, 1978), 82.

16. Yuri Corrigan similarly identifies the transgressive desire for knowledge as Stepan Trofimovich's original sin, although he emphasizes Stepan Trofimovich's desire to know other people, his "hungry, invasive intimacy" (*Dostoevsky and the Riddle of the Self* [Evanston, Ill.: Northwestern University Press, 2017], 100).

17. By middle age, Stepan Trofimovich's ambitions have become comically deflated. In lieu of godlike omniscience, he satisfies himself with provincial rumors: "He absolutely had to be told some gossip, something interesting that was going on in town, and it had to be something new every day besides" (*D*, 69; *PSS*, 10:52).

18. Paul J. Griffiths, *Intellectual Appetite: A Theological Grammar* (Washington, D.C.: Catholic University of America Press, 2009), 9. I would like to thank Paul Contino for introducing me to Griffiths's work.

19. Griffiths, *Intellectual Appetite*, 20.

20. Griffiths, *Intellectual Appetite*, 143.

21. Griffiths, *Intellectual Appetite*, 21.

22. Griffiths, *Intellectual Appetite*, 188.

23. Griffiths, *Intellectual Appetite*, 198–99.

24. Rowan Williams argues that the pathologies of the characters in *Demons* "can be traced to an inability or unwillingness to become visible." This is especially true of Pyotr Verkhovensky, whom Williams calls "a character in flight from visibility" (*Dostoevsky*, 117, 122).

25. Jackson, *Dialogues with Dostoevsky*, 41.

26. M. V. Jones, "The Narrator and Narrative Technique in Dostoevsky's *The Devils*," in *Dostoevsky's "The Devils": A Critical Companion*, ed. W. J. Leatherbarrow (Evanston, Ill.: Northwestern University Press, 1999), 101.

27. Slobodanka B. Vladiv, *Narrative Principles in Dostoevskij's "Besy": A Structural Analysis* (Las Vegas: Lang, 1979), 84.

28. As Adam Weiner has noted, even Liputin's language seems to infect G——v, who adopts some of the gossip's favorite words, such as *frappirovat'* (*By Authors Possessed: The Demonic Novel in Russia* [Evanston, Ill.: Northwestern University Press, 1998], 129).

29. I. S. Zil'bershtein and L. M. Rozenblium, eds., *F. M. Dostoevskii: Novye materialy i issledovaniia*, Literaturnoe nasledstvo 86 (Moscow: Nauka, 1973), 488. The accusation was unfounded: the delay was owing to the fact that Dostoevsky himself was behind schedule.

30. Gene M. Moore describes the narrative structure of *Demons* as an "*epistemological* palimpsest composed of multiple and often contradictory layers of rumor, speculation, and eyewitness testimony" ("The Voices of Legion: The Narrator of *The Possessed*," *Dostoevsky Studies* 6 [1985]: 53).

31. This scene has inspired several interpretations that complement my own. Slobodanka Vladiv-Glover, for example, uses it as a primary example of what she calls the "impressionistic" structure of meaning in the novel, which emphasizes the impossibility of ever reaching one, definitive account of historical truth (*Narrative Principles*, 82–84). Gary Saul Morson claims the passage as an example of what he calls narrative "sideshadowing": it gives readers "not one but *many possible stories*" about what happened (*Narrative and Freedom*, 122).

32. Iu. F. Kariakin, "Zachem Khroniker v 'Besakh'?," in *Dostoevskii: Materialy i issledovaniia*, vol. 5, ed. G. M. Fridlender (Leningrad: Nauka, 1983), 124; Victor Terras, *Reading Dostoevsky* (Madison: University of Wisconsin Press, 1998), 97.

33. Weiner, *By Authors Possessed*, 109–23.

34. David Stromberg, "The Enigmatic G——v: A Defense of the Narrator-Chronicler in Dostoevsky's *Demons*," *Russian Review* 71, no. 3 (July 2012): 463. Stromberg elaborates his argument in his recent book *Narrative Faith: Dostoevsky, Camus, and Singer* (Newark: University of Delaware Press, 2018), 1–38.

35. Joseph Frank, *Dostoevsky: The Miraculous Years, 1865–1871* (Princeton, N.J.: Princeton University Press, 1995), 473.

36. Wayne C. Booth, *The Rhetoric of Fiction*, 2nd ed. (Chicago: University of Chicago Press, 1983), 285.

37. Gérard Genette, *Narrative Discourse: An Essay in Method*, trans. Jane E. Lewin (Ithaca, N.Y.: Cornell University Press, 1980), 195.

38. James Phelan, "Implausibilities, Crossovers, and Impossibilities: A Rhetorical Approach to Breaks in the Code of Mimetic Character Narration," in *A Poetics of Unnatural Narrative*, ed. Jan Alber, Henrik Skov Nielson, and Brian Richardson (Columbus: Ohio State University Press, 2013), 174.

39. Phelan, "Implausibilities, Crossovers, and Impossibilities," 174. Paul Dawson has argued that even overtly omniscient first-person narration need not strike readers as particularly unnatural; instead, it can be used to highlight "the fact that telling one's story is as much an act of imaginative reconstruction as it is a narrative report by someone who knows." In G——v's case, however, such highlighting would seriously undermine the authority of his account, which he presents as documentary fact (*The Return of the Omniscient Narrator: Authorship and Authority in Twenty-First Century Fiction* [Columbus: Ohio State University Press, 2013], 209).

40. Weiner calls such moments in G——v's narrative evidence of his "excess pride of authorship": G——v is so demonically proud of the scenes he has thought up that he cannot help but draw attention to his own inventiveness, even if it hurts his reliability (*By Authors Possessed*, 119).

41. Dorrit Cohn, *Transparent Minds: Narrative Modes for Presenting Consciousness in Fiction* (Princeton, N.J.: Princeton University Press, 1978).

42. Scholars have long drawn comparisons between nineteenth-century om-

niscient narrators and God. According to Susan Lanser, for example, "It is only a slight exaggeration to suggest that upon this narrator rested the demands and powers of divinity itself, trusted at once to know all and to judge aright" (*Fictions of Authority: Women Writers and Narrative Voice* [Ithaca, N.Y.: Cornell University Press, 1992], 85). In her interesting book chapter on *Demons*, Susanna Lee also describes the novel's narrator as a "human-God" or "God-human" whose "oscillations between hesitation and boldness, scrupulousness and grandiosity, limited and unlimited perceptual and creative capacities, are of more than technical narratological interest. These oscillations can suggest a fusion or confusion of the human and the superhuman, a fusion with considerable political, social, and spiritual resonance" (*A World Abandoned by God: Narrative and Secularism* [Lewisburg, Pa.: Bucknell University Press, 2006], 142).

43. Ruediger Heinze has argued that (sometime) omniscient character narrators almost *always* resist easy classification: "As readers we realize that our reevaluation cannot reach closure, that on the level of narrative, reliability cannot be decided" ("Violations of Mimetic Epistemology in First-Person Narrative Fiction," *Narrative* 16, no. 3 [2008]: 291).

44. For a detailed account of the composition and publication history of "At Tikhon's," see *PSS*, 12:237–46. For a history of Dostoevsky's long, fraught relationship with Katkov, see Susanne Fusso, *Editing Turgenev, Dostoevsky, and Tolstoy: Mikhail Katkov and the Great Russian Novel* (DeKalb: Northern Illinois University Press, 2017), 98–162.

45. W. J. Leatherbarrow, "*The Devils* in the Context of Dostoevsky's Life and Works," in Leatherbarrow, *Dostoevsky's "The Devils,"* 43.

46. In and of itself, Stavrogin's confession is neither clear nor straightforward. In fact, it is so vague and internally contradictory that some scholars suspect him of inventing the entire thing. See Carol Apollonio, *Dostoevsky's Secrets: Reading Against the Grain* (Evanston, Ill.: Northwestern University Press, 2009), 136–41, and Amy D. Ronner, "Is Stavrogin Leading Us by the Nose? The Nihilistic Confession," *Dostoevsky Studies* 20 (2016): 71–101.

47. Peter Brooks, *Reading for the Plot: Design and Intention in Narrative* (Cambridge, Mass.: Harvard University Press, 1984), 61, xiii. According to D. A. Miller, suspense "constitutes the narratable" (*Narrative and Its Discontents: Problems of Closure in the Traditional Novel* [Princeton, N.J.: Princeton University Press, 1981], 265).

48. Lorri Nandrea, "Objectless Curiosity: *Frankenstein*, *The Station Agent*, and Other Strange Narratives," *Narrative* 15, no. 3 (October 2007): 339.

49. As Melissa J. Sokol has argued, readers of *Demons* (simply by virtue of being readers of *Demons*) cannot help but participate in the networks of gossip that dominate the novel ("Rumor and Gossip in 19th-Century Russian Literature: Griboedov, Pushkin, Gogol, and Dostoevsky" [Ph.D. diss., Brown University, 2007], 161, ProQuest [UMI 3272058]). Similarly, Tatiana Pirusskaia em-

phasizes the self-referential quality of gossip in *Demons*, and the similarities between gossip and novel writing as such ("Spletnia kak mekhanizm avtorefleksii v romanakh Dostoevskogo 'Besy' i Dzhordzh Eliot 'Midlmarch,'" *Voprosy literatury*, no. 2 [2015]: 193–216).

50. Neil Kenny, *Curiosity in Early Modern Europe: Word Histories* (Wiesbaden: Harrassowitz Verlag, 1998), 14.

51. On the enormous symbolic importance of the heart in Dostoevsky's ethics and fiction, see Evgenia Cherkasova, *Dostoevsky and Kant: Dialogues on Ethics* (Amsterdam: Rodopi, 2009), 7–27.

52. Barbara M. Benedict, *Curiosity: A Cultural History of Early Modern Inquiry* (Chicago: University of Chicago Press, 2001), 2. Hilary M. Schor discusses other benefits of curiosity, especially for those "great experimenters"—Victorian heroines (*Curious Subjects: Women and the Trials of Realism* [Oxford: Oxford University Press, 2013]).

53. Note that Shatov both looks at *and* listens to his wife's pain with compassion. In *Demons*, Dostoevsky does not emphasize the differences between watching, listening to, or even listening to stories *about* human suffering. To the contrary, he tends to group these three actions together. Verkhovensky both dreams of "overhearing" Stavrogin's private conversations and of "peeking" at what Stavrogin is doing behind closed doors; Liputin is called both a "gossip" and a "spy"; and the townsfolk who enjoy watching their neighbors' houses burn love listening to juicy rumors about them as well. In this novel, Dostoevsky is less concerned with the manner in which characters learn about one another's suffering than with the emotional attitude they adopt toward that suffering.

54. Here I quote Faye Halpern's recent discussion of the "messy, unhygienic" nature of narrative sympathy and empathy ("Closeness Through Unreliability: Sympathy, Empathy, and Ethics in Narrative Communication," *Narrative* 26, no. 2 [May 2018]: 126).

55. Wyman, *The Gift of Active Empathy*, 117. Wyman argues that, for Dostoevsky, truly understanding other people *means* acknowledging that there are some things about them we will never know. Recognizing that we cannot perfectly read other people's hearts and minds is a "necessary precondition for, rather than an insurmountable obstacle to, morally productive understanding, always based on *partial* knowledge in Dostoevsky" (272n24).

56. Kathleen Lundeen has called "forever finding oneself either too close or not close enough to the object of self-identification" the "ethical dilemma inherent in empathy" ("Who Has the Right to Feel? The Ethics of Literary Empathy," *Style* 32, no. 2 [Summer 1998]: 270).

57. Wyman, *The Gift of Active Empathy*, 141–75. Scholars have pointed to still other ways that compassion (or emotions masquerading as compassion) can go wrong in Dostoevsky's works. According to Anna Schur, Dostoevsky questions "not only the possibility but also the authenticity and the moral force of indiscrim-

inate compassion," especially among jury members, who may be tempted to empathize with the criminal at the expense of the victim ("The Limits of Listening: Particularity, Compassion, and Dostoevsky's 'Bookish Humaneness,'" *Russian Review* 72, no. 4 [October 2013]: 589). See also Gary Rosenshield's analysis of "the perils of narrative empathy" in writings by Dostoevsky (and others) about the law (*Western Law, Russian Justice: Dostoevsky, the Jury Trial, and the Law* [Madison: University of Wisconsin Press, 2005], 105–30). For a broad discussion of empathy's many pitfalls, see Fritz Breithaupt, "The Bad Things We Do Because of Empathy," *Interdisciplinary Science Reviews* 43, no. 2 (April 2018): 166–74.

58. Moreover, Tikhon knows that no matter how compassionate his interest may be, it will not always be *perceived* as compassionate by the sufferer himself. As if trying to save Stavrogin from the discomfort of being so clearly seen, Tikhon initially avoids meeting his gaze. When Tikhon finally does look at Stavrogin "with curiosity," he does so as gently as possible, "his eyes soft and seemingly rather shy" (*D*, 758; *PSS*, 11:10). Even this "soft" interest turns out to be more than Stavrogin can bear, however: he accuses Tikhon of "spying," "psychologizing," and "monkish curiosity" (*D*, 760; *PSS*, 11:11). Being the object of someone else's empathy is not always a pleasant experience. To quote Amy Shuman, it can feel like "the colonization of the mind, the imagination," and create "misunderstanding and mistrust exactly at the rhetorical moment when empathy promises the opposite" (*Other People's Stories: Entitlement Claims and the Critique of Empathy* [Urbana: University of Illinois Press, 2005], 8).

59. Here Dostoevsky is probably drawing, once again, on Schiller, who wrote extensively about the mixed feelings that scenes of violence and horror can evoke. Like Dostoevsky, Schiller was especially interested in how our response to real-world horror—including public executions—corresponds to our response to the horrible in works of art; see, for example, Schiller's 1792 essay "On the Art of Tragedy."

60. Stavrogin is often described as moving, speaking, or even *living* "indolently" (*vialo*).

61. This is not the only time in the novel that a character uses someone else's suicide as a cure for boredom. The lady voyeur I discussed earlier in this chapter wants to go see the young man's corpse precisely *because* "everything's become so boring" (*D*, 362; *PSS*, 10:254).

62. Stavrogin's body language resembles Virginsky's, who similarly stands "on tiptoe" while curiously looking down at the corpse of someone he helped kill (*D*, 669; *PSS*, 10:461).

63. Pyotr Verkhovensky is well aware of Stavrogin's need for continual excitement and tries his best to take advantage of it. In a last-ditch effort to curry Stavrogin's favor, he helps arrange the rendezvous with Liza, as he explains, "to give you a bit of amusement and to demonstrate that you wouldn't be bored with me [*so mnoiu vam skuchno ne budet*]; I can prove useful for this sort of thing three hundred times" (*D*, 587; *PSS*, 10:406).

64. Martha C. Nussbaum, *Love's Knowledge: Essays on Philosophy and Literature* (Oxford: Oxford University Press, 1990).

65. Suzanne Keen, *Empathy and the Novel* (Oxford: Oxford University Press, 2007), 88–92. As Keen argues elsewhere, whether or not a reader empathizes with a particular character depends not only on the author's narrative strategies but also on that reader's unique emotional and psychological makeup. ("Readers' Temperaments and Fictional Character," *New Literary History* 42, no. 2 [Spring 2011]: 295–314).

66. Amy Coplan, "Empathic Engagement with Narrative Fictions," *Journal of Aesthetics and Art Criticism* 62, no. 2 (Spring 2004): 141–52. The word "empathy" is a relatively recent coinage. Derived from the German *Einfühlung*, it originated in late nineteenth-century theories of aesthetics; see Lauren Wispé, "History of the Concept of Empathy," in *Empathy and Its Development*, ed. Nancy Eisenberg and Janet Strayer, 17–37 (Cambridge: Cambridge University Press, 1987); Meghan Marie Hammond and Sue J. Kim, introduction to *Rethinking Empathy through Literature*, ed. Meghan Marie Hammond and Sue J. Kim (New York: Routledge, 2014), 1–18.

67. See, among others, Mary-Catherine Harrison, "The Paradox of Fiction and the Ethics of Empathy: Reconceiving Dickens's Realism," *Narrative* 16, no. 3 (October 2008): 256–78, Mary-Catherine Harrison, "How Narrative Relationships Overcome Empathic Bias: Elizabeth Gaskell's Empathy across Social Difference," *Poetics Today* 32, no. 2 (Summer 2011): 255–88; and Rae Greiner, *Sympathetic Realism in Nineteenth-Century British Fiction* (Baltimore: Johns Hopkins University Press, 2012).

68. Patricia Meyer Spacks, *Gossip* (New York: Knopf, 1985), 22. Spacks emphasizes gossip's threatening aspect but also its potential to lead to moral growth: in her account, gossiping implies a "will to control," but it can also signify a "desire for alliance and for moral exploration" (49, 60).

69. Blakey Vermeule, *Why Do We Care about Literary Characters?* (Baltimore: Johns Hopkins University Press, 2010), 164. Ned Schantz likewise argues that "narrative interest since the novel has been above all an interest in the private lives of other people—the interest of gossip" (*Gossip, Letters, Phones: The Scandal of Female Networks in Film and Literature* [Oxford: Oxford University Press, 2008], 4).

70. Thomas Pavel, "Safely Watching Wild Adventures," *Narrative* 24, no. 1 (January 2016): 7.

71. M. M. Bakhtin, "Forms of Time and of the Chronotope in the Novel," in *The Dialogic Imagination: Four Essays*, ed. Michael Holquist, trans. Caryl Emerson and Michael Holquist (Austin: University of Texas Press, 1981), 123.

72. Jeremy Hawthorn, "Reading Fiction: Voyeurism without Shame?," in *Narrative Ethics*, ed. Jakob Lothe and Jeremy Hawthorn, 73–88 (Amsterdam: Rodopi, 2013). John Vernon points out the connections between novel reading, novel writing, and the curiosity that drives the eavesdropper and the gos-

sip ("Reading, Writing, and Eavesdropping: Some Thoughts on the Nature of Realistic Fiction," *Kenyon Review* 4, no. 4 [Fall 1982]: 44–54). Ann Gaylin similarly argues that "[e]avesdropping gives concrete form to readerly desire," which is driven by the "primal human curiosity to know, and to know those aspects of others' lives that we are not supposed to know, those that they wish to keep hidden from us" (*Eavesdropping in the Novel from Austen to Proust* [Cambridge: Cambridge University Press, 2002], 6, 7). (My thanks to Sarah Young for introducing me to Vernon's and Gaylin's work.)

73. V. I. Ivanov, *Sobranie sochinenii*, ed. D. V. Ivanova and O. Deshart, 4 vols. (Brussels: Foyer Oriental Chrétien, 1971–87), 4:419, 420.

74. Bakhtin almost acknowledges that the narrator of *Demons* represents an exception to his rule. He admits that G——v seems to tell his story "as if from a certain temporal perspective," only to insist that he in fact "structures his narration without any significant perspective at all" (*PDP*, 225; *SS*, 251–52). In a fascinating article in progress (to be published in the upcoming volume *Dostoevsky at 200*), Sarah Young challenges Bakhtin's claim from a different angle. Focusing on *Crime and Punishment*, Young argues that the "indirect witnessing" of "nonparticipating third persons" not only plays an essential role in Dostoevsky's novels, it sometimes even plays a positive one ("Deferred Senses and Distanced Spaces: Embodying the Boundaries of Dostoevskii's Realism" [unpublished manuscript, February 8, 2019]).

75. Coplan, "Empathic Engagement with Narrative Fictions," 149. Keith Oatley makes a similar point in "Meetings of Minds: Dialogue, Sympathy, and Identification, in Reading Fiction," *Poetics* 26 (1999): 439–54.

76. Keen, "Readers' Temperaments and Fictional Character," 304–7.

77. The novel's second epigraph introduces the question, how should we respond to tales of suffering and violence? Its first epigraph introduces an equally important theme—the difficulty of tolerating uncertainty. The first epigraph consists of two stanzas from Alexander Pushkin's poem "Demons" ("Besy"), which tells the story of travelers who get lost in a snowstorm and start to wonder if supernatural forces are leading them astray. Structured as a series of unanswered questions, it describes a scene of visual confusion as disorienting as any in the novel: the travelers look out into the swirling darkness and cannot tell road from field, spirits from snow.

78. The instruction really is *indirect*. Because "At Tikhon's" was suppressed, the description of the "pure souls" and their self-aware response never appeared in the novel proper (at least not during Dostoevsky's lifetime). For more on Dostoevsky's preference for indirect moral instruction over explicit didacticism, see Miller, *Dostoevsky and "The Idiot."*

79. Malcolm V. Jones, *Dostoyevsky: The Novel of Discord* (New York: Barnes and Noble Books, 1976), 148.

80. René Girard, *The Scapegoat*, trans. Yvonne Freccero (Baltimore: Johns Hopkins University Press, 1986), 167–83.

CHAPTER TWO

1. Wayne C. Booth, "Are Narrative Choices Subject to Ethical Criticism?," in *Reading Narrative: Form, Ethics, Ideology*, ed. James Phelan (Columbus: Ohio State University Press, 1989), 63.

2. The influence of this aspect of Bakhtin's argument has been far-reaching. Viktor Shklovsky's claim that Dostoevsky "didn't like finishing manuscripts" bears its impact (*Za i protiv: Zametki o Dostoevskom* [Moscow: Sovetskii pisatel', 1957], 171). Gary Saul Morson builds upon it in his study of how Dostoevsky models contingency, personal freedom, and "the openness of time" in narrative form (*Narrative and Freedom*), and it contributes to Ksana Blank's compelling analysis of Dostoevsky's dialectics (*Dostoevsky's Dialectics and the Problem of Sin* [Evanston, Ill.: Northwestern University Press, 2010], 16–18).

3. V. V. Timofeeva, "God raboty s znamenitym pisatelem," in *F. M. Dostoevskii v vospominaniiakh sovremennikov*, ed. V. V. Grigorenko et al., 2 vols. (Moscow: Khudozhestvennaia literatura, 1964), 2:170.

4. Peter Sekirin, ed., *The Dostoevsky Archive: Firsthand Accounts of the Novelist from Contemporaries' Memoirs and Rare Periodicals* (Jefferson, N.C.: McFarland, 1997), 227.

5. For other scholars who have noted this weakness in Bakhtin's argument, see Caryl Emerson, "Word and Image in Dostoevsky's Worlds: Robert Louis Jackson on Readings That Bakhtin Could Not Do," in *Freedom and Responsibility in Russian Literature: Essays in Honor of Robert Louis Jackson*, ed. Elizabeth Cheresh Allen and Gary Saul Morson (Evanston, Ill.: Northwestern University Press, 1995), 256–57, 263–64; Jones, *Dostoyevsky after Bakhtin*, xiv; and David M. Bethea, *The Shape of the Apocalypse in Modern Russian Fiction* (Princeton, N.J.: Princeton University Press, 1989), 102–4.

6. Frank Kermode, *The Sense of an Ending: Studies in the Theory of Fiction; With a New Epilogue* (Oxford: Oxford University Press, 2000), 54.

7. Kermode, *The Sense of an Ending*, 6. According to A. A. Mendilow, "time affects every aspect of fiction: the theme, the form, and the medium—language," and so novels by necessity model their authors' conceptions of time (*Time and the Novel* [New York: Nevill, 1952], 31). Ursula K. Heise makes a related claim, calling the novel "a genre whose organizational structures necessarily embody specific conceptions of time" (*Chronoschisms: Time, Narrative, and Postmodernism* [Cambridge: Cambridge University Press, 1997], 6).

8. Peter J. Rabinowitz, *Before Reading: Narrative Conventions and the Politics of Interpretation* (Ithaca, N.Y.: Cornell University Press, 1987), 164.

9. David H. Richter, *Fable's End: Completeness and Closure in Rhetorical Fiction* (Chicago: University of Chicago Press, 1974), 166.

10. Tzvetan Todorov, "Structural Analysis of Narrative," trans. Arnold Weinstein, *Novel: A Forum on Fiction* 3, no. 1 (Autumn 1969): 75.

11. Rabinowitz, *Before Reading*, 164. Umberto Eco usually uses the terms

"open" and "closed" in the second sense; see, for example, Umberto Eco, "The Poetics of the Open Work," in *The Role of the Reader: Explorations in the Semiotics of Texts* (Bloomington: Indiana University Press, 1979), 47–66. Like Rabinowitz, H. Porter Abbott has attempted to distinguish between these two types of closure, but using different terminology. He argues that narrative closure can occur "at the level of expectations" (about the plot) or "at the level of questions" (about meaning) (*The Cambridge Introduction to Narrative*, 2nd ed. [Cambridge: Cambridge University Press, 2008], 58–65).

12. Nathan Rosen, "Breaking Out of the Underground: The 'Failure' of 'A Raw Youth,'" *Modern Fiction Studies* 4, no. 3 (Fall 1958): 233. Edward Wasiolek argues that in attempting to depict social disorder, Dostoevsky "disorders" his novel itself (introduction to *The Notebooks for "A Raw Youth,"* by Fyodor Dostoevsky, ed. Edward Wasiolek, trans. Victor Terras [Chicago: University of Chicago Press, 1969], 16). My own view is in line with that of Kate Holland, who argues that "*The Adolescent* seeks to represent the contingent, open, unformed nature of the contemporary moment while also answering the demands of narrative form and closure" (*The Novel in the Age of Disintegration*, 130). Jacques Catteau contends that, in both form and content, *The Adolescent* does not model disorder so much as the protagonist's "uncertain struggle" against disorder's forces (*Dostoyevsky and the Process of Literary Creation*, trans. Audrey Littlewood [Cambridge: Cambridge University Press, 1989], 289–90).

13. On the enormous social, political, and economic changes Russia was undergoing during these decades, see Ben Eklof, John Bushnell, and Larissa Zakharova, eds., *Russia's Great Reforms, 1855–1881* (Bloomington: Indiana University Press, 1994).

14. Here, and in the title of this subsection, I am, of course, referencing Robert Louis Jackson's classic study *Dostoevsky's Quest for Form.*

15. As Kate Holland puts it, "Narrating his protagonist's development as an author allows Dostoevsky to lay bare his own novelistic process; the text turns out to be not only an attempt to represent the moment of social transition in all its fragmentation, but also a novelistic meditation on whether and how such representation can be possible within the form of the novel" (*The Novel in the Age of Disintegration*, 104).

16. Yuri Corrigan describes Arkady's plot as "the search for a more robust theory of personhood" (*Dostoevsky and the Riddle of the Self*, 105).

17. For the origins of Arkady's prophecy in nineteenth-century scientific discourse, see Liza Knapp, *The Annihilation of Inertia: Dostoevsky and Metaphysics* (Evanston, Ill.: Northwestern University Press, 1996), 131–71.

18. Aleksandr Babuk, "The Myth of Childhood as an Embodiment of the Golden Age in Dostoevsky's Oeuvre," trans. Liv Bliss, *Russian Studies in Literature* 51, no. 2 (Spring 2015): 50; Tat'iana Kasatkina, "Dostoevsky's *Raw Youth*: The 'Idea' of the Hero and the Idea of the Author," trans. Liv Bliss, *Russian Studies in Literature* 40, no. 4 (Fall 2004): 56.

19. The hopelessness of Versilov's vision is brought into sharp relief by the way he addresses the second half of Arkady's question (how will the social world be "renewed" [*obnovitsia*]?). Rather than responding directly, Versilov absorbs the verb into his account, revising its meaning. The only "renewal" that Versilov predicts for human society during this final cataclysm is that all nations "will be renewed [*obnovit'sia*] in a general bankruptcy" (*A*, 210; *PSS*, 13:172).

20. Barbara Herrnstein Smith, *Poetic Closure: A Study of How Poems End* (Chicago: University of Chicago Press, 1968), 13.

21. Caroline Levine, *Forms: Whole, Rhythm, Hierarchy, Network* (Princeton, N.J.: Princeton University Press, 2015), 28.

22. W. J. Leatherbarrow, *A Devil's Vaudeville: The Demonic in Dostoevsky's Major Fiction* (Evanston, Ill.: Northwestern University Press, 2005), 15.

23. Tatiana Kasatkina discusses the significance of this intertext as well ("Dostoevsky's *Raw Youth*," 47).

24. If Versilov does not live up to the ideal of Christ in this scene, then Arkady does not live up to the model of the wealthy young man either. The young man in Matthew 19 asks what "good" he can do to win "eternal life"; Arkady mentions neither the good (his "what I'm to do" is ethically neutral) nor heaven (his question about the end of the world has no explicit religious overtones), and he dismisses Versilov's advice to follow the Ten Commandments.

25. A. S. Dolinin notes these changes to the endings of *Faust* and *The Old Curiosity Shop*, but he attributes the revision to Dostoevsky himself. I would argue that in this instance it is important to separate the character from his creator. Trishatov wants to reform himself, but he is not willing to undertake the hard work of doing so, and the particular ways in which he misappropriates Dickens and Goethe attest to his weakness (*Poslednie romany Dostoevskogo*, 179–84).

26. Charles Dickens, *The Old Curiosity Shop*, ed. Norman Page (London: Penguin Books, 2000), 390.

27. Dickens, *The Old Curiosity Shop*, 401.

28. Unlike Trishatov, Dostoevsky knew the plot of *The Old Curiosity Shop* very well. He found Little Nell's death so moving that he re-created it in *The Insulted and the Injured*, a novel that ends with the death of a Russian-British prepubescent girl named Nellie. Indeed, Susanne Fusso has called Trishatov's story a "double type of quotation," which refers simultaneously to *The Old Curiosity Shop* and to Dostoevsky's own earlier work (*Discovering Sexuality in Dostoevsky* [Evanston, Ill.: Northwestern University Press, 2006], 65).

29. Dostoevsky expressed his own opinion about Gretchen's crime in an 1876 issue of his *Writer's Diary*. He imagines what Russian jurors—who had a habit of acquitting violent criminals—would say when asked to convict a young woman of infanticide: "You can't even pass judgment on one like that; she's a poor, deceived, sympathetic girl; she ought to be eating candies, but suddenly she has a fainting fit, and besides, if you think of Marguerite in *Faust* (some of these jurors are uncommonly well educated), then there is simply no way one

can pass judgment on her; one even ought to take up a subscription for her" (*WD1*, 493; *PSS*, 23:21).

30. Less typical is Trishatov's (hinted at but never clearly stated) choice of employment. As Susanne Fusso has shown, he almost certainly makes his living seducing and blackmailing wealthy homosexual men (*Discovering Sexuality in Dostoevsky*, 42–68).

31. If Gretchen had failed to win salvation, it would have had a cascading negative effect on the rest of the plot. In part 2, Faust is finally redeemed, thanks partly to his famous striving but also, Goethe implies, because Gretchen's soul has been interceding on his behalf, asking the Virgin Mary leave "to teach him!" In the concluding lines of the play, Mary allows Gretchen to pull Faust higher up into heaven: "Come! Into higher spheres / outreach him! / He must sense you to find the way." Faust will fly only as high as Gretchen does; if she sinks, so will he (Johann Wolfgang von Goethe, *Faust: Part Two*, trans. David Luke [Oxford: Oxford University Press, 1994], 239).

32. The image of a ray of light slanting through clouds serves as an apt metaphor for the relationship between the triumphant conclusion toward which Makar believes human history is moving and the present day. Liza Knapp notes that Makar is closely associated with light—both material and divine—throughout the novel (*The Annihilation of Inertia*, 157–60).

33. In *Demons*, the similarly morally authoritative Tikhon admits to a similar degree of imperfection. He acknowledges that even he may not believe in God "perfectly" (*v sovershenstve*) (*PSS*, 11:10).

34. Diane Oenning Thompson, *"The Brothers Karamazov" and the Poetics of Memory* (Cambridge: Cambridge University Press, 1991), 69. Rowan Williams has argued that Dostoevsky's "theology of writing" *requires* resisting easy narrative closure (*Dostoevsky*, 46). Russell Reising makes a related point about literary fiction in general: "No novel, no social text, can resolve in its imaginative work the crises, tensions, and vexations that characterize the social and cultural world of its genesis, [. . .] any appearance of having done so is tantamount to political, moral, and rhetorical bad faith" (*Loose Ends: Closure and Crisis in the American Social Text* [Durham, N.C.: Duke University Press, 1996], 2–3).

35. On Dostoevsky's debt to the French utopian socialists, see V. L. Komarovich, "Iunost' Dostoevskogo" and "Mirovaia garmoniia Dostoevskogo," in *O Dostoevskom: Stat'i*, ed. Donald Fanger, 75–115, 119–49 (Providence, R.I.: Brown University Press, 1966). Dostoevsky's vision of the end of time generally does not include the Last Judgment, which he rarely mentions except to accuse Catholics of being overly fixated on it. According to A. G. Gacheva, Dostoevsky—like his theological fellow travelers Nikolai Fyodorov and Vladimir Solovyov—may have considered the Last Judgment a *possibility* rather than an inevitability. Fyodorov, for example, considered it just one potential—and highly undesirable—outcome to human history. He believed that if humankind came

together in love, resolved their differences, and established universal harmony on earth, the Last Judgment could be avoided and salvation would come to all ("Problema vseobshchnosti spaseniia v romane 'Brat'ia Karamazovy' [v kontekste eskhatologicheskikh idei N. F. Fedorova i V. S. Solov'eva]," in Kasatkina, *Roman F. M. Dostoevskogo*, 226–82). For more on Fyodorov's and Solovyov's thoughts about the Last Judgment, see Irene Masing-Delic, *Abolishing Death: A Salvation Myth of Russian Twentieth-Century Literature* (Stanford, Calif.: Stanford University Press, 1992), 84–85, 106. For a contemporary Orthodox theological justification of the "hope that all *may* be saved," see Timothy Ware, *The Orthodox Church* (London: Penguin Books, 1997), 261–63.

36. Gary Saul Morson, "Introductory Study: Dostoevsky's Great Experiment," in *WD1*, 29.

37. Holland, *The Novel in the Age of Disintegration*, 152.

38. It is perhaps largely *because* Dostoevsky's eschatological thought is imbued with chauvinism that so many of his admirers downplay its influence on his fiction. Rowan Williams, for example, contends that despite "the regular apocalyptic *reference* in the novels" Dostoevsky's novels "are not themselves vehicles of apocalyptic imagination" (*Dostoevsky*, 60).

39. For a history of Dostoevsky's anti-Polish sentiments and how they were related to his deep, paranoiac suspicion of Catholicism, see Elizabeth A. Blake, *Dostoevsky and the Catholic Underground* (Evanston, Ill.: Northwestern University Press, 2014).

40. For an account of Dostoevsky's antisemitism, see Susan McReynolds, *Redemption and the Merchant God: Dostoevsky's Economy of Salvation and Antisemitism* (Evanston, Ill.: Northwestern University Press, 2008), esp. 15–16.

41. As Gary Saul Morson puts it, "Once Dostoevsky sees history in terms of a single story he adopts conspiracy logic to explain all resistance to his utopian dreams" ("Introductory Study," 37).

42. George Eliot, *The George Eliot Letters: Volume 2, 1852–1858*, ed. Gordon S. Haight (New Haven, Conn.: Yale University Press, 1955), 324.

43. This quote helps clarify a paradox Gary Rosenshield identifies in Dostoevsky's vision of personal moral resurrection, which is both an "'event' that occupies no space in real time" and "also a process, and often a slow and arduous one" ("The Realization of the Collective Self: The Rebirth of Religious Autobiography in Dostoevskii's *Zapiski iz Mertvogo Doma*," *Slavic Review* 50, no. 2 [Summer 1991]: 323). It also helps reconcile two contradictory models of personal transformation that Ilya Kliger traces throughout *Crime and Punishment*: Sonya's belief in instantaneous conversion and salvation versus Razumikhin's insistence that the human soul can change only gradually, over time (*The Narrative Shape of Truth: Veridiction in Modern European Literature* [University Park: Pennsylvania State University Press, 2011], 114–44). Here Dostoevsky suggests that both are true. One can indeed experience a sudden insight and instanta-

neous conversion to the path of right. *Maintaining* that newfound faith, however, requires long-term effort.

44. William James, *The Varieties of Religious Experience: A Study in Human Nature*, ed. Matthew Bradley (Oxford: Oxford University Press, 2012), 150. Robin Feuer Miller clarifies his point: in a Jamesian conversion, "evil is not destroyed, undone, or rendered impotent, but it is incorporated, miraculously, into a sense of divine harmony" (*Dostoevsky's Unfinished Journey* [New Haven, Conn.: Yale University Press, 2007], 153).

45. Old Prince Sokolsky *does* mention Anna Andreevna once more. Right before his death, he bequeaths her sixty thousand rubles. In general, he comes closer to reaching balance and harmony in his personal relationships than Versilov does. (Anna Andreevna refuses the money, however. She finds it difficult to come to terms with her past as well. When she and Arkady spend time together, they "don't mention the old times at all" [*A*, 557; *PSS*, 13:45].)

46. Tatiana Kasatkina provides, in "Dostoevsky's *Raw Youth*," 45–49, an in-depth analysis of the connections between Arkady's original "idea" of amassing wealth and the habits of Christian devotion.

47. Lina Steiner, *For Humanity's Sake: The Bildungsroman in Russian Culture* (Toronto: University of Toronto Press, 2011), 148–49.

48. Smith, *Poetic Closure*, 188.

49. Dostoevsky's tragic endings balance openness and closure as well, but in different proportions. The dark conclusion to *The Idiot*, for example, which leaves Nastasya Filippovna dead, Rogozhin in Siberia, Myshkin sunk in a state of irremediable idiocy, and Aglaya married to a Pole (a fate practically worse than death in Dostoevsky's eyes), is lightened by the budding relationship between Radomsky and Vera Lebedeva. The hopeful open-endedness of their incipient friendship counteracts the hopeless closure of the major plotlines. As Olga Matich has argued, however, this hopefulness seems insignificant by comparison with the terrible tragedies that surround it ("Time and Memory in Dostoevsky's Novels, *or* Nastasya Filippovna in Absentia," *Slavic and East European Journal* 60, no. 3 [Fall 2016]: 412).

50. G. M. Fridlender has noted this similarity as well ("Romany Dostoevskogo," in *Istoriia russkogo romana v dvukh tomakh*, ed. B. P. Gorodetskii et al., 2 vols. [Moscow: Nauka, 1962–64], 2:246).

51. Kliger, *The Narrative Shape of Truth*, 39. Michael Holquist and Harriet Murav have made complementary claims. According to Holquist, Dostoevsky "was among the first to recognize that the question of what a man might be could not be separated from the question of what might constitute an authentic history" (*Dostoevsky and the Novel* [Princeton, N.J.: Princeton University Press, 1977], 194). Harriet Murav has likewise argued that "for Dostoevsky individual identity and national identity, autobiography and history are mutually interdependent" (*Holy Foolishness: Dostoevsky's Novels and the Poetics of Cultural Critique* [Stanford, Calif.: Stanford University Press, 1992], 100).

52. Robert Louis Jackson, "Alyosha's Speech at the Stone: 'The Whole Picture,'" in *A New Word on "The Brothers Karamazov,"* ed. Robert Louis Jackson (Evanston, Ill.: Northwestern University Press, 2004), 246. Multiple references to the resurrection of the dead solidify the parallels between this final scene and the end of time as Dostoevsky envisioned it.

53. My reading of Dostoevsky's future-oriented endings resonates with Joseph Frank's description of Dostoevsky's unusual brand of realism. According to Frank, Dostoevsky "looks for the essence of the passing and the contemporary by projecting it into the future and *imagining* its completion (which makes it 'fantastic'), but then, with an unflinching moral-social and psychological realism, dramatizing all the consequences of this future, as if it had already occurred" (*Dostoevsky: The Mantle of the Prophet, 1871–1881* [Princeton, N.J.: Princeton University Press, 2002], 112). Similarly, James P. Scanlan dubs Dostoevsky a "prophetic" realist, because for Dostoevsky "all genuinely realistic art is essentially projective, for it discerns the seeds of future developments in the reality, past or present, that it depicts" (*Dostoevsky the Thinker* [Ithaca, N.Y.: Cornell University Press, 2002], 144).

CHAPTER THREE

1. Forster, *Aspects of the Novel*, 78, 68. Forster includes "all the Dostoevsky characters" in the round category (77). Indeed, Dostoevsky criticizes other authors for creating characters that Forster would call flat (and that Dostoevsky calls types rather than real persons). According to Dostoevsky, Gogol is a chief offender: "Gogol's Sobakevich is only Sobakevich, Manilov is only Manilov. We do not see real people in them, but only those features that the artist wished to highlight [. . .] There is nobody in the whole world who is a scoundrel and nothing more" (*PSS*, 26:312–13).

2. David Galef, *The Supporting Cast: A Study of Flat and Minor Characters* (University Park: Pennsylvania State University Press, 1993), 1, 16–20.

3. Boris Uspensky, *A Poetics of Composition: The Structure of the Artistic Text and Typology of a Compositional Form*, trans. Valentina Zavarin and Susan Wittig (Berkeley: University of California Press, 1973), 159. Robert Higbie argues that, in its most fundamental form, a narrative resembles a sentence, complete with subject, verb, and object. Some characters occupy the "subject" position in the narrative: readers imaginatively inhabit their psyches and act in (and on) the fictional world through them. Other characters occupy the "object" position, and we think of them "in terms of their relation to the subject. We see them as outside the self, to some extent therefore opposed to it, existing to be acted on by it" (*Character and Structure in the English Novel* [Gainesville: University of Florida Press, 1984], 21).

4. According to Forster, in Russian novels flat characters "so seldom occur, they would be a decided help" (*Aspects of the Novel*, 69).

5. V. P. Burenin, review of *The Idiot*, by Fedor Dostoevskii, *Sankt-Peterburgskie vedomosti*, September 13, 1868, no. 250, quoted in *PSS*, 9:415.

6. D. D. Minaev, "Prazdnichnye podarki 'Iskry,'" *Iskra*, April 15, 1873, no. 19, quoted in *PSS*, 12:260.

7. Nikolai Strakhov to Fedor Dostoevskii, April 12, 1871, *Russkii sovremennik* 1 (1924): 199–200.

8. Matich, "Time and Memory in Dostoevsky's Novels," 404. As Malcolm Jones puts it, the narrator of *The Idiot* "dwells equally on trivial and serious topics, sometimes abandoning matters of life and death to pursue some apparently sordid episode" (*Dostoyevsky after Bakhtin*, 139). Alyson Tapp makes an especially interesting argument. She suggests that the novel's structural "inclusiveness that does not know such hierarchical distinctions as those between background and foreground, between major or minor characters, springs from Myshkin's vision." It reflects the hero's own sense that *everyone* matters ("Embarrassment in *The Idiot*," 430).

9. This "rule" gave Dostoevsky yet another reason to make Arkady Dolgoruky a first-person narrator: when the hero tells his own story, he necessarily centers the action around himself. Dostoevsky says as much in another note: "If it's from the first person there will undoubtedly be more unity and less of *that* which Strakhov reproached me with; i.e., a multitude of characters and plotlines" (*PSS*, 16:87).

10. Baruch Hochman, *Character in Literature* (Ithaca, N.Y.: Cornell University Press, 1985), 107–8.

11. Alex Woloch, *The One vs. the Many: Minor Characters and the Space of the Protagonist in the Novel* (Princeton, N.J.: Princeton University Press, 2003), 13, 15, 21, 20.

12. During the investigation, Dmitry makes a similar statement, with similar metaliterary overtones. When the prosecutor asks him how he suddenly came up with thousands of rubles (when he apparently had none at all just a few hours earlier), Dmitry answers, "Eh, gentlemen, why pick on such little things [*ne nado by melochi*]: how, when, and why, and precisely this much money and not that much, and all that claptrap . . . if you keep on, it'll take you three volumes and an epilogue to cram it all in" (*BK*, 466; *PSS*, 14:420). Dmitry and the prosecutor have very different ideas about what counts as a "little thing," however. By refusing to say where he got the money for last night's spree, Dmitry gives the appearance of stalling for time, which makes the truth seem less plausible when he finally agrees to tell it. By ignoring this seemingly "little thing," Dmitry ends up doing serious damage to his case. It is always dangerous to overlook the apparently minor and insignificant in this novel.

13. Robin Feuer Miller, *"The Brothers Karamazov": Worlds of the Novel* (New Haven, Conn.: Yale University Press, 2008), 16–17.

14. Vetlovskaia, *Roman F. M. Dostoevskogo*, 27. According to Victor Terras,

all of Dostoevsky's narrators are partisan: "They will always find ways, direct or indirect, to express their sympathies and antipathies" (*Reading Dostoevsky*, 102).

15. While the narrator tends to devote little attention to peasants and servants, he is willing to spend much more time on socially significant characters. For example, he carefully describes the meeting of two secondary characters: Madame Khokhlakova and the ambitious Perkhotin. Although he initially apologizes for expanding on "such petty and incidental details," he justifies the digression by explaining that, thanks to this meeting, Perkhotin would soon become a very important person. The encounter "served as the foundation for the whole life's career of that precise and accurate young man, which is still recalled with astonishment in our town, and of which we, too, shall perhaps have a special word to say, once we have concluded our long story of the Karamazov brothers" (*BK*, 450–51; *PSS*, 14:406).

16. N. V. Gogol', *Polnoe sobranie sochinenii*, ed. N. L. Meshcheriakov et al., 14 vols. (Moscow: Izdatel'stvo AN SSSR, 1937–52), 6:20.

17. Gogol', *Polnoe sobranie sochinenii*, 6:19.

18. Both Robert L. Belknap, *The Structure of "The Brothers Karamazov"* (Evanston, Ill.: Northwestern University Press, 1989), 83, and Meerson, *Dostoevsky's Taboos*, 184, point out this intertext.

19. Meerson, *Dostoevsky's Taboos*, 203–7, and "Chetvertyi brat ili kozel otpushcheniia ex machina?"

20. George Gibian, "Dostoevskij's Use of Russian Folklore," *Journal of American Folklore* 69, no. 273 (July 1956): 240–41, compares Alyosha Karamazov to "Ivan the Fool." Vetlovskaia, *Roman F. M. Dostoevskogo*, 230–36, makes the comparison as well.

21. The consequences of Alyosha's forgetfulness are dire. If he had found Dmitry, he might have put a halt to the chain of events that led to his father's death. As Carol Apollonio puts it, "No less than Ivan's departure before the murder, Alyosha's negligence brings about Fedor Pavlovich's death" (*Dostoevsky's Secrets*, 163).

22. Thompson, *"The Brothers Karamazov,"* 160.

23. The novel's characters have difficulty sharing in matters great and small. In one scene, the boy Ilyusha's half-mad mother insists that his new toy cannon go exclusively to her: "No, I don't want it to be both of ours, no, I want it to be just mine and not Ilyusha's" (*BK*, 547; *PSS*, 14:493). While the example may seem trivial, it only demonstrates how omnipresent battles for dominance and ownership are in this novel.

24. V. S. Dorovatovskaia-Liubimova, "Dostoevskii i shestidesiatniki," in *Dostoevskii* (Moscow: Gosudarstvennaia akademiia khudozhestvennykh nauk, 1928), 14.

25. Victor Terras similarly calls Rakitin a "stock character" (*A Karamazov Companion: Commentary on the Genesis, Language, and Style of Dostoevsky's*

Novel [Madison: University of Wisconsin Press, 1981], 63). It is important to note, however, that Ivan and Dmitry *treat* Rakitin as a type (thereby helping to establish his status as one). Dmitry often refers to Rakitin as "they" or one of "them." To use Sarah Young's terminology, Dmitry "scripts" Rakitin into the "stock character" role (*Dostoevsky's "The Idiot"*).

26. Grushenka's use of the demeaning label "lackey" to describe Rakitin creates yet another association between him and Smerdyakov, who is called a "lackey" by the narrator, Ivan, and even by Alyosha.

27. Robert L. Belknap, *The Genesis of "The Brothers Karamazov": The Aesthetics, Ideology, and Psychology of Making a Text* (Evanston, Ill.: Northwestern University Press, 1990), 144–46. Nina Perlina has pointed out similarities between Rakitin's language and ideas and those of Ivan's devil, a comparison that makes the prospect of Rakitin's rise to journalistic prominence all the more worrisome (*Varieties of Poetic Utterance: Quotation in "The Brothers Karamazov"* [Lanham, Md.: University Press of America, 1985], 139–40).

28. Gary Saul Morson, "Verbal Pollution in *The Brothers Karamazov*," in *Critical Essays on Dostoevsky*, ed. Robin Feuer Miller (Boston: Hall, 1986), 235.

29. Olga Meerson analyzes the conflicting connotations in Smerdyakov's provocative statement to Ivan: "Forgive me, sir [*Prostite-s*], I thought you were like I am" (*BK*, 608; *PSS*, 15:46). Smerdyakov's language underscores the power imbalance between the two likely brothers: Ivan addresses Smerdyakov in the informal register, *ty*, and Smerdyakov answers in the formal, *vy*, emphasizing Ivan's social superiority by adding the servile *slovoers*. Yet the grammatical trappings of inferiority do not distract from Smerdyakov's radical message: the servant says to the nobleman, "I thought you were like I am" ("Chetvertyi brat," 593–94).

30. Morson, "Verbal Pollution in *The Brothers Karamazov*," 240.

31. Belknap, *The Structure of "The Brothers Karamazov,"* 62.

32. Maxim D. Shrayer, "Metamorphoses of 'Bezobrazie' in Dostoevskij's *The Brothers Karamazov*: Maksimov—Von Sohn—Karamazov," *Russian Literature* 37 (1995): 103.

33. Belknap, *The Structure of "The Brothers Karamazov,"* 34.

34. It is wise to remember that we may be a little smelly, too. Even Father Zosima's body gives off an "odor of corruption" after his death. He may be good, but he is still mortal and therefore both subject to earthly degradation and implicated in the sins of his community.

35. In one of his notebooks, Dostoevsky writes about the necessity of excluding criminals from the community (but also the necessity of leaving a door open for their return) in much the same terms that Zosima does: "The expulsion from society by the entire collective (the only punishment, but without torture) and his certain return to society if he is worthy of it, in order not to leave his soul in despair—these are the principles that should be adopted without fail" (*PSS*, 24:207). Anna Schur discusses the significance of this note in *Wages of Evil: Dos-*

toevsky and Punishment (Evanston, Ill.: Northwestern University Press, 2012), 57–58.

36. See Eric Naiman, "Kalganov," *Slavic and East European Journal* 58, no. 3 (Fall 2014): 394–418.

37. When Kalganov turns away from Maksimov, he also turns away from engagement with life in general. We next hear of him from Lise, who reports that Kalganov "walks about and dreams. He says: why live in reality, it's better to dream. One can dream up the gayest things, but to live is boring" (*BK*, 581; *PSS*, 15:22).

38. Grushenka's statement is made even more ambivalent by her very next words: "I wish that the Pole wasn't here at all [*ne bylo etogo poliaka vovse*], Alyosha, he decided to get sick today" (*BK*, 566; *PSS*, 15:8). Pevear and Volokhonsky interpret her expression charitably. It could also be taken to mean "I wish this Pole didn't *exist* at all."

39. Woloch, *The One vs. the Many*, 38.

40. For more on Dostoevsky's attitude toward the honor code, and its significance to this scene in particular, see Irina Reyfman, *Ritualized Violence Russian Style: The Duel in Russian Culture and Literature* (Stanford, Calif.: Stanford University Press, 1999), 248–52.

41. Anne Hruska, "The Sins of Children in *The Brothers Karamazov*: Serfdom, Hierarchy, and Transcendence," *Christianity and Literature* 54, no. 4 (Summer 2005): 483.

42. A. K. Baiburin, *Zhilishche v obriadakh i predstavleniiakh vostochnykh slavian* (Leningrad: Nauka, 1983), 149–50. Another important difference between Smerdyakov and Ilyusha is how each character relates to the icon corner. For Ilyusha, it is a place of healing. Smerdyakov, by contrast, treats it cynically, using this otherworldly space to hide money—the ultimate symbol of worldliness.

43. Even this harmonious scene includes references to the difficulty of sharing. Ilyusha's mother asks for a flower from the dead boy's hands, and her husband angrily refuses, reminding her of the time she demanded Ilyusha's toy cannon.

44. On the significance of this nickname, see Vetlovskaia, *Roman F. M. Dostoevskogo*, 147. For a study of the important difference between fatherly and brotherly love in *The Brothers Karamazov*, see Anna A. Berman, *Siblings in Tolstoy and Dostoevsky: The Path to Universal Brotherhood* (Evanston, Ill.: Northwestern University Press, 2015), 114–32. In her memoirs, Dostoevsky's wife, Anna, laments that financial hardship, the need to write quickly and publish constantly, prevented her husband from reaching his full artistic potential: "And how my husband's work would have gained in the artistic sense if he had not had those self-imposed debts and could have written without hurry, looking over and rewriting his work before handing it over to the printer. Frequent comparisons are made, in literature and in society, between Dostoevsky's work and the work

of other gifted writers, and Dostoevsky is criticized for excessive complexity, intricacy and accumulation of detail, whereas the work of others is polished" (*Dostoevsky: Reminiscences*, ed. and trans. Beatrice Stillman [New York: Liveright, 1975], 181–82). She need not have worried. The revealing inconsistency concerning the landladies shows that even Dostoevsky's "mistakes" were artistically productive. (My thanks to Eric Naiman for reminding me of this quotation.)

45. Hruska, "The Sins of Children," 489.

46. Jackson, "Alyosha's Speech at the Stone," 238.

47. See, for example, Jackson, "Alyosha's Speech at the Stone," 246, and Thompson, *"The Brothers Karamazov,"* 325.

48. Apollonio, *Dostoevsky's Secrets*, 164; Joe Andrew, "For Men Only? Dostoevskii's Patriarchal Vision in *The Brothers Karamazov*," in *Aspects of Dostoevskii: Art, Ethics, and Faith*, ed. Robert Reid and Joe Andrew (Amsterdam: Rodopi, 2012), 230.

49. In *The Brothers Karamazov*, Dostoevsky's own prejudices are on full display. They come through especially clearly in his depiction of Grushenka's former Polish lover, a ridiculous, pompous nationalist who pretends to speak Russian less fluently than he really does. Even more disturbing are the novel's references to Jews, who are accused of kidnapping and murdering Christian children on Passover—an accusation that Alyosha will neither confirm nor deny (*BK*, 583; *PSS*, 15:24).

50. Meerson, "Chetvertyi brat," 568.

51. Bakhtin, "Toward a Reworking," in *PDP*, 297; *SS*, 5:355.

52. Bakhtin, "Toward a Reworking," *PDP*, 300; *SS*, 5:360.

53. Chloë Kitzinger observes that Bakhtin's argument *itself* relies on major and minor characters, as it were. Bakhtin's representation of Dostoevsky's characters as bearers of their own word "becomes convincing, in part, because it is juxtaposed with the specter of other characters who are only the passive objects of authorial language. Ironically, insofar as it relies on this authoritative act of characterization, Bakhtin's argument is itself structured rather like a novel—and importantly, structured more like Tolstoy's novels than like Dostoevsky's" ("Illusion and Instrument: Problems of Mimetic Characterization in Dostoevsky and Tolstoy" [Ph.D. diss., University of California, Berkeley, 2016], 178–79, ProQuest [10150919]).

CONCLUSION

1. Gogol', *Polnoe sobranie sochinenii*, 4:5.

2. Mikhailovskii, *Literaturno-kriticheskie stat'i*, 211.

Selected Bibliography

Abbott, H. Porter. *The Cambridge Introduction to Narrative*. 2nd ed. Cambridge: Cambridge University Press, 2008.

Alter, Robert. *The Five Books of Moses*. New York: Norton, 2004.

Andrew, Joe. "For Men Only? Dostoevskii's Patriarchal Vision in *The Brothers Karamazov*." In *Aspects of Dostoevskii: Art, Ethics, and Faith*, edited by Robert Reid and Joe Andrew, 187–240. Amsterdam: Rodopi, 2012.

Apollonio, Carol. *Dostoevsky's Secrets: Reading Against the Grain*. Evanston, Ill.: Northwestern University Press, 2009.

Babuk, Aleksandr. "The Myth of Childhood as an Embodiment of the Golden Age in Dostoevsky's Oeuvre." Translated by Liv Bliss. *Russian Studies in Literature* 51, no. 2 (Spring 2015): 33–53.

Baiburin, A. K. *Zhilishche v obriadakh i predstavleniiakh vostochnykh slavian*. Leningrad: Nauka, 1983.

Bakhtin, M. M. "Forms of Time and of the Chronotope in the Novel." In *The Dialogic Imagination: Four Essays*, edited by Michael Holquist, translated by Caryl Emerson and Michael Holquist, 84–258. Austin: University of Texas Press, 1981.

———. *Problems of Dostoevsky's Poetics*. Edited and translated by Caryl Emerson. Minneapolis: University of Minnesota Press, 1984.

———. *Sobranie sochinenii v semi tomakh*. Edited by S. G. Bocharov et al. 6 vols. Moscow: Russkie slovari, 1996–.

Belknap, Robert L. *The Genesis of "The Brothers Karamazov": The Aesthetics, Ideology, and Psychology of Making a Text*. Evanston, Ill.: Northwestern University Press, 1990.

———. *Plots*. New York: Columbia University Press, 2016.

———. *The Structure of "The Brothers Karamazov."* Evanston, Ill.: Northwestern University Press, 1989.

Benedict, Barbara M. *Curiosity: A Cultural History of Early Modern Inquiry*. Chicago: University of Chicago Press, 2001.

Berman, Anna A. *Siblings in Tolstoy and Dostoevsky: The Path to Universal Brotherhood*. Evanston, Ill.: Northwestern University Press, 2015.

Bethea, David M. *The Shape of the Apocalypse in Modern Russian Fiction*. Princeton, N.J.: Princeton University Press, 1989.

Blake, Elizabeth A. *Dostoevsky and the Catholic Underground*. Evanston, Ill.: Northwestern University Press, 2014.

Blank, Ksana. *Dostoevsky's Dialectics and the Problem of Sin*. Evanston, Ill.: Northwestern University Press, 2010.

Bocharov, Sergey. "Conversations with Bakhtin." Translated by Stephen Blackwell and Vadim Liapunov. *PMLA* 109, no. 5 (October 1994): 1009–24.

Booth, Wayne C. "Are Narrative Choices Subject to Ethical Criticism?" In *Reading Narrative: Form, Ethics, Ideology*, edited by James Phelan, 57–78. Columbus: Ohio State University Press, 1989.

———. *The Rhetoric of Fiction*. 2nd ed. Chicago: University of Chicago Press, 1983.

Breithaupt, Fritz. "The Bad Things We Do Because of Empathy." *Interdisciplinary Science Reviews* 43, no. 2 (April 2018): 166–74.

Brooks, Peter. *Reading for the Plot: Design and Intention in Narrative*. Cambridge, Mass.: Harvard University Press, 1984.

Burry, Alexander. *Multi-Mediated Dostoevsky: Transposing Novels into Opera, Film, and Drama*. Evanston, Ill.: Northwestern University Press, 2011.

Catteau, Jacques. *Dostoyevsky and the Process of Literary Creation*. Translated by Audrey Littlewood. Cambridge: Cambridge University Press, 1989.

Cherkasova, Evgenia. *Dostoevsky and Kant: Dialogues on Ethics*. Amsterdam: Rodopi, 2009.

Coates, Ruth. *Christianity in Bakhtin: God and the Exiled Author*. Cambridge: Cambridge University Press, 2004.

Cohn, Dorrit. *Transparent Minds: Narrative Modes for Presenting Consciousness in Fiction*. Princeton, N.J.: Princeton University Press, 1978.

Coplan, Amy. "Empathic Engagement with Narrative Fictions." *Journal of Aesthetics and Art Criticism* 62, no. 2 (Spring 2004): 141–52.

Corrigan, Yuri. *Dostoevsky and the Riddle of the Self*. Evanston, Ill.: Northwestern University Press, 2017.

Davidovich, M. G. "Problema zanimatel'nosti v romanakh Dostoevskogo." In *Tvorcheskii put' Dostoevskogo: Sbornik statei*, edited by N. L. Brodskii, 104–30. Leningrad: "Seiatel'" E. V. Vysotskogo, 1924.

Dawson, Paul. *The Return of the Omniscient Narrator: Authorship and Authority in Twenty-First Century Fiction*. Columbus: Ohio State University Press, 2013.

Dickens, Charles. *The Old Curiosity Shop*. Edited by Norman Page. London: Penguin Books, 2000.

Dolinin, A. S. *Poslednie romany Dostoevskogo: Kak sozdavalis' "Podrostok" i "Brat'ia Karamazovy."* Moscow: Sovetskii pisatel', 1963.

Dorovatovskaia-Liubimova, V. S. "Dostoevskii i shestidesiatniki." In *Dostoevskii*, 5–60. Moscow: Gosudarstvennaia akademiia khudozhestvennykh nauk, 1928.

Dostoevsky, Anna. *Dostoevsky: Reminiscences*. Edited and translated by Beatrice Stillman. New York: Liveright, 1975.

[Dostoevskii, F. M.] *Polnoe sobranie sochinenii v tridtsati tomakh*. Edited by V. G. Bazanov, V. V. Vinogradov, F. Ia. Priima, G. M. Fridlender, and M. B. Khrapchenko. 30 vols. Leningrad: Nauka, 1972–90.

Dostoevsky, Fyodor. *The Adolescent*. Translated by Richard Pevear and Larissa Volokhonsky. New York: Vintage Classics, 2003.

———. *The Brothers Karamazov*. Translated by Richard Pevear and Larissa Volokhonsky. New York: Farrar, Straus and Giroux, 1990.

———. *The Idiot*. Translated by Richard Pevear and Larissa Volokhonsky. New York: Vintage Classics, 2003.

———. *A Writer's Diary*. Translated by Kenneth Lantz. 2 vols. Evanston, Ill.: Northwestern University Press: 1993–94.

Dostoyevsky, Fyodor. *Crime and Punishment*. Translated by Oliver Ready. London: Penguin Books, 2014.

———. *Demons*. Translated by Robert A. Maguire. Edited by Ronald Meyer. London: Penguin Books, 2006.

Eco, Umberto. "The Poetics of the Open Work." In *The Role of the Reader: Explorations in the Semiotics of Texts*, 47–66. Bloomington: Indiana University Press, 1979.

Eklof, Ben, John Bushnell, and Larissa Zakharova, eds. *Russia's Great Reforms, 1855–1881*. Bloomington: Indiana University Press, 1994.

Eliot, George. *The George Eliot Letters*. Edited by Gordon S. Haight. 9 vols. New Haven, Conn.: Yale University Press, 1954–58.

Emerson, Caryl. *The First Hundred Years of Mikhail Bakhtin*. Princeton, N.J.: Princeton University Press, 1997.

———. "Problems with Baxtin's Poetics." *Slavic and East European Journal* 32, no. 4 (Winter 1988): 503–25.

———. "Word and Image in Dostoevsky's Worlds: Robert Louis Jackson on Readings That Bakhtin Could Not Do." In *Freedom and Responsibility in Russian Literature: Essays in Honor of Robert Louis Jackson*, edited by Elizabeth Cheresh Allen and Gary Saul Morson, 245–66. Evanston, Ill.: Northwestern University Press, 1995.

Forster, E. M. *Aspects of the Novel*. London: Harcourt, 1927.

Frank, Joseph. *Dostoevsky: The Mantle of the Prophet, 1871–1881*. Princeton, N.J.: Princeton University Press, 2002.

———. *Dostoevsky: The Miraculous Years, 1865–1871*. Princeton, N.J.: Princeton University Press, 1995.

Fridlender, G. M. "Romany Dostoevskogo." In *Istoriia russkogo romana v dvukh tomakh*, edited by B. P. Gorodetskii et al., 2 vols., 2:193–269. Moscow: Nauka, 1962–64.

Fusso, Susanne. *Discovering Sexuality in Dostoevsky*. Evanston, Ill.: Northwestern University Press, 2006.

———. *Editing Turgenev, Dostoevsky, and Tolstoy: Mikhail Katkov and the Great Russian Novel*. DeKalb: Northern Illinois University Press, 2017.

Gacheva, A. G. "Problema vseobshchnosti spaseniia v romane 'Brat'ia Karamazovy' (v kontekste eskhatologicheskikh idei N. F. Fedorova i V. S. Solov'eva)." In *Roman F. M. Dostoevskogo "Brat'ia Karamazovy": Sovremennoe sostoianie izucheniia*, edited by T. A. Kasatkina, 226–82. Moscow: Nauka, 2007.

Galef, David. *The Supporting Cast: A Study of Flat and Minor Characters*. University Park: Pennsylvania State University Press, 1993.

Gaylin, Ann. *Eavesdropping in the Novel from Austen to Proust*. Cambridge: Cambridge University Press, 2002.

Genette, Gérard. *Narrative Discourse: An Essay in Method*. Translated by Jane E. Lewin. Ithaca, N.Y.: Cornell University Press, 1980.

Gibian, George. "Dostoevskij's Use of Russian Folklore." *Journal of American Folklore* 69, no. 273 (July 1956): 239–53.

Girard, René. *The Scapegoat*. Translated by Yvonne Freccero. Baltimore: Johns Hopkins University Press, 1986.

Goethe, Johann Wolfgang von. *Faust: Part Two*. Translated by David Luke. Oxford: Oxford University Press, 1994.

Gogol', N. V. *Polnoe sobranie sochinenii*. Edited by N. L. Meshcheriakov et al. 14 vols. Moscow: Izdatel'stvo AN SSSR, 1937–52.

Greiner, Rae. *Sympathetic Realism in Nineteenth-Century British Fiction*. Baltimore: Johns Hopkins University Press, 2012.

Griffiths, Paul J. *Intellectual Appetite: A Theological Grammar*. Washington, D.C.: Catholic University of America Press, 2009.

Grigorenko, V. V., et al., eds. *F. M. Dostoevskii v vospominaniiakh sovremennikov*. 2 vols. Moscow: Khudozhestvennaia literatura, 1964.

Grossman, Leonid. *Poetika Dostoevskogo*. Moscow: Gosudarstvennaia akademiia khudozhestvennykh nauk, 1925.

Halpern, Faye. "Closeness Through Unreliability: Sympathy, Empathy, and Ethics in Narrative Communication." *Narrative* 26, no. 2 (May 2018): 125–45.

Hammond, Meghan Marie, and Sue J. Kim, eds. *Rethinking Empathy through Literature*. New York: Routledge, 2014.

Harrison, Mary-Catherine. "How Narrative Relationships Overcome Empathic Bias: Elizabeth Gaskell's Empathy across Social Difference." *Poetics Today* 32, no. 2 (Summer 2011): 255–88.

———. "The Paradox of Fiction and the Ethics of Empathy: Reconceiving Dickens's Realism." *Narrative* 16, no. 3 (October 2008): 256–78.

Hawthorn, Jeremy. "Reading Fiction: Voyeurism without Shame?" In *Narrative Ethics*, edited by Jakob Lothe and Jeremy Hawthorn, 73–88. Amsterdam: Rodopi, 2013.

Heinze, Ruediger. "Violations of Mimetic Epistemology in First-Person Narrative Fiction." *Narrative* 16, no. 3 (2008): 279–97.

Heise, Ursula K. *Chronoschisms: Time, Narrative, and Postmodernism*. Cambridge: Cambridge University Press, 1997.

Higbie, Robert. *Character and Structure in the English Novel*. Gainesville: University of Florida Press, 1984.

Hochman, Baruch. *Character in Literature*. Ithaca, N.Y.: Cornell University Press, 1985.

Holland, Kate. *The Novel in the Age of Disintegration: Dostoevsky and the Problem of Genre in the 1870s*. Evanston, Ill.: Northwestern University Press, 2013.

Holquist, Michael. *Dostoevsky and the Novel*. Princeton, N.J.: Princeton University Press, 1977.

Hruska, Anne. "The Sins of Children in *The Brothers Karamazov*: Serfdom, Hierarchy, and Transcendence." *Christianity and Literature* 54, no. 4 (Summer 2005): 471–95.

Ivanov, V. I. *Sobranie sochinenii*. Edited by D. V. Ivanova and O. Deshart. 4 vols. Brussels: Foyer Oriental Chrétien, 1971–87.

Jackson, Robert Louis. "Alyosha's Speech at the Stone: 'The Whole Picture.'" In *A New Word on "The Brothers Karamazov,"* edited by Robert Louis Jackson, 234–53. Evanston, Ill.: Northwestern University Press, 2004.

———. *Dialogues with Dostoevsky: The Overwhelming Questions*. Stanford, Calif.: Stanford University Press, 1993.

———. *Dostoevsky's Quest for Form: A Study of His Philosophy of Art*. New Haven, Conn.: Yale University Press, 1966.

James, William. *The Varieties of Religious Experience: A Study in Human Nature*. Edited by Matthew Bradley. Oxford: Oxford University Press, 2012.

Jones, Malcolm V. *Dostoyevsky: The Novel of Discord*. New York: Barnes and Noble Books, 1976.

———. *Dostoyevsky after Bakhtin: Readings in Dostoyevsky's Fantastic Realism*. Cambridge: Cambridge University Press, 1990.

———. "The Narrator and Narrative Technique in Dostoevsky's *The Devils*." In *Dostoevsky's "The Devils": A Critical Companion*, edited by W. J. Leatherbarrow, 100–118. Evanston, Ill.: Northwestern University Press, 1999.

Kariakin, Iu. F. "Zachem Khroniker v 'Besakh'?" In *Dostoevskii: Materialy i issledovaniia*, vol. 5, edited by G. M. Fridlender, 113–31. Leningrad: Nauka, 1983.

Kasatkina, Tat'iana. "Dostoevsky's *Raw Youth*: The 'Idea' of the Hero and the Idea of the Author." Translated by Liv Bliss. *Russian Studies in Literature* 40, no. 4 (Fall 2004): 38–68.

Keen, Suzanne. *Empathy and the Novel*. Oxford: Oxford University Press, 2007.

———. "Readers' Temperaments and Fictional Character." *New Literary History* 42, no. 2 (Spring 2011): 295–314.

Kenny, Neil. *Curiosity in Early Modern Europe: Word Histories*. Wiesbaden: Harrassowitz Verlag, 1998.

Kermode, Frank. *The Sense of an Ending: Studies in the Theory of Fiction; With a New Epilogue*. Oxford: Oxford University Press, 2000.

Kitzinger, Chloë. "Illusion and Instrument: Problems of Mimetic Characterization in Dostoevsky and Tolstoy." Ph.D. diss., University of California, Berkeley, 2016. ProQuest (10150919).

Kliger, Ilya. *The Narrative Shape of Truth: Veridiction in Modern European Literature*. University Park: Pennsylvania State University Press, 2011.

Knapp, Liza. *The Annihilation of Inertia: Dostoevsky and Metaphysics*. Evanston, Ill.: Northwestern University Press, 1996.

Kokobobo, Ani. *Russian Grotesque Realism: The Great Reforms and the Gentry Decline*. Columbus: Ohio State University Press, 2018.

Komarovich, V. L. "Iunost' Dostoevskogo." In *O Dostoevskom: Stat'i*, edited by Donald Fanger, 75–115. Providence, R.I.: Brown University Press, 1966.

———. "Mirovaia garmoniia Dostoevskogo." In *O Dostoevskom: Stat'i*, edited by Donald Fanger, 119–49. Providence, R.I.: Brown University Press, 1966.

Lanser, Susan Sniader. *Fictions of Authority: Women Writers and Narrative Voice*. Ithaca, N.Y.: Cornell University Press, 1992.

Leatherbarrow, W. J. "*The Devils* in the Context of Dostoevsky's Life and Works." In *Dostoevsky's "The Devils": A Critical Companion*, edited by W. J. Leatherbarrow, 3–62. Evanston, Ill.: Northwestern University Press, 1999.

———. *A Devil's Vaudeville: The Demonic in Dostoevsky's Major Fiction*. Evanston, Ill.: Northwestern University Press, 2005.

Lee, Susanna. *A World Abandoned by God: Narrative and Secularism*. Lewisburg, Pa.: Bucknell University Press, 2006.

Levine, Caroline. *Forms: Whole, Rhythm, Hierarchy, Network*. Princeton, N.J.: Princeton University Press, 2015.

———. *The Serious Pleasures of Suspense: Victorian Realism and Narrative Doubt*. Charlottesville: University of Virginia Press, 2003.

Lossky, Vladimir. *Orthodox Theology: An Introduction*. Translated by Ian and Ihita Kesarcodi-Watson. Crestwood, N.Y.: Saint Vladimir's Seminary Press, 1978.

Lundeen, Kathleen. "Who Has the Right to Feel? The Ethics of Literary Empathy." *Style* 32, no. 2 (Summer 1998): 261–71.

Lyngstad, Alexandra H. *Dostoevskij and Schiller*. The Hague: Mouton, 1975.

Maikov, V. N. *Literaturnaia kritika: Stat'i, retsenzii*. Leningrad: "Khudozhestvennaia literatura," 1985.

Martinsen, Deborah A. *Surprised by Shame: Dostoevsky's Liars and Narrative Exposure*. Columbus: Ohio State University Press, 2003.

Masing-Delic, Irene. *Abolishing Death: A Salvation Myth of Russian Twentieth-Century Literature*. Stanford, Calif.: Stanford University Press, 1992.

Matich, Olga. "Time and Memory in Dostoevsky's Novels, *or* Nastasya Filippovna in Absentia." *Slavic and East European Journal* 60, no. 3 (Fall 2016): 397–421.

McReynolds, Susan. *Redemption and the Merchant God: Dostoevsky's Economy of Salvation and Antisemitism*. Evanston, Ill.: Northwestern University Press, 2008.

Mendilow, A. A. *Time and the Novel*. New York: Nevill, 1952.

Meerson, Olga. "Chetvertyi brat ili kozel otpushcheniia ex machina?" In *Roman Dostoevskogo "Brat'ia Karamazovy": Sovremennoe sostoianie izucheniia*, edited by T. A. Kasatkina, 565–604. Moscow: Nauka, 2007.

———. *Dostoevsky's Taboos*. Dresden: Dresden University Press, 1998.

———. *Personalizm kak poetika: Literaturnyi mir glazami ego obitatelei*. Saint Petersburg: Izdatel'stvo "Pushkinskii dom," 2009.

Merezhkovskii, D. S. *L. Tolstoi i Dostoevskii*. Edited by E. A. Andrushchenko. Moscow: Nauka, 2000.

Mikhailovskii, N. K. *Literaturno-kriticheskie stat'i*. Moscow: Gosudarstvennoe izdatel'stvo khudozhestvennoi literatury, 1957.

Miller, D. A. *Narrative and Its Discontents: Problems of Closure in the Traditional Novel*. Princeton, N.J.: Princeton University Press, 1981.

Miller, Robin Feuer. *"The Brothers Karamazov": Worlds of the Novel*. New Haven, Conn.: Yale University Press, 2008.

———. *Dostoevsky and "The Idiot": Author, Narrator, and Reader*. Cambridge, Mass.: Harvard University Press, 1981.

———. *Dostoevsky's Unfinished Journey*. New Haven, Conn.: Yale University Press, 2007.

Mochulsky, Konstantin. *Dostoevsky: His Life and Work*. Translated by Michael A. Minihan. Princeton, N.J.: Princeton University Press, 1967.

Moore, Gene M. "The Voices of Legion: The Narrator of *The Possessed*." *Dostoevsky Studies* 6 (1985): 51–66.

Morson, Gary Saul. "Introductory Study: Dostoevsky's Great Experiment." In Fyodor Dostoevsky, *A Writer's Diary*, translated by Kenneth Lantz, 2 vols., 1:1–117. Evanston, Ill.: Northwestern University Press, 1993–94.

———. "Misanthropology." *New Literary History* 27, no. 1 (Winter 1996): 57–72.

———. *Narrative and Freedom: The Shadows of Time*. New Haven, Conn.: Yale University Press, 1994.

———. "Return to Process: The Unfolding of *The Idiot*." *New Literary History* 40, no. 4 (Autumn 2009): 843–65.

———. "Verbal Pollution in *The Brothers Karamazov*." In *Critical Essays on Dostoevsky*, edited by Robin Feuer Miller, 234–42. Boston: Hall, 1986.

Murav, Harriet. *Holy Foolishness: Dostoevsky's Novels and the Poetics of Cultural Critique*. Stanford, Calif.: Stanford University Press, 1992.

Naiman, Eric. "Kalganov." *Slavic and East European Journal* 58, no. 3 (Fall 2014): 394–418.

Nandrea, Lorri. "Objectless Curiosity: *Frankenstein, The Station Agent*, and Other Strange Narratives." *Narrative* 15, no. 3 (October 2007): 335–56.

Newton, Adam Zachary. *Narrative Ethics*. Cambridge, Mass.: Harvard University Press, 1995.

Nussbaum, Martha C. *Love's Knowledge: Essays on Philosophy and Literature*. Oxford: Oxford University Press, 1990.

Oatley, Keith. "Meetings of Minds: Dialogue, Sympathy, and Identification, in Reading Fiction." *Poetics* 26 (1999): 439–54.

Pavel, Thomas. "Safely Watching Wild Adventures." *Narrative* 24, no. 1 (January 2016): 1–12.

Perlina, Nina. *Varieties of Poetic Utterance: Quotation in "The Brothers Karamazov."* Lanham, Md.: University Press of America, 1985.

Phelan, James. "Implausibilities, Crossovers, and Impossibilities: A Rhetorical Approach to Breaks in the Code of Mimetic Character Narration." In *A Poetics of Unnatural Narrative*, edited by Jan Alber, Henrik Skov Nielson, and Brian Richardson, 167–84. Columbus: Ohio State University Press, 2013.

———. *Narrative as Rhetoric: Technique, Audiences, Ethics, Ideology*. Columbus: Ohio State University Press, 1996.

———. "Narrative Ethics." In *The Living Handbook of Narratology*, edited by Peter Hühn et al. Hamburg: Universität Hamburg. Last modified December 9, 2014. http://www.lhn.uni-hamburg.de/article/narrative-ethics.

Phelan, James, and Peter J. Rabinowitz. "Narrative as Rhetoric." In *Narrative Theory: Core Concepts and Critical Debates*, edited by David Herman et al. Columbus: Ohio State University Press, 2012.

Pirusskaia, T. "Spletnia kak mekhanizm avtorefleksii v romanakh Dostoevskogo 'Besy' i Dzhordzh Eliot 'Midlmarch.'" *Voprosy literatury*, no. 2 (2015): 193–216.

Plutarch. *Selected Essays and Dialogues*. Translated by Donald Russell. Oxford: Oxford University Press, 1993.

Poluboyarinova, Larisa. "Impello–Impuli–Impulsum: Dostoevsky and Schiller between Logos and Pathos." *Dostoevsky Studies* 20 (2016): 31–46.

Rabinowitz, Peter J. *Before Reading: Narrative Conventions and the Politics of Interpretation*. Ithaca, N.Y.: Cornell University Press, 1987.

Reed, Natalia. "The Philosophical Roots of Polyphony: A Dostoevskian Reading." In *Critical Essays on Mikhail Bakhtin*, edited by Caryl Emerson, 117–52. New York: Hall, 1999.

Reising, Russell. *Loose Ends: Closure and Crisis in the American Social Text*. Durham, N.C.: Duke University Press, 1996.

Reyfman, Irina. *Ritualized Violence Russian Style: The Duel in Russian Culture and Literature*. Stanford, Calif.: Stanford University Press, 1999.

Richter, David H. *Fable's End: Completeness and Closure in Rhetorical Fiction*. Chicago: University of Chicago Press, 1974.

Ronner, Amy D. "Is Stavrogin Leading Us by the Nose? The Nihilistic Confession." *Dostoevsky Studies* 20 (2016): 71–101.

Rosen, Nathan. "Breaking Out of the Underground: The 'Failure' of 'A Raw Youth.'" *Modern Fiction Studies* 4, no. 3 (Fall 1958): 225–39.

Rosenshield, Gary. "The Realization of the Collective Self: The Rebirth of Religious Autobiography in Dostoevskii's *Zapiski iz Mertvogo Doma*." *Slavic Review* 50, no. 2 (Summer 1991): 317–27.

———. *Western Law, Russian Justice: Dostoevsky, the Jury Trial, and the Law*. Madison: University of Wisconsin Press, 2005.

Saltykov-Shchedrin, M. E. *Sobranie sochinenii v dvadtsati tomakh*. Edited by S. A. Makashin et al. 20 vols. Moscow: Izdatel'stvo "Khudozhestvennaia literatura," 1965–77.

Scanlan, James P. *Dostoevsky the Thinker*. Ithaca, N.Y.: Cornell University Press, 2002.

Schantz, Ned. *Gossip, Letters, Phones: The Scandal of Female Networks in Film and Literature*. Oxford: Oxford University Press, 2008.

Schor, Hilary M. *Curious Subjects: Women and the Trials of Realism*. Oxford: Oxford University Press, 2013.

Schur, Anna. "The Limits of Listening: Particularity, Compassion, and Dostoevsky's 'Bookish Humaneness.'" *Russian Review* 72, no. 4 (October 2013): 573–89.

———. *Wages of Evil: Dostoevsky and Punishment*. Evanston, Ill.: Northwestern University Press, 2012.

Sekirin, Peter, ed. *The Dostoevsky Archive: Firsthand Accounts of the Novelist from Contemporaries' Memoirs and Rare Periodicals*. Jefferson, N.C.: McFarland, 1997.

Shklovskii, Viktor. *Za i protiv: Zametki o Dostoevskom*. Moscow: Sovetskii pisatel', 1957.

Shrayer, Maxim D. "Metamorphoses of 'Bezobrazie' in Dostoevskij's *The Brothers Karamazov*: Maksimov—Von Sohn—Karamazov." *Russian Literature* 37 (1995): 93–107.

Shuman, Amy. *Other People's Stories: Entitlement Claims and the Critique of Empathy*. Urbana: University of Illinois Press, 2005.

Smith, Barbara Herrnstein. *Poetic Closure: A Study of How Poems End*. Chicago: University of Chicago Press, 1968.

Sokol, Melissa J. "Rumor and Gossip in 19th-Century Russian Literature: Griboedov, Pushkin, Gogol, and Dostoevsky." Ph.D. diss., Brown University, 2007. ProQuest (UMI 3272058).

Spacks, Patricia Meyer. *Gossip*. New York: Knopf, 1985.

Spektor, Alexander. "From Violence to Silence: Vicissitudes of Reading (in) *The Idiot*." *Slavic Review* 72, no. 3 (Fall 2013): 552–72.

———. *Reader as Accomplice: Narrative Ethics in Dostoevsky and Nabokov*. Evanston, Ill.: Northwestern University Press, forthcoming.

Steiner, Lina. *For Humanity's Sake: The Bildungsroman in Russian Culture*. Toronto: University of Toronto Press, 2011.

Sternberg, Meir. *Expositional Modes and Temporal Ordering in Fiction*. Bloomington: Indiana University Press, 1978.

Stromberg, David. "The Enigmatic G——v: A Defense of the Narrator-Chronicler in Dostoevsky's *Demons*." *Russian Review* 71, no. 3 (July 2012): 460–81.

———. *Narrative Faith: Dostoevsky, Camus, and Singer*. Newark: University of Delaware Press, 2018.

Tapp, Alyson. "Embarrassment in *The Idiot*." *Slavic and East European Journal* 60, no. 3 (Fall 2016): 422–46.

Terras, Victor. *A Karamazov Companion: Commentary on the Genesis, Language, and Style of Dostoevsky's Novel*. Madison: University of Wisconsin Press, 1981.

———. *Reading Dostoevsky*. Madison: University of Wisconsin Press, 1998.

Thompson, Diane Oenning. *"The Brothers Karamazov" and the Poetics of Memory*. Cambridge: Cambridge University Press, 1991.

Tihanov, Galin. *The Master and the Slave: Lukács, Bakhtin, and the Ideas of Their Time*. Oxford: Oxford University Press, 2000.

Tikhon Zadonskii. *Uchenie Sviatitelia Tikhona ob istinakh very i tserkvi*. Saint Petersburg, 1864.

Todd, William Mills, III. "'To Be Continued': Dostoevsky's Evolving Poetics of Serialized Publication." *Dostoevsky Studies* 18 (2014): 23–33.

Todorov, Tzvetan. "Structural Analysis of Narrative." Translated by Arnold Weinstein. *Novel: A Forum on Fiction* 3, no. 1 (Autumn 1969): 70–76.

Tolstoi, L. N. *Polnoe sobranie sochinenii*. Iubileinoe izdanie. 90 vols. Moscow: Gosudarstvennoe izdatel'stvo khudozhestvennoi literatury, 1928–64.

Uspensky, Boris. *A Poetics of Composition: The Structure of the Artistic Text and Typology of a Compositional Form*. Translated by Valentina Zavarin and Susan Wittig. Berkeley: University of California Press, 1973.

Vermeule, Blakey. *Why Do We Care about Literary Characters?* Baltimore: Johns Hopkins University Press, 2010.

Vernon, John. "Reading, Writing, and Eavesdropping: Some Thoughts on the Nature of Realistic Fiction." *Kenyon Review* 4, no. 4 (Fall 1982): 44–54.

Vetlovskaia, V. E. *Roman F. M. Dostoevskogo "Brat'ia Karamazovy."* Saint Petersburg: Izdatel'stvo "Pushkinskii dom," 2007.

Vladiv, Slobodanka B. *Narrative Principles in Dostoevskij's "Besy": A Structural Analysis*. Las Vegas: Lang, 1979.

Ware, Timothy. *The Orthodox Church*. London: Penguin Books, 1997.

Wasiolek, Edward. Introduction to *The Notebooks for "A Raw Youth,"* by Fyodor Dostoevsky, edited by Edward Wasiolek, translated by Victor Terras, 1–19. Chicago: University of Chicago Press, 1969.

Weiner, Adam. *By Authors Possessed: The Demonic Novel in Russia*. Evanston, Ill.: Northwestern University Press, 1998.

Williams, Rowan. *Dostoevsky: Language, Faith, and Fiction*. Waco, Tex.: Baylor University Press, 2011.

Wispé, Lauren. "History of the Concept of Empathy." In *Empathy and Its Development*, edited by Nancy Eisenberg and Janet Strayer, 17–37. Cambridge: Cambridge University Press, 1987.

Woloch, Alex. *The One vs. the Many: Minor Characters and the Space of the Protagonist in the Novel*. Princeton, N.J.: Princeton University Press, 2003.

Wyman, Alina. *The Gift of Active Empathy: Scheler, Bakhtin, and Dostoevsky*. Evanston, Ill.: Northwestern University Press, 2016.

Young, Sarah J. *Dostoevsky's "The Idiot" and the Ethical Foundations of Narrative: Reading, Narrating, Scripting*. London: Anthem Press, 2004.

Zil'bershtein, I. S., and L. M. Rozenblium, eds. *F. M. Dostoevskii: Novye materialy i issledovaniia*. Literaturnoe nasledstvo 86. Moscow: Nauka, 1973.

Index